HEARTS

Rob Robertson and Paul Kiddie

HEARTS

Great Tynecastle Tales

MAINSTREAM
PUBLISHING

EDINBURGH AND LONDON

First published in Great Britain in 2005 by
MAINSTREAM PUBLISHING COMPANY (EDINBURGH) LTD
7 Albany Street
Edinburgh EH1 3UG

ISBN 1 84596 003 3

A catalogue record for this book is available from the British Library

Typeset in Baskerville Book and Stone Sans
Printed and bound in Great Britain by
William Clowes Ltd, Beccles, Suffolk

For Margaret Kiddie, without whom this book would never have seen the light of day. Also to our children, Kirsten and Clare Robertson and Caitlin Kiddie, for lighting up our lives.

CONTENTS

ACKNOWLEDGEMENTS

Thanks to Mark Douglas Home, the editor of the *Herald* newspaper, the paper's sports editor, Donald Cowey, and his deputy, Hugh MacDonald. Thanks to the *Edinburgh Evening News* and also to Scotsman Publications Ltd for access to their extensive pictorial library.

Dan Brennan of Libero Language Lab provided his translation expertise and top-class knowledge of Eastern European football, while Davy Allan of London Hearts provided the electronic know-how and links with the fans. Also, thanks to Clare Cowan and Charlie Mann for their help and Bill Smith and David Speed for their statistical expertise.

Most importantly, we thank the Hearts players past and present as well as the fans who gave their time so gracefully to make this project happen.

Yours in sport,

Rob Robertson and Paul Kiddie

FOREWORD

It gives me great pleasure to have been asked to write the foreword to *Hearts: Great Tynecastle Tales*, a book which celebrates one of the greatest football grounds in the world. Such a publication is long overdue considering the great memories that the famous stadium has given everyone for more than 100 years.

For me, this publication could not come at a more suitable time. The threat of Tynecastle being sold for housing has finally been lifted and the Hearts supporters who campaigned long and hard to stop the sale and the proposed move to Murrayfield should give themselves a round of applause.

Hearts belong at Tynecastle; the ground is part of the community of Gorgie and a major landmark in the city of Edinburgh. Ask any football supporter, regardless of which team they follow, and they will tell you they love going there to watch matches. As a player, running out onto the pitch used to make the hairs on the back of my neck stand up; the atmosphere was always electric and the crowd always loud and supportive. I know for a fact that having thousands of Hearts supporters baying for blood intimidated many an opposition player.

Tynecastle was my second home for 17 great years and I loved every minute of my time at the club. I was signed as a teenager by

Bobby Moncur and, as a lifelong Hearts supporter and former pupil of Tynecastle High School, that was a dream come true. I loved the stadium as a player and still retain the same feelings every time I go back as a fan.

It would have been a disgrace for the ground to be bulldozed, as it holds a special place in the history of Scottish football. Tynecastle is steeped in memories and, thankfully, this book captures many of them for posterity. Generation after generation have come through the turnstiles to pay homage to the team which has meant so much to them and it is only right that their thoughts are captured in print.

As for all the great players who played for Hearts through the years, their words in the book show how much of an honour it was for them to play for the club. It was certainly an honour for me to play for Hearts and I am proud to call myself a fan. I hope you enjoy this book, which pays tribute to Tynecastle, the ground we all love. Long may it remain!

Gary Mackay

INTRODUCTION

DANCING IN THE STREETS OF GORGIE

'Save our Hearts!' was the cry – and save them they did.

March 2004 was a defining period in the history of the famous Gorgie club, as it was the month in which supporters took it upon themselves to halt the controversial sale of Tynecastle and thwart the proposed move to Murrayfield. Galvanised by the fear of seeing their beloved club threatened with extinction by such a move, the Federation of Hearts Supporters' Clubs and the Supporters' Trust combined to launch the Save Our Hearts (SOH) campaign. The aim was to raise enough money to buy a stake in the club – Scottish Media Group's (SMG) near 20 per cent stake was the number one target – while the removal of Chris Robinson from the board was also a priority.

Hearts legend Gary Mackay became the campaign figurehead and demonstrated his commitment to the cause with a £10,000 donation. Campaign headquarters were set up in a dedicated shop in Gorgie Road and support quickly grew, with cash flooding in from fans desperate to play their part in keeping Hearts in their spiritual home.

Just a month after its formation, the campaign was celebrating its first victory with the resignation of Doug Smith as chairman.

Veteran Labour MP George Foulkes was appointed as his successor and he immediately announced a year's postponement of the ground-share proposal with Scottish Rugby Union.

With some 1,300 contributors raising £650,000 and protests grabbing the headlines, the campaign was voted a resounding success. Although there were two aborted attempts to buy out SMG, Save Our Hearts got the result they wanted when Robinson was removed from his position as chief executive and major shareholder by Lithuanian Vladimir Romanov at the start of February 2005. Murrayfield was off the agenda – almost a year to the day after the group was founded.

Although the Baltic millionaire's involvement was unconnected to SOH's drive to oust Robinson, campaign organisers feel proud of their efforts to safeguard the future of the club. 'The official launch of the Save Our Hearts campaign was in March 2004,' said group secretary John Borthwick. 'The group was formed by the Supporters' Trust and the Federation of Hearts Supporters' Clubs and came about as the result of a conversation between myself and Derek Watson from the Trust the previous month. As far as we were concerned, when Chris Robinson announced that the club was going to sell Tynecastle and move to Murrayfield, it would have meant the death of Hearts. There was no "plan B" and it was suggested the choice would be Murrayfield or bust. I said at the time I thought it would be Murrayfield *and* bust. A lot of fans envisaged the club losing its SPL status and maybe even ending up in the Second Division, and then finding it difficult to re-establish itself. That was the whole reason behind the formation of Save Our Hearts. We couldn't just sit back and do nothing. We tried to galvanise the fans and things gradually gathered pace.

'Doug Smith eventually resigned, as he knew the club wouldn't take the fan base to Murrayfield; George Foulkes came in to replace him and immediately announced that the club would be staying at Tynecastle for at least another year. That was a major announcement as far as we were concerned and he also said that a working party would be set up to explore all the viable options for a new long-term home – that was basically all we were asking for at the time.

'As far as Chris Robinson was concerned, it was Murrayfield and nothing else, whereas George was at least willing to look at the options. When we heard a deal had been agreed with Mr Romanov to buy out Chris Robinson, we were all ecstatic. He has been like a breath of fresh air. Comparing the situation at the start of 2004 to the possibilities we may have under Mr Romanov is like comparing night and day.

'I am convinced that had it not been for the Save Our Hearts campaign, Hearts would have been playing at Murrayfield and staring disaster in the face.'

Martin Laidlaw, chairman of the Supporters' Trust, echoed those sentiments. 'As a trust, we had known for some time that things were wrong. The reason we initially set up the Trust was to establish a structure to try to influence what was going on. It was clear from the publication of Mr Robinson's "Not Fit For Purpose" document that things were a lot more serious than we thought.

'The Trust launched "Keep Hearts in Gorgie" in January 2004, as we thought his plans were fundamentally wrong. There was a board meeting at which it was agreed that something needed to be done to bring everyone together on the issue and we decided to approach the Federation. Save Our Hearts was set up and the campaign showed that supporters were absolutely committed to staying at Tynecastle and getting rid of Chris Robinson. It also gave others the confidence to know the fans were behind what they wanted to do. Peter McGrail, for example, would never have done all his work on a plan for Tynecastle to be part of a regeneration of Gorgie had he not met us.

'A string of things happened which showed we were being taken seriously, including the talks with SMG, Doug Smith's resignation and a survey which revealed that 97 per cent of supporters would not buy a season ticket for Murrayfield.

'One of the things which really was quite remarkable was seeing the 5,000 people walk along from Saughton Park to Tynecastle on 19 March 2004. We didn't dwell too much on it at the time but on reflection it really was quite amazing. We are just proud to have played a part. If we are brutally honest about it, the two organisations merging together have saved Hearts, simple as that.'

Former Scottish Rugby Union figurehead Phil Anderton was Romanov's number one target to replace Robinson as chief executive. He assumed his role in March 2005 and stressed the importance of the fans in the development of the club in the new era.

'There is no doubt the supporters have a key role to play in the future of Hearts,' said Anderton when he was appointed. 'We need to make them feel they are being listened to and ultimately give them value for money. We have to listen to fans all the time, especially those who have supported the club through thick and thin.

'There are a lot of people who say Hearts have no chance of challenging Celtic and Rangers but this isn't a club starting from scratch. This is a club with a great tradition and pedigree.

'There is a sleeping giant here. If you look across the UK, all the major cities such as Liverpool, Manchester, Birmingham and Glasgow have clubs challenging right up there. Why not Edinburgh?

'Just look at the history of the club. We won the league in the 1950s, came close again in the '80s and won the Scottish Cup in the '90s. People, though, start accepting that it can't be done.

'When I was a kid, I remember Dundee United and Aberdeen challenging and winning things. I don't think it is impossible. I am similar to Mr Romanov in that I am ambitious with a "can do" mentality. If everyone works together instead of fighting each other, then there is every chance. I want to ensure we are dynamic and challenging the status quo. With a lot of hard work and maybe a bit of good fortune, I'm confident we can do that.

'Increasing the revenue stream is vital but the supporters need to know it is not about raising money to make a few people rich. It is about raising money to make the club more successful and that is what we all want.'

The Save Our Hearts campaign was wound up in mid-June

2005, with contributors to the fund either taking their money back or having it transferred into a share-purchase scheme administered by the Supporters' Trust.

Much to the fans' angst, Robinson was still involved at boardroom level during the early summer, albeit in a non-executive capacity. He finally severed his official ties with the club by resigning as a director on Monday, 18 July 2005, although he was involved on an informal basis in the early days of the plans to redevelop Tynecastle, a fact which further dismayed supporters. He was paid for his work directly by Vladimir Romanov rather than by the club. He was finally sidelined when George Foulkes, the popular Hearts chairman, was put in personal charge of the redevelopment of Tynecastle.

'The day that Chris resigned as a director was one we had waited a long time for and to say we were absolutely delighted would have been an understatement,' said Borthwick. 'It was good to see him out of the boardroom at last.'

CHAPTER ONE

TYNECASTLE: A NATIONAL MONUMENT
by Hugh MacDonald of *The Herald*

If football is the beautiful game, the more grizzled among us could be forgiven for muttering in the past, 'What's a sexy sport like you doing in a place like this?'

Old football stadiums were wondrous places. But they were not pretty. Never sanitary, barely safe and hardly comfortable, they were always noisy, always full of pith and patter. The bucket seat now rules but the terracings were once the place we dinosaurs loved to roam. I had my favourite spot in a stadium in Glasgow but I was promiscuous. I was an easy one day stand on grounds throughout Scotland. Each stadium left its own mark. Tannadice, I remember, had unusually large terracings steps. The sea poked its nose over Gayfield on a windy day. East Stirling seemed situated up a close. Boghead needed the builders in. And Tynecastle?

Well, Tynecastle had its own unique charms. As a Glaswegian studying in Edinburgh (an absurd proposition, I concede), I was a regular visitor to Gorgie Road in the 1970s. I grazed contentedly on the terraces. I was incognito. No colours, no bias, no worries. I could watch the Hearts without having to suffer with them. I formed a loose attachment with Rab Prentice but that's not criminal and they can't do you for it.

I also became inordinately fond of the stadium, which was but a bracing walk from my digs up Lothian Road. It was great to mingle with the Hearts fans, keeping my dulcet Glaswegian tones to a minimum while listening to the massed growls and roars. It was even better when my own mob came to town. Then Tynecastle was revealed in all its grandeur. There is nothing like a full stadium. Even better, there is nothing like a full stadium that glowers over the pitch with only a strip of dirty ash separating bile-filled fan and ball-carrying player. Magic.

Tynecastle trembled when the massed armies of two sets of fans faced each other down. It also offered an interesting entrance. As I remember it, the road from every pub converged into a sharp left off Gorgie Road, when the entire population of Glasgow heading for the away end attempted to squeeze between tenements and towards turnstiles manned by two pensioners, one of whom never seemed to know what he was doing and the other with an attitude problem borrowed from Genghis Khan.

The slowly clanking turnstiles defiantly made fun of the gathering mass tilted towards them. The air was heavy with beer-soaked obscenity before finally, gratefully, you were thrown upon the terracings much in the same way that Jonah escaped from the whale. There it was 'rerr', to use the weegie vernacular. Hearts, whether it was Prentice or McCann, whether it was Busby or Robertson, or whether it was MacDonald or Mackay, always dished it up hot and heavy. The fans, too, were hardly demure. It all added up to a substantial dish best devoured on a wintry afternoon as the sun dimmed and the floodlights illuminated a theatre of thrills and spills, roars and glaur, and the odd bit of fitba'.

It may have been the same scenario all over Scotland but each ground had its different plot, twists and special settings. Tynecastle had its own peculiarities, its own atmosphere and its own glories, the last burned into the hearts and souls of its supporters. You may have heard there was talk of selling Tynecastle. But it couldn't have been true. How can you put a price on memories? And how can you flog a national monument?

CHAPTER TWO

THE HEARTBEAT OF GORGIE

Gorgie on a match day is a joy to behold. Bustling with supporters, local pubs full to bursting and the noise of the Hearts faithful filling the air as they make their way to Tynecastle, it is one of the most exhilarating places to go to watch football.

The pilgrimage to Tynecastle is a ritual that began back in 1886, 12 years after the Heart of Midlothian Football Club was founded. There are two theories as to how the world-famous name was thought up and how the club, Hearts, came into being.

One theory is that youths used to play around the old Tolbooth jail on the Royal Mile, which was nicknamed the 'Heart of Midlothian' after Walter Scott's novel. The local authority regarded the footballers as a public nuisance because their regular games took place in an area where there were a number of public hangings. In a show of defiance, the players took their ball to the Meadows and started up their team, which they called the Heart of Midlothian after the nickname of the jail next to which they were forbidden to play. Others believe the club got its name from a dance hall called Heart of Midlothian, which had also been named after Scott's novel.

Tom Purdie, the first captain of Hearts, is given credit for making sure the name of Heart of Midlothian stuck. Purdie won the captaincy after a one-on-one game against the other leading player of the time, Jake Reid, and agreed with the vast majority of people at the time that the name of Heart of Midlothian should be adopted.

Whichever story you believe, the club has gone from strength to strength, becoming one of Britain's greatest sporting institutions. Heart of Midlothian is part of Scottish culture and is an Edinburgh tradition that is as much a part of the capital city as the castle or Princes Street. The team's exploits on the field have brought both joy and heartache to millions through the decades.

It's hard to imagine nowadays but when the club was starting out they played in red, white and blue hoops before switching to their famous maroon in 1878. Once the club started to grow they moved from the Meadows to Powburn and later to Powderhall. In 1881, they moved to 'Old Tynecastle', which was close to the present ground, and stayed there until they made the short trip to Gorgie Road to take up residence in their current location.

Their final match at Old Tynecastle was on 27 February 1886 when a crowd of 2,000 saw them beat Sunderland 2–1. Two months later, on 10 April 1886, Bolton Wanderers travelled to Edinburgh to be the first opponents at the new ground. Around 6,000 turned up for what was a carnival occasion. Hearts beat Bolton 4–1, with Tommy Jenkinson, Hearts' first Scotland international player, scoring the first goal at the new ground.

The interest in Hearts was growing. It was clear they needed to increase the capacity of the ground. In 1888, two years after Tynecastle was opened, two new stands and a pavilion were built on the east side of the stadium, which took the capacity up to 10,000. Four years later, a roof was put over the south-east stand and in 1894 Hearts built refreshment kiosks all over the ground to cater for their hungry and thirsty supporters.

Building work continued apace. In 1901, another covered stand, this time replacing the north-east stand, was built and the banking around the pitch was extended to take the capacity up to 20,000. The north and south stands were combined in 1903 and a cycle track that had run around the pitch was taken away as the capacity grew. By the end of 1911, a covered enclosure with a capacity of 4,500 was added, which became known to that generation as the 'Iron Stand'.

The Main Stand, under which the dressing-rooms were located, was built just before the outbreak of war in 1914 and cost £12,178. In 1925, the club bought the ground from Edinburgh Corporation at a cost of £5,000. There was a clause that allowed the corporation to buy it back whenever it wanted, although that was never enforced and it was finally bought out by the club in 1977, giving them control of their own ground.

In 1926, Hearts spent £18,000 building a new entrance at Wheatfield Street and added more terracings after they demolished the Iron Stand. By 1930, the capacity at Tynecastle was an impressive 55,842, with that figure nearly reached for a Scottish Cup tie against Rangers two years later.

During the Second World War, match attendances were restricted to 8,000 due to the threat of air raids. Many among that generation remember being part of bigger crowds during the war years. It seems the police used their discretion to let as many people in as possible.

With the war over, safety work was carried out after a disaster at Burnden Park, the home of Bolton Wanderers, when 33 fans were crushed to death. The terracings were concreted at a cost of £1,700 and the work took four years to complete. The capacity was reduced from 55,842 to 49,000 for safety reasons.

In 1957, floodlights were erected at a cost of £14,000, with a match against Hibs arranged to christen them. It was a big boost to Hearts, as, up until that point, they'd had to hire Easter Road for winter evening matches. Newcastle and Manchester City were among the clubs who played floodlit 'friendlies' within the first few months of the Tynecastle floodlights being installed.

In the late 1950s, the average home gate at Tynecastle was around 20,000, but in a match against Raith Rovers on 29 March 1958 only 9,000 were allowed in after a freak rainstorm made the terraces too dangerous. That was the last straw for the club's board, which, by the end of the decade, had spent a further £23,000 on a covered enclosure for 15,000 on the distillery side of the ground. The costs of the floodlights and the ground improvements were taken from a year-to-year profit of £13,000, with around £10,000 of that coming from their European Cup tie against Standard Liège in September 1958. Around £15,000 from the 1958 Scottish League Cup final win also helped balance the books.

The ground remained relatively the same for many years after but with violence affecting football across the globe Hearts put up security fences and introduced segregation barriers in 1978.

The early 1980s were the Wallace Mercer years and he brought flamboyance to the club, introducing marketing initiatives that helped bring in much-needed cash. For selected matches, he introduced half-time draws for cars that were supplied by Alexander's, the Ford dealers, who had the honour of being Hearts' first shirt sponsors. The supporters also played their part and 30 volunteers repaired the terraces and repainted the ground to help cut maintenance costs.

With money from corporate hospitality vital for the survival of every football club, Hearts under Mercer opened their own boxes in 1984. A new Executive Business Club, a Sponsors' Lounge and a restaurant were created at Tynecastle and were hugely successful. The floodlights were also upgraded to European standard and a family enclosure with seating for 1,000 opened as the club realised the need to attract the next generation of football fans to Tynecastle.

The Hillsborough tragedy of 1989 affected every football club and the Hearts board decided they had to leave Tynecastle. They looked at 14 possible sites and considered a controversial ground-sharing scheme with Hibs but no agreement was reached. A plan to leave Gorgie for Millerhill on the south-east of the city did not receive planning permission and after that it was clear Tynecastle would remain home.

In 1993, Mercer unveiled proposals to buy the stadium for £2.7 million, upgrade it and then lease it back to the club for 50 years. However, shareholders and supporters were unhappy with the plan and it was scrapped. Instead, the '500 Club' was set up, whereby supporters each gave £500 to allow work to begin on a new 5,902-seat Wheatfield Stand, which was opened in 1994. The Roseburn Stand at the School End was opened a year later.

A share scheme failed to raise the cash needed to build the Gorgie Stand, but the finance was put in place in 1996 when new revenue was released after Hearts were placed on the Stock Exchange. It was completed in September 1997, adding another 3,300 seats, which took the capacity up to 17,702, and created an even more atmospheric ground. Looking from the centre circle you are surrounded by the Roseburn, Gorgie and Wheatfield stands. All are good-sized single-tiered stands, similar in design and height. Only the Main Stand remains of the 'old' Tynecastle and it looks somewhat out of place amongst its shiny new neighbours. It is two-tiered, smaller than the other stands and has a fair few supporting pillars, which do spoil the view for some.

Away fans for big matches are housed in the Roseburn Stand at one end of the ground, which can accommodate around 3,500 supporters. Clubs with a smaller following may find only a portion of this stand is allocated to them. The steep slope of the new stands ensures a good view of the pitch wherever you are and those who have been to Tynecastle never forget the experience.

JAMES CLYDESDALE, ARCHITECT

James Clydesdale was the man behind the three Tynecastle stands which were built in the mid-1990s and the Wheatfield, Gorgie and Roseburn stands received major plaudits for their construction and design. In 2004, Clydesdale was a leading light on the Stadium Working Group, which recommended that for just £100,000 Hearts could upgrade Tynecastle to ensure its survival for at least another five years. He is still a keen Hearts supporter and his design of the three stands with their steep sides and magnificent views of the pitch is a contributory factor to the great atmosphere at Tynecastle on match days.

'I was first taken to Tynecastle by Wallace Mercer in 1982 when he asked me how to improve facilities there. My first memory of walking in the door was seeing a young John Robertson and a similarly youthful Gary Mackay sitting in a room called Mary's cupboard, where the players used to go for a cup of tea. It was a tiny room and they were sitting next to the sink trying to get some warmth from a portable heater. Gary, tongue in cheek, told me these were the players' entertainment facilities.

'Tynecastle back then was, to say the least, quaint. The notion of sponsorship or match-day entertainment was in its infancy. For instance, in the middle of the players' lounge was a snooker table, which on match days was covered with a piece of hardboard and had a white table cover thrown over it so the room could become the special place for sponsors. As I kept trying to improve things, I ended up with the reputation of someone who every time he looked in a cupboard turned it into a bar or lounge.

'The club spent years looking at moving away from Gorgie but after abortive planning applications the only option left was to stay put and improve Tynecastle. Three new stands were needed and it was difficult, in terms of planning and construction, to create them in such a tight, urban area. The site could not be made any bigger, as no extra land was available at the time.

'The Wheatfield Stand was the first to be built and cost around £2.4 million. Work started on it in the spring of 1993 with the removal of the cowshed and part of the School End terracing. Dispensation was sought from the council to fit the Gorgie Road end out with open-air seats, while the School End was removed and used as a walkway to get from McLeod Street to the Wheatfield Stand.

'There was huge interest from Hearts fans in what we were doing. We set up a viewing gallery at the end of Tynecastle Terrace so people could see how work was progressing. It was there I met a supporter who was aghast that the steelwork was to be pink, as he thought it would bring ridicule on the club. He didn't seem to see the irony in the fact he was wearing a pink polo shirt that day. Personally, I thought pink brought panache to the stadium and the maroon cladding brought balance.

'After the Wheatfield Stand was built, the Roseburn Stand was completed in August 1995 at a cost of around £1.4 million and then the Gorgie Road Stand followed. Replacing the Main Stand would be a good move if possible, as it would finish the ground off and provide an even more exciting amphitheatre for football.

'I was part of the Stadium Working Group which recommended that the club should stay at Tynecastle and make improvements in the short term to allow its continued use for, say, five years. It would cost around £100,000, which would mostly be spent on work on the Main Stand. The group also said that the club should take formal advice from UEFA and that it would be possible to make the pitch the correct size to allow European matches to be played at Tynecastle rather than at Murrayfield. We also felt that the club should apply for planning permission to redevelop Tynecastle for the best economic use possible. I have always felt staying at Tynecastle made sense and I still do.'

CHAPTER THREE

MERCER MAGIC

Wallace Mercer was the most charismatic chairman Hearts have ever had. He was only 33 years old when he took over the club and was the first to realise that football was part of the entertainment industry. His style and flamboyance brought the club into the public eye and he introduced several off-the-field innovations to bring in cash.

He stayed in charge for 13 years before selling out to Leslie Deans and Chris Robinson for more than £2 million. He retired to recharge his batteries, first to Jersey and then to his villa in the south of France before returning to his business career with his new company Almondale Investments.

'I got involved with Hearts in May 1981, just after they had been relegated from the First Division. We were known as the yo-yo team because we were too good for the Second but not good enough for the First. It was a frustrating time.

'They were on their knees financially when I got involved and it was Donald Ford who brought me to the club. Hearts were trying to raise £500,000 through a share issue, as they were nearly bust. Kenny Waugh, who went on to become chairman of Hibs and who was a well-known supporter of the Easter Road club, wrote a cheque for £500,000, taking up the share issue. Donald phoned me in a panic when I was down at Wembley to see the Scotland–England game, as he wanted me to take over the club and thought I would be the best man to take the club forward. I got so romantically carried away by Scotland's performance that on the plane home I decided I would try to match Kenny Waugh's commitment.

'I put together a consortium overnight along with some other wealthy Hearts supporters. At a public meeting at the Locarno ballroom on Gorgie Road, I was cross-examined by Donald Ford in front of the supporters about my plans. I told the hundreds who turned up I would put up £350,000, which was a lot of money for my wife Anne and I back then, as I was only 33 years old. The fans pitched in £150,000 and we were off and running.

'It was up to the Hearts board to choose between me or Kenny Waugh. They were split but I won the vote 3–2 and the two who voted against me resigned. Ten days after my romantic trip to Wembley, I had inherited the controlling shareholding in Hearts.

'At the first board meeting, I realised how difficult a job we had to turn the club around financially. Ian Watt, a well-respected banker, was on the board at the time and he told me that we could afford seven and a half professional players.

'Indeed, I lost manager Bobby Moncur within seven days of taking over when he left for Plymouth Argyle. We didn't have time to fall in, let alone fall out! Tony Ford, who had been Bobby's assistant, became the new manager. I always remember a week after he got the job he started coming to see me in the boardroom wearing a white jacket. He looked like a dance-band leader. It was no surprise when he only lasted about four months.

'When he left, we didn't have any money for a big managerial appointment. I came to the conclusion the only logical thing to do was to sit down with the captain, Alex MacDonald, to try to establish a plan for a way forward. I asked him did he fancy becoming player/manager of Hearts. One, I thought it was a good idea, and two, I felt it was a good business option. I believe we were the first British team to have a player/manager.

'I couldn't sit across the table from Alex when we met in a boss and employee context, as people forgot that the chairman and the new manager of Hearts were the same age. I was just 34 years old when I appointed him.

'I had great respect for Alex and he'd had a great career with Rangers. With no money, we managed to cobble together two or three new signings, like Jimmy Bone, who was magnificent for us, and we just missed promotion to the top league by one point. In Alex's second full season, which was 1982–83, we had a good mix of youth and experience in the team, with players like John Robertson making the breakthrough and gaining experience in the team with players such as Sandy Jardine, Willie Pettigrew and my own personal favourite Willie Johnston.

'I brought in the bus company owner Douglas Park as a director and it was a good move. He came up with the idea of low-cost travel for our supporters. We were making things up as we went along and learning all the time.

'Pilmar Smith was appointed as my vice-chairman, as I wanted a director to be responsible for the fans. Soon afterwards we started Scotland's first junior club for families and we were coming up with inventive ideas. We had a young chairman and a young manager, and although it was hard work, it was great fun. We wanted to make it fun because it was a hard time for a section of our supporters. This was the time of the miners' strike and we drew a lot of support from the east-coast mining communities. Because of that we were the first British club to let the unemployed in for nothing.

'In the first season of being promoted to the new Premier League [1983–84] we managed to achieve a European place and got to fifth in the league, which astounded everyone. We had some great players at Tynecastle and our defenders like Craig Levein and Sandy Jardine were the rock on which we built the team.

'Goalkeeping-wise I felt we needed to strengthen and the cheapest signing I ever made was Henry Smith for £1,000 from Leeds United. We had John Brough, who I felt was dreadful at cross balls but a great shot stopper. I wanted someone who was good at both and Henry fitted the bill. I felt we were really on the up with our blend of youth and experience.

'The young players, like Robertson and Mackay, were getting better and better and we had some good times. In May 1981, the business had been nearly bust but by May 1986 we only lost the league on the final day and lost the cup final. I was always the optimist and thought we'd win them both!

'I'd commissioned a book which took just a few weeks to print and produce to celebrate that season on the assumption we would win something. It was called *The Boys in Maroon*, by John Fairgrieve, the well-known journalist who was also a keen Hearts fan. It was a good read and centred on the fact that we had gone 30 games undefeated that season. I remember meeting a group of journalists who were out in Los Angeles and presenting the book to them in the Polo Lounge of the Beverly Hills Hotel.

'When I returned, we made Sandy Jardine co-manager along with Alex but, as history has shown with other clubs, that set-up never works. You can only have one boss at a football club.

'We had a great pool of players from the mid to late 1980s. I remember going to see Scotland against Germany in Glasgow and we had six players in the squad: Henry Smith, John Colquhoun, John Robertson, Dave McPherson, Gary Mackay and Alan McLaren. But of all the players I had at Tynecastle, Sandy Jardine was the most influential. The way he handled himself was magnificent and it was one of the saddest days of my footballing life when we came to the conclusion he had to move on. We also lost Alex MacDonald as manager. What caused part of the problem with Alex was that I had tried to tap Alex Ferguson from Manchester United just before the World Cup in Italy. We thought he was going to get sacked if he lost the FA Cup final to Crystal Palace on 12 May 1990. Alex MacDonald got to hear about that and obviously wasn't happy. I didn't blame him, as I didn't want the story to get out.

'When Alex left, we brought in Joe Jordan, who was the most difficult man I had to deal with at Hearts. Joe was difficult to communicate with and would growl at you. For me, he was a cross between Bill Shankly and Tommy Docherty in his approach to motivating players but was not one of the world's great communicators. As a player, though, I accept he had done great things.

'Through all of this I wanted to improve Hearts. I wanted to take us to the next level and I thought I had the answer when I was offered shares in Hibs. I remember the events that split Edinburgh as if they were yesterday.

'I was approached to see if I would be interested in taking an option on 35 per cent of Hibs shares, which were owned by the multimillionaire David Rowland. He said I was the man to buy Hibs. It was worth pursuing.

'I went to his office in London after doing a deal with the Bank of Scotland for £7.5 million to make it happen. Nobody knew about it. We had kept it tight. The Hibs board were invited down to meet Rowland at his office in Mayfair and told they were about to meet the new owner of Hibernian Football Club. They were all sitting there drinking champagne thinking they were going to get Robert Maxwell or some other multimillionaire from down south. Then I walked out of the private lift! Their faces were a picture.

'Not surprisingly, my plan to merge Hearts and Hibs leaked out. I had the biggest press conference of my life at the Caledonian Hotel in Edinburgh and there were media representatives there from all over the world. It was an amazing occasion, as nobody had come up with the idea of merging two clubs.

'The reason I did it was because I was sick of Hearts being the nearly men, getting to second in the league, second in the cup but not quite making that step up. We had come to the conclusion we needed economies of scale and the plan was to move the new team to a new stadium at Hermiston Gate.

'The backlash against the plan made me realise social engineering is not a wise move. Dealing with that had taken a lot out of me and the end of the road was near.

'I decided to take a break from Scottish football and moved abroad to France in April 1993. I did not sell the business for a full season and by that time Joe Jordan had been dismissed and Sandy Clark had come in as manager.

'Just before I left Tynecastle, my wife Anne and I gave 100 shares each to the players and the staff, and that was the end of the era for me. They were 13 great, eventful years but they had taken their toll on my health. I was trying to run Hearts and my property business at the same time. It was very tiring. I used to be in the offices of my business, Dunedin Properties, in the morning and at 3 p.m. on the dot go to Tynecastle. I always said I would only be there for a little while. Invariably I would be there for hours. I was 33 when I started at Hearts and 46 when I finished. I needed a break, as physically and emotionally I was very tired.

'Did I enjoy it all? You bet I did. I had real fun on every level. I got christened "Wireless Mercer", as I had my own radio show and the BBC let me have a television chat show where I interviewed people like Sir Clive Sinclair, Jimmy Gulliver and Anita Roddick.

'I'm always proud of the fact if you had taken 100 shares for £100 in Hearts back in 1981 these would be worth £750 in 1993 when we left. We did make the occasional loss but the shareholders had a good run.

'When I packed it in, Hearts had a great group of Scottish international players and good facilities in place. There were borrowings of approximately £3.5 million, which was within the plan agreed by the Bank of Scotland. We also had a credit facility of £3.6 million, which was in place to build the first two stands at Tynecastle. This was structured in that we had £500,000 from the 500 Club, £200,000 from my purchase of the offices at McLeod Street, £700,000 from the pre-sale of Alan McLaren to Rangers, £1.2 million from the Football Trust and £1 million extra lending from the bank, which was personally guaranteed by me for four years.

'During my 13 years, I like to think I raised the profile of Hearts and was respected for what I tried to do for the club. It was a form of fellowship we all formed at Tynecastle and along the way the team competed well. We had some great times. The board named me Honorary Life President in May 1994, which was a great gesture and kept my link with the club.

'When I stepped down at Hearts, I was approached to take a role at Falkirk or Livingston. With all due respect to those clubs, it would have been like leaving a residency at the London Palladium to join an end-of-pier show.

'With hindsight, the unhappiness of the planned merger between Hearts and Hibs suggests I could have done things differently on that front. The way that panned out was my biggest regret during my time at Hearts. The debacle surrounding that era didn't please me. Maybe it was not thought through as much as it should have been. We had the resources to do it and the positive thing that came out of it was the fact that Sir Tom Farmer became involved in Scottish football, as he became the white knight for Hibs.

'Obviously the Scottish Cup win in 1998 was fantastic but off the field things went from bad to worse for Hearts with mounting debts and I think the club lost its soul when the Scottish Media Group invested its cash. Those in charge now have to restore some pride in the club and put the smiles back on the faces of the fans.

'I have homes in North Berwick and Mougins in the south of France and both places have pictures of my Hearts days on the walls. I have also kept Edinburgh Crystal glasses that were cut every time Hearts played a European match. I have great Tynecastle memories, as have our supporters. They deserve to smile and have a successful team.'

CHAPTER FOUR

HOME DRESSING-ROOM

PLAYERS
Stephane Adam (striker, 1997–2002)
'There were highs and lows for me during my time at the club. The start was much better than the finish because of the many injuries I picked up towards the end of my time at Tynecastle and the tough situation when Jim Jefferies left. In general, though, it was good, as it was my first and only experience of football in a foreign country. I said to my friends afterwards that looking back I wish I had gone to Scotland earlier in my career.

'I appreciated the time I spent in my own country but the five years I played in Edinburgh were special. The football was different and the passion of the supporters was very different to what I had been used to. I wasn't too nervous about coming over, as it was the time of my career when I needed a change. I was looking for something else after playing in the second and third division in France and Hearts provided me with that after signing from Metz. It was the right time for a new experience and after a trial period I felt it would be a good move for me, so I was very confident when I arrived at Tynecastle and was motivated to do well.

'I was ambitious and relished the challenge of making a mark on Hearts' history. I have absolutely no regrets at all about coming to

Scotland and the Scottish Cup final in 1998 was an obvious highlight. Nobody in France will ever appreciate just how good that was to bring the trophy back to Tynecastle and the scenes we all enjoyed afterwards. It was absolutely fantastic and the best memories I have of football. I won the League Cup with Metz and that was a great time also but it didn't compare to '98. I still look at the videotapes of everything that weekend and it's very emotional. People were crying and for days afterwards folk kept coming to my house in Stockbridge to ring the bell and ask to have their photograph taken with me. Others came round just to say thank you. It was incredible.

'It was a tough challenge for me as a foreign player to make my mark in the game in Scotland but I was determined to do something special and scoring the winning goal in the cup final fulfilled a burning ambition of mine to give something back to the club. Of course, I am proud to have helped write a new chapter in Hearts' history. I had already settled into the team quite quickly but that day changed my life, as it gave me the chance to be accepted by all the fans in Edinburgh and helped me enjoy five years in Scotland.

'I had a great understanding with Jim Jefferies. He was a tough guy but someone who treated you with respect. As a foreigner in a strange country for me that was even more important than someone's coaching qualities. When I first came over, I didn't speak English at all and it wasn't easy to settle in but Jim and Billy Brown were always there for myself and the other foreigners like Thomas Flogel and Gilles Rousset when we had any problems. I think that was part of the reason for our success as well, the fact that Jim and Billy were so helpful to us.

'When the day came to leave Tynecastle, of course I was sad. I was still looking to play but I had struggled with a few injuries and I also understood the financial problems the club was experiencing. Five years is quite a long time at one club and it was a wrench to leave what had really become my second home. My little boy Arthur was born in Simpson's in September 1999, so he has a little bit of Scottish in him.'

Alan Anderson (centre-half, 1963–76)

'I saw a few managers in my time at Tynecastle. Tommy Walker signed me in 1963 and then Johnny Harvey, who had been the trainer, took over for a short spell. Bobby Seith then took over and I was still there when John Hagart was in charge. I played one season in the Premier League and then retired at the age of 36. Hearts actually got relegated the year after I stopped playing and I'd like to think that had something to do with me not being in the team!

'I was just happy to be playing for Hearts but throughout the years I was at the club we always seemed to be the bridesmaid. We were runners-up in the league in 1964–65 when we were beaten by Kilmarnock on goal average and then we lost the Scottish Cup final against Dunfermline in 1968.

'Jock Wallace made a big impression when he was assistant to Johnny Harvey, who was getting on a bit when he was in charge. He allowed Jock to run the thing, really, and it was when Jock left that Bobby Seith came in. Johnny then got pushed to the side a wee bit and became chief scout.

'Big Jock was a great motivator and won the respect of all the players. His training techniques were well known and we were a very fit side. He put us through the mill, that's for sure. While it was hard work, I think he actually helped me get another couple of seasons of playing as I was so fit. There were times when I felt I could take on King Kong out on the park.

'There used to be a hill at Gullane in East Lothian which we had to run up and down goodness knows how many times. I had the best ever time amongst all the players Jock took down there. I couldn't run on the park but I could run in the sand! He used to have a stopwatch to time you and at the start of the season he would ask the young lads who had signed for the club that summer to do the runs. They just couldn't cope with it and would be crawling up on their knees and Jock would still be there, shouting at them to get to the top.

'When he took us on a Tuesday and a Thursday, we knew we were going to get gutted. On the way out to training you could have heard a pin drop, as everyone was dreading what was coming up. He might have just trained us for 45 minutes but it was non-stop. It was tough but I always regarded it as similar to taking a dose of medicine. You didn't like it but it was meant to be good for you. It worked for us, as we were so fit that we used to run all over the top of the other teams.

'He took us down to Gullane before he went to Rangers. From when I can remember, ever since the days of Tommy Walker and Johnny Harvey, Hearts have always trained down there. We were doing it long before Rangers players even knew there was a place called Gullane. It was when big Jock went to Ibrox and took the Rangers players there that they got all the publicity about running up and down the sand dunes.

'What could have been but never was always stuck in my mind about my spell with the club. It was so close yet so far but I also had a lot of happy memories of my years at Tynecastle. The camaraderie in the squad back in those days was brilliant and I think things are more serious in the modern era. I still go to Tynecastle to watch the games but I can't say I enjoy watching Scottish football.

'I'm from Leith and, while I was always a Hearts man, I did watch Hibs and I was fortunate that both Hearts and Hibs had such good sides back then. I used to go with my pals to Easter Road and it would cost us something like nine pence in the old money to get in the boys' gate. Then my dad used to take me to Tynecastle when Hearts were at home, so I was able to see a lot of good football. When the trains were running in the 1950s, my dad used to take my brother and me down to Leith Caledonian Station and we'd get the train to Dalry and then walk to Tynecastle. When Hearts had the Terrible Trio of Conn, Bauld and Wardhaugh, and Hibs had the Famous Five, we were spoilt with the football we could watch but didn't realise it at the time.

'Being captain was an honour but I was just proud to pull a Hearts jersey on all the time. Back in those days a lot of the guys really did play for the jersey, certainly more so than now, as players are a lot more mercenary with the freedom of contract which we never had.

'Wee Donald Ford was a great one for pulling a few stunts with the guys. He was a wee bit naughty and used to tell some of his teammates that certain clubs were interested in them and he'd arrange to meet the player at a certain place and when the guy did turn up there would be a bunch of Hearts players there ready to take the mickey out of him.

'Towards the end of my career in 1976, I was offered the manager's job but knocked it back and I sometimes think back and wonder how I would have got on had I taken the job. I was only 33 at the time and I didn't feel as if I wanted to be a player/manager.

'Bobby Seith was the manager at the time and we were having a bad run. I'd bought a pub in Infirmary Street called The Royal Oak, which I renamed The Pivot. One night Johnny Harvey, the chief scout, wandered in and asked to speak to me. We had a drink in the lounge downstairs and he explained that the directors of the club had told him to approach me with a view to taking over the manager's job. It came right out of the blue and I didn't know what to say, to be honest. I asked for a week to think it over but the club was struggling a bit at the time and I went in to see Johnny and told him I had decided not to take it. It is still in the back of my mind what might have happened.

'I was friendly with Alex Ferguson and look at how he has got on! I am not sure how the change from being a player one day to being the manager the following week would have worked out. Sometimes I can't help thinking, "Christ, I might have done well." But I had three kids at the time and a couple of businesses and I thought it better to give it a body swerve.

'After I knocked it back, Bobby Seith got the sack and the job went to John Hagart. He was interim boss for a spell before getting it permanently but he ended up being the first manager in the history of Hearts to get the club relegated.

'It was the players who took him down but you don't want that kind of thing on your CV. I had seen the way the club was going and that was also behind my reason to reject the chance to manage the club I had supported as a boy.'

Eamonn Bannon
(midfielder, 1976–79 and 1988–93; assistant manager, 1994–95)

'In terms of a football ground, Tynecastle was always one of the better ones in Scotland. I think most people in the game would agree that Parkhead is the best arena followed by Ibrox. But the third one in my book would be Tynecastle. It is a very good place to watch and play football, and possibly because the pitch is that bit smaller the games were a bit more intense. The stands were right up to the edge of the pitch, stacked high because of the lack of space, and that all added to the atmosphere. It was as good for the players as it was for the fans.

'Another good thing about Tynecastle was there was never a predominant slope like at Easter Road or even Fir Park. It was a nice, compact flat pitch and you never seemed bothered by any severe winds there either.

'That was from purely a player's perspective. As a spectator, it was a great place to watch football as well, although the pillars in the Main Stand could be a damn pest.

'One of my special memories was the night we beat the mighty Bayern Munich at Tynecastle on 28 February 1989. That sticks in the mind as there was such a big build-up and they were such a big team. The stadium was packed to the gunnels and we thrived on the atmosphere. The crowd was breathing down the players' necks and when the Germans were taking throw-ins, the supporters were right at them. It really was quite intimidating for them.

'When I first went to Tynecastle to join Hearts in 1976, I had just come into the professional ranks. Back then, the Hearts fans used to march from one end of the ground to the other at half-time, as they always wanted to be behind the "home" goal. Quite often, if the captain won the toss at kick-off he would choose to shoot away from the Shed in the first half to have the benefit of shooting into that end after the break, as that was when the crowd really got going.

'Initially, both dressing-rooms were large but the away one was chopped dramatically, as I think there was a feeling it was too luxurious for the opposition. I spent a while with Dundee United and the home dressing-room at Tannadice was quite small, while the away one was worse, like a cupboard, and it was a real squash in there. To be honest, it was just ridiculous and when I went back there with Hearts such a small dressing-room made me think there should be some sort of minimum-size rule.

'A lot of my other memories of Tynecastle involve the time I used to spend up in the brown gymnasium or running up and down the steps during training. If the ground outside was rock solid with frost in the winter, many a day would be spent playing head tennis or two-a-side football, as there weren't really any other facilities.'

Neil Berry (defender/midfielder, 1984–96)

'When I joined Hearts, Tynecastle was a really old stadium, although it was later brought up to standard. To be honest, I don't think it has changed for the better. When I go to games, I prefer to stand, as there is a better atmosphere with people standing. If you're sitting down and something happens, you all end up standing anyway, which seems to defeat the whole purpose.

'I remember the dressing-rooms being a bit dated and there was this one huge bath which we all used to jump into after a game. We would be covered in muck but just dived in. It was minging and I think we were actually dirtier getting out than when we went in.

'The European game against Bayern Munich was one of the biggest matches I played in, although it was also great to be part of the side that went 22 games unbeaten against Hibs. It's funny how things work in a derby because there were a number of times Hibs actually did well but didn't get a result. Not that we would let that bother us.

'One of the biggest characters I remember from my time at Tynecastle was Willie Johnston. He was a great player and really quick but he was just ridiculous when it came to training sometimes. We always used to get a tough session on a Tuesday, which normally involved long runs. We would have to do about four laps of the park but Willie would start to tail off after about a hundred yards! The flip side of that, though, was that over a 30-yard sprint he could hammer you.

'Wee Robbo, or wee Ceefax as he was known then, was another one. He seemed to know everything, the wee git. It didn't have to be just quizzes; everything we talked about he seemed to know about. He was just a mine of useless information.

'Hearts did well getting into Europe under Craig Levein as manager but if that team came up against the team I was in, at our best we'd easily have come out on top. With the likes of Gary Mackay, Kenny Black and Robbo there was a good core of players.

'One of the highlights of my career with Hearts was the season we did so well in getting so close to the League Championship and reaching the Scottish Cup final but the biggest downer ever was losing them both in the space of a week.

'It was disappointing that the European games had to be moved to Murrayfield in 2004. I went along to watch and felt there was no atmosphere whatsoever. If the matches had been played at Tynecastle, I am sure we would have seen different results.

'I spent 12 years at Tynecastle, which is a long time, and served under a host of managers such as Alex MacDonald, Sandy Jardine, Tommy McLean, Joe Jordan, Sandy Clark and finally Jim Jefferies. I have happy memories of the place, as I was well looked after by Hearts when I had my serious knee injury. For example, they sent me away on holiday to help me recover, which was a great gesture. I fought my way back but didn't play in the first team for 14 months, even though I was fit. Joe Jordan had something to do with that, though.

'Even when you weren't playing through injury there was still a bonus system in place, which helped ease the pain a bit. In general, Hearts looked after the first-team players when I was at Tynecastle, which wasn't always the case with football clubs. And that was good to see.'

Jim Bett (midfielder, 1994–95)

'Tynecastle will always be a special place for Hearts. I remember going there in my Aberdeen days and there was always a fantastic atmosphere inside the stadium because it was so enclosed, with the fans right next to you. Having Tynecastle as their home was a major bonus for the players and it was never an easy place to go to and win games.

'I was going to hang up my boots in 1994 when I came back from Iceland, where I had played for a few months after leaving Aberdeen. I had just had a knee operation and wee Tommy McLean called me to ask about going to Hearts. I said no at first but he was always on the phone pestering me to sign. He persuaded me to come down for a month to see how I liked it and I ended up staying for a year.

'I was only there a year or so but I enjoyed myself immensely and would have been there longer had wee Tommy stayed on as manager. After playing alongside him at Rangers, I enjoyed working with him as a manager. The writing was on the wall, though, when he left and a new management team came in who wanted to build a younger side. I ended up at Dundee United in the First Division but we won promotion that season and I called it quits after that. It was a nice way to finish playing football.

'I thoroughly enjoyed my time at Tynecastle. Some of the players were getting on a bit but the likes of John Robertson, John Colquhoun and Gary Mackay were all great professionals.

'One of the special games I remember was the night we defeated Rangers 4–2 in the Scottish Cup at Tynecastle. The stadium was packed, the atmosphere was fantastic and I think the match was on television as well. It was a great win for us, as Rangers were favourites for the cup that year. It proved what the team could do in a one-off situation at Tynecastle. The only disappointing thing was that we went all the way to the semi-final but lost to Airdrie at Hampden Park in a match most people were expecting us to win.

'While I was at Rangers and Aberdeen, we were always wary of going to Tynecastle. Obviously Ibrox and Parkhead were difficult places for teams to go to but Tynecastle also had that reputation. Time seemed to catch up with it, though, and if they could somehow rebuild the Main Stand, it would be a great stadium. There is loads of history attached to the place and when you're inside the ground you can just imagine all the great names from the past that have played there.'

Dave Bowman (midfielder, 1980–84)

'Tynecastle itself is so full of history and holds many great memories for me. I made my league debut there as a 16 year old against Airdrie. My dad Andy, who had also played for Hearts in the 1950s, was there that day and that was a very special moment for both of us. I think his parting shot to me was along the lines of, "None of you would have got a game in the reserves when I played."

'Having supported the club as a boy, it was a dream come true to actually play for Hearts. I just wish I had appreciated it more or taken in more at the time instead of letting it all go by without giving it much of a thought. Looking back, I realise they were great times but I took them for granted and didn't regard what happened as anything special. It was just what people did, or so I thought. Now I know differently.

'I grew up with John Robertson and Gary Mackay, and to actually end up playing in the same Hearts team as them was great. Wee Robbo and I used to live about 200 yards apart in Paisley Avenue when we went to Parson's Green Primary School. I played with Robbo from day one at school and Gary from the age of ten. Robbo and I actually went to the same classes as well, although I was cleverer than him. We actually spent so much time together that he referred to my dad as "Father".

'Despite how he looks having gone into management, I still think he appears lighter than he was at school, where he was just like a wee fat ball! We came up through the ranks together. He used to score all the goals and I used to get sent off – so things didn't change much over the years! It is a bit surreal how the three of us grew up together and then played for Hearts at the same time. It felt like I was just playing with my mates.

'There were some great times under Alex MacDonald when we were there. He took Hearts into Europe for the first time in a good few years and my one experience of European football with

"Doddie" against Paris St Germain brought home to me just what Hearts should be all about. He was one of the real characters of Tynecastle and it was great to work with him and the likes of Sandy Jardine, Jimmy Bone and Willie Johnston. They liked to burn the candle at both ends but they were also great professionals and I think that stood myself, wee Robbo and Gary in good stead. Much of our development at Tynecastle was down to guys like Doddie, Jimmy and Willie. They trained hard. In fact, the best thing they used to say to us was, "You should train the way you play. " They didn't want performances to be like a light switch that could be flicked on and off. It was a great lesson to learn early on in our careers.

'I left Hearts towards the end of 1984 when Coventry City made an offer for me which the club accepted. It is strange but even back then the club needed the money. I remember sitting talking to wee Robbo at the time and we knew that somebody was going to have to move. It was difficult to leave at first but I just had to get on with it. I had always wanted to try England, although maybe under different circumstances.

'It would have been great to have spent longer at Tynecastle. The team went on a decent run under Alex MacDonald and qualified for Europe again, and that is something I would like to have savoured again with Hearts.

'At the start of my career at Tynecastle I was always referred to as "Andy Bowman's son" and was never really known by my own name. When I left, though, I was my own person. I was recognised as Dave Bowman, which pleased me.

'I think Tynecastle was one of the best "new" grounds after it had been upgraded. The likes of my old club Dundee United, Dundee and Motherwell have all done well with their improvements over the years but for me Tynecastle was always a great venue for a football match. I went back there as a United player and it was great to come up against wee Robbo. I knew when he was going to dive, so I just stood out of the way.

'I lost a few cup finals while I was at Tannadice but did win the Scottish Cup. That was a great day but seeing Hearts lift the same trophy in 1998 gave me just as big a thrill, even though I wasn't involved with the club. I still enjoy going back now and again and I must admit I envy the guys I see playing there. I often wish I could do it all over again. The mind is willing but the body isn't. One thing is for sure, though, Tynecastle still has a special place in my heart.'

Jimmy Brown (goalkeeper, 1942–52)

'We were playing Queen of the South at Tynecastle when I dislocated my right shoulder. I remember our defence had been caught square by a through pass and I was in a race with Billy Houliston to get to the bouncing ball first. Billy was a nice chap and a good pal of mine but he certainly made his presence felt. I had to dive and punch clear because had I held the ball I would have carried it outside my area.

'As the ball flew in the air I kept looking to see where it was going and as a result I landed on my right side. As soon as I hit the ground, I knew something bad had happened. It was very painful and while you could usually move these things back into place, the Hearts trainer Johnny Torbett couldn't do it on the pitch on this occasion.

'I eventually walked off with Johnny's assistance and went back into the dressing-room before an ambulance took me to hospital, where the shoulder was reset under anaesthetic. That is one of my more painful memories of Tynecastle and ever since then my movement has been restricted a bit. That put me out of the game for a wee while and had I not been injured I think I could have stayed at Hearts.

'Tommy Walker took over from Dave McLean and he released me after a while. For a goalkeeper a shoulder dislocation is dodgy and with mine being a recurring injury, Tommy maybe had that in mind when he allowed me to leave.

'I signed for Malcolm McDonald at Kilmarnock and it turned out to be a good move for me, although I didn't think so at the time as I had wanted to end my career at Tynecastle. I won promotion with Killie to the First Division and while leaving Tynecastle was initially disappointing I was actually very fortunate, as I managed to play for a good number of years after that.

'I had started my footballing days at Bayview Youth Club, which used East Fife's pitch. Dave McLean was manager at East Fife and eventually went to Hearts. He was the main reason I moved to Tynecastle, as had he stayed at East Fife, I am sure I would have signed for them.

'Tynecastle was a great ground for us, although I am not sure if outsiders appreciated it in the same way as we did. Top of the list of games must be the derbies against Hibs – they were great occasions. Although they had a great side with the likes of Jimmy Kerr, Eddie Turnbull and Gordon Smith, we always seemed to have the sign over them and kept beating them.'

Drew Busby (striker, 1973–79)

'The greatest player I ever played with at Tynecastle was Rab Prentice. He supplied some fantastic crosses for me to score from. My favourite game, which showed Tynecastle in its true light, was when Willie Bauld turned up for a match against Kilmarnock after being away from the place for years.

'It was a midweek match, the place was packed and I scored with a header. There was a real special atmosphere and probably the fact Bauld was there contributed to it but, whatever the reason, it was a great night.

'We had some great European nights at Tynecastle and I scored against Lokomotiv Leipzig when we won 5–1 on 29 September 1976. I enjoyed taking penalties and got 12 out of 12 before missing my 13th at Tynecastle. It was a penalty shoot-out against Dundee United in the League Cup on 16 November 1977 and I was taking the fourth kick. I ran up and slipped, and the ball didn't even reach the goals. Not my best effort, although we won the shoot-out 4–3.

'I don't get along to Tynecastle much now. But when I do go, I enjoy it. Playing for Hearts was a good period of my career and we had an excellent side.'

Sandy Clark
(striker, 1984–89, coach 1990–93, manager, 1993–94)

'Growing up, I was very much an Airdrie fan, so even before I joined Hearts I had been used to going along to Tynecastle as an opposition supporter and it was a place I always enjoyed. Although I had a real feel for the ground, I never at that point expected to spend ten years of my career there. I thoroughly enjoyed my time as a player, coach and a manager, and I still enjoy going back, although it is a completely different environment stadium-wise.

'Alex MacDonald signed me from Rangers in 1984 and if I can remember correctly the fee was £35,000. At the time, though, Hearts were in a very poor financial position and, while it was a good deal for Hearts, the payment was made in 14 instalments of £2,500. That's how skint the club was.

'I was lucky in that I had an affiliation with the fans right away; maybe it was my style of play, but I know the supporters appreciated guys who played for the jersey. I was good to them and they were good to me.

'The next period of time, through '85–'86, was probably the most enjoyable of my playing career. We put in a lot but ended up with nothing. I remember playing Clydebank on 26 April 1986 and we struggled to win 1–0, Gary Mackay scoring the winner. At that stage, a lot of fans had come back to the club because of the run we had been on and the relief both on and off the park was incredible. Tynecastle at that time really did have a superb atmosphere and it was a great place to play your football.

'Alex gave me the chance to be a coach there in the spring of 1990 and it was an easy decision for me to make. It was very much a happy place and there was a good social scene at the club. Les Porteous was the secretary and his door was always open to everybody. There was a good bond between the directors, the manager and the players, and a lot of it took place in his room. Everybody was just happy to be at their work.

'Three years later, I became manager and it was a real privilege for me to accept that position. I took over from Joe Jordan and knew the club inside out. My previous job was coaching the reserves and the youths, and I knew the playing staff well. The transition was therefore very easy to make. Joe had decided not to play too many of the promising youngsters coming through. Maybe he didn't know them as well as I did but I was certainly more than happy to play guys like Allan Johnston, Gary Locke and Kevin Thomas.

'The young players who were there proved something of a salvation. But it turned out to be a bad time for me to take over.

'It was quite hurtful the way things finished when my contract was terminated. I had a massive chip on my shoulder for a long time, as I felt the rug had been pulled from under my feet through no fault of my own. That was hard to take but at least I was young enough to bounce back from it. The daft thing is that every time I went back to Tynecastle after that as a manager, I never lost a game. The biggest piece of revenge I enjoyed against Robinson was when St Johnstone beat Hearts 3–0 in the League Cup semi-final at Easter Road. That gave me immense satisfaction.

'I actually could have been back at Tynecastle as manager. After Jim Jefferies and Billy Brown left the club, Chris Robinson approached the St Johnstone chairman Geoff Brown and asked him for permission to speak to me. I told Geoff that I wasn't interested – I just couldn't go back and work for the person who had put me and my family through so much heartbreak. I suppose I could have bitten the bullet and taken the job. But knowing my nature, at some point in time the past would have come up and it might not have been very pleasant. I couldn't go back when he was still there and I don't think I am alone in saying I am quite happy he has now gone.'

Alfie Conn Jnr (striker, 1980–81)

'My first memory of Tynecastle isn't so much about the ground but the excitement I felt crossing the Forth Rail Bridge on a steam train on my way there. I was about six and my grandfather Willie Baxter used to take me from our home in Fife to Edinburgh to see my dad play. I can't remember much about the games he played in but I do remember the steam train. For a six-year-old boy it was a great thrill being in one.

'With my dad such a Hearts legend, I always had a soft spot for them. I started out playing football with Musselburgh Windsor in the same team as Jim Jefferies and Billy Brown. As a schoolboy, I started training with Hearts but ended up signing for Rangers instead.

'To be honest, out of all the grounds I played at during my career Tynecastle was always my bogey one, which is ironic considering my dad had his best footballing experiences there.

'I always used to have a rotten game there when I played against Hearts. Even after I signed for them, I don't think the fans saw the best of me. I must admit when I did play for them it was difficult. I was 28 when Bobby Moncur signed me but I only played at Tynecastle for nine months.

'It was hard because when things weren't going right the fans always compared me with my dad and said I wasn't as good as him. Dad was a Hearts legend and obviously was a hard act to follow but I'm pleased I played for the same club as him all the same.'

Alfie Conn Snr (inside-right, 1944–58)

'It was a great club to be with, and to be in the same team as Willie Bauld and Jimmy Wardhaugh was a tremendous privilege. We made our first appearance together on 9 October 1948 and marked the occasion in style with a 6–1 hammering of East Fife in a League Cup tie at Tynecastle. I scored two, Willie got a hat-trick and Davie Laing scored with a penalty.

'They were great guys and, my goodness, could they play football. Jimmy did all the hard work for the three of us. He just never stopped running and was a very hard worker for the team. Me and Willie were just there for passing and scoring, whereas Jimmy did it all on his own with his hard graft.

'As far as I was concerned, they were two fabulous players. Willie looked a lazy type but his brain was working all the time. People may have thought he was slow but his brain was quick. It was a great trio, although the name "terrible" stuck after it was used in the papers. It was marvellous to play alongside them and I thoroughly enjoyed it. We were lucky as the side was packed full of good players from Jimmy Brown in goal right through the side. The fact so much attention was paid to the three of us maybe took some praise away from the rest of the lads and Willie tended to be the centre of the attraction with his marvellous ability with his head as well as his feet.

'I was a miner in Prestonpans when I signed for Hearts and when I joined, I thought I'd won a million dollars. I just drifted into the club, met the boys and they were all pals. It was all marvellous stuff. I can't really recall how much I was paid at Tynecastle but, to be honest, I'd have been happy to have played for nothing. If Hearts had asked me to play but told me I wasn't going to get any money, I'd have been delighted. I say that without hesitation and I think most of the players back then would have been the same.

'Apart from the changes to the stands, I don't think the stadium has altered that much since I was there. There were always big crowds watching us but, to be honest, we never paid much attention to the fans. I never thought about them during games. Thirty thousand was maybe the normal attendance back then but we weren't really aware of the supporters because when we didn't have the ball we were looking at the opposition and when we did have possession we were trying to score. Sometimes you might have heard somebody shout something at you but that didn't happen very often.

'Dave McLean wasn't just a manager, he was a great manager, and I'd imagine that everybody in the team enjoyed every second they were there. And then Tommy Walker came in and carried on his good work.

'Brown, Parker, McKenzie, Cox, Dougan, Laing, Sloan, Conn, Bauld, Wardhaugh and Urquhart. I can remember the names vividly and I'm sure a lot of the supporters will remember them, too. There is no doubt in my mind Hearts will come back again to be as good as we were back in those days. Tynecastle was a great place to play and a great team to be in. It was such an enjoyable time and, let's face it, when you are enjoying your football, you play better.'

Scott Crabbe (striker, 1985–92)

'There were a few characters around the club when I signed, with the likes of Willie Johnston and Jimmy Bone already there. I'd come in straight from school and wee Robbo was my boyhood hero.

'Wee Bud and Jimmy were unbelievable. I remember one day when I hadn't long started and I was told to stay behind to do the washing while the guys went training. I was waiting on the machine finishing when I heard these feet running along the corridor. The door was barged open and there was Kenny Black and Dave Bowman. They didn't know my name and just looked at me and said, "Don't say anything about this, wee man."

'Bow then proceeded to get a hold of Bud's beige flannels – Willie was a wee bit older than the rest of the players – held them tight and Kenny Black cut them right across the knees. Bow then stapled them back up at the knee and ran out again. I couldn't believe it and thought to myself, "What's going on here?" There was no way I was going to tell anybody, so I watched them all come back from training and spotted Willie looking at his trousers. He wasn't saying much so I began to wonder if that sort of thing happened every day.

'Blacky and Bow were nowhere to be seen but came in about half an hour later and started to look about for Willie. They soon saw him sitting in the old big bath in the dressing-room with their gear on! He thought they must have thought he was stupid but he quickly sussed them out, as they were the only two who were left behind for treatment when the rest went out training! He knew it was either them or me who had stayed to do the washing. There was obviously no chance of it being me, as I had just been in the door for two minutes. Wee Bud then tore his trousers off at the staples and wore the cut-down version and his brogues on the train back to Kirkcaldy that day! Seeing him walk out of Tynecastle like that was absolutely hilarious. It was just his way of making a point that he was the experienced pro and nothing would bother him. That was one of my first experiences of Tynecastle and I wondered what I'd let myself in for.

'I used to go in and make the boys' tea in the morning and wee Willie and Jimmy Bone would be in there having a cuppa with wee Mary, the tea woman. There was one toilet in her room and the first week I was there I walked in to get the teapot and cups and saw smoke coming up from behind the closed toilet door. It was wee Bud having a quick fag before he went out training!

'From the playing side, I have some great memories. I made my debut at 17 against Clydebank at Tynecastle under Alex MacDonald and Sandy Jardine. I was putting tape around my finger when Malcolm Murray asked me if I was all right. I assured him I was fine, only to look down and see my hand absolutely shaking!

'I remember scoring the first goal in a 2–1 win over Celtic at Parkhead – John Millar scored the other one – around the festive period. We were top of the league and had a big party at Dave McPherson's house that night as we thought it could be our year, but Rangers came and pipped us after we suffered a horrendous run of results.

'The end of my time at Hearts was very emotional. I made my last appearance for the club on the bench against Slavia Prague on 30 September 1992 but very few people knew that I had already signed for Dundee United. We had been staying in the Marine Hotel in North Berwick but I had gone to Dundee to talk to Jim McLean and signed for United. Joe Jordan needed me for the bench but United wanted the signing to go through so I could play for them on the Saturday. If I remember rightly, the Prague game was on a Wednesday and I'd put pen to paper the day before. The form was dated for the Friday. Had I been needed that night, I could have played for Hearts having already signed for United.

'I came back up the road and was scared to speak to anyone, even Robbo or Gary [Mackay]. I couldn't bring myself to say anything, knowing I was going to be on the bench and maybe have to come on. I kept the whole thing to myself, although the manager knew I had signed. I was only ever going to be needed in an emergency and as it transpired we won 4–2 and I didn't play.

'At the final whistle, I'll always remember running on to the pitch and the first person I went to was wee Robbo. I told him, "Listen, wee man, I'm away." He just looked at me and replied, "What do you mean?" It was at that point I told him I'd signed for United and that I wanted to throw my strip to the crowd. He told me to go ahead and do it.

'I have to admit I cried all night. Joe was still speaking after the match but I went into the old kit room next to the dressing-room and was down on my knees crying my eyes out when Bert Logan and George McNeill came in. It was such a wrench and it really was a nightmare. Wallace Mercer was in a different class, though. He walked me out to the centre of the park after everything had died down and had a quiet word with me to settle me down. He said I'd been a great servant to Hearts and was quite sincere with everything he said.

'He made me think about just what I had done for the club and insisted it was a good move for me and urged me to go and better myself as a player. It was really good of him but at the same time it was strange being out there knowing that I wouldn't be wearing a Hearts jersey again.

'I went home to my dad, who hadn't been at the game, and just grabbed him. To leave the club I had supported as a boy and then played for had a huge effect on me and I never anticipated being so upset. So much had gone on in the previous two weeks that I think the build-up just got to me in the end.

'Funnily enough, I was back at Tynecastle about three weeks later with United. Jim had asked me on the Friday if I wanted to play and stressed to me that he'd seen it all before where players had gone back to their old clubs and ended up not doing well as they had been trying too hard. I was desperate to play but it turned out he was bang on – I had a nightmare! I had a total shocker in the first half because I was trying too hard and he came up to me in the dressing-room and said, "You've got five minutes; it's not happening for you out there." I said, "Yeah, fair enough." But he was adamant, "You've got five minutes." And guess what? I was off after five minutes! It's fair to say I learned never to doubt his judgement.'

Jim Cruickshank (goalkeeper, 1960–77)

'I spent 17 years with Hearts and the first year I was there I think I only played four league games, the first against Ayr United at

Somerset Park on 15 October 1960. One game I remember playing well in was in the East of Scotland Shield against Hibs, which we won 3–1.

'I also enjoyed our good run in the Texaco Cup in the 1970–71 season. To have the teams from Scotland playing the English ones was a good idea but the tournament eventually died a death. I remember playing Burnley down there and before the game the referee told me he was the best friend I had and that nobody could touch me. Well, the first corner came in and I went to get the ball and this guy came in and put me in the back of the net. The next ball came in and the same thing happened, and the ball hit the back of the net. I asked the ref, "What's the story here?" to which he replied, "You should have got out of the way!" We lost the first leg 3–1 to Burnley but we won the second leg 4–1 and went all the way to the final, where we lost to Wolves.

'People made a lot about my penalty save from Joe Davis in the New Year's Day derby against Hibs when I also stopped two rebounds. I have always thought I should have held the first shot, though, rather than taking three attempts. I think the problem was the ground was brick hard except for the goalmouths. They had a crazy idea back then of putting boards down in the goal so for a yard the pitch was soft and elsewhere it was solid. Once I came off that I was all over place! Joe Davis hit it to the left and instead of holding it I only succeeded in pushing it back out to him. He hit again and I blocked it and then it went out to someone else and I stopped it again.

'One thing that upset me was that John Hagart had asked me which of the two goalkeepers he was looking at should he go for. I liked the look of this guy we had over from Hong Kong and told him he was different class. He then went and signed the other one from Arbroath on a free transfer!

'I remember spending a night with Pat Stanton and talking about who our favourite player was in our teams of the time. He picked Jimmy O'Rourke and I always went for George Fleming. Fleming went on to really make his name with Dundee United but he was the hardest working wee man we had in our team for years.

'The best captain we had for cup matches was George Miller. As soon as he arrived from Dunfermline, we started to get to the finals or semi-finals quite regularly. The best defence I had in front of me was Davie Holt at left-back, Chris Shevlane at right-back and Willie Polland at centre-half. We had a great rapport and were a really solid unit.

'I left in the summer of 1977, two years after the supporters held a gala night for me in an Edinburgh cinema. Somebody had gone out and filmed me in training and it was quite funny. That wasn't anything to do with the club, which did nothing for me. I got absolutely nothing from them. I was supposed to get a testimonial but it never happened. I wanted it in writing but they wouldn't do that. We had got to the 1975–76 Scottish Cup final and were due to go on a tour round the world. But I wasn't going to go unless I got some guarantees over a testimonial. John Hagart said he was 99 per cent sure I'd get one and would think about it. I told him to think about it otherwise I wouldn't go on the tour and, indeed, I didn't bother with the trip. The club had freed David Graham and had to bring him back and take him! The following season I was in the team and played against Lokomotiv Leipzig and assumed I'd be in the side for the next Euro match. That wasn't the case, though, and I didn't play again until we faced Dumbarton in the Scottish Cup something like five months later.

'At the end I was called in and told the board wanted to thank me for my services and that was it. I said I would never go back and I never did. Some players say that, like Willie Bauld, but do end up going back. Not me, though. Why should I go to Tynecastle? I played plenty of times there. I've been there, done it and got the T-shirt.'

Iain Ferguson (striker, 1988–90)

'Those lucky enough to be there on 28 February 1989 will never forget how Hearts nearly put the mighty Bayern Munich to the sword at Tynecastle.

'Nobody had given us much chance in the first-leg clash against the Bundesliga giants. However, football's history is potted with fairytales and my goal, which won the game, was one of my greatest moments in football.

'I have great memories of the night at Tynecastle and to win the first leg was a great achievement. It was a shame we lost over in Germany and subsequently the tie over two legs.

'It was a big occasion for the club and to score the winner like I did was a bit special. It was all the more memorable as I didn't even know I was playing until the morning of the game. I'd even given away my complimentary tickets, as I didn't think I was going to be involved. But it turned out to be a terrific evening for everyone connected with Hearts. I was lucky enough to enjoy scoring goals on a number of big occasions and I certainly enjoyed facing European opposition.'

Thomas Flogel (midfielder, 1997–2002)

'The first time I saw Tynecastle was with Jim Jefferies, who showed me around the place after I had turned down the chance to join Dundee following a trial with them. I basically fell in love as soon as I walked out of the tunnel and saw the two huge Hearts signs in the stand facing me.

'Tynecastle was different from the stadiums in Austria which I had been used to and I knew that I wanted to play my football there. Within a couple of hours, I had signed a contract and that was the beginning of five very happy years in Edinburgh.

'I was surprised at how close the supporters were to the pitch and, with the team doing so well, there was a brilliant atmosphere in my first season. I started up front then moved slowly backwards into almost every position apart from goalkeeper.

'One thing which sticks in my mind is when I brought my son Alec, who was born in Edinburgh, to Tynecastle to see a game. He was born in 2000 and he was maybe six months old at the time. I was playing that afternoon and he was sitting in the crowd with my wife cheering me on. He was sitting there clapping his hands. It was unbelievable. Normally he would have been upset because of the noise of the crowd but he was quite happy clapping away.

'When he was a bit older, I took him to an open day at the club and to see my son run about the pitch was brilliant. We actually gave Alec a second name of Scott in honour of the country where he was born and we always feel welcome when we come back.'

Donald Ford (striker, 1964–76)

'Tynecastle is a magnificent ground and I got very angry when it was suggested the club would have to move away from it. It is their home and always should be. As a player, the backing you got from the crowd was fantastic and the opposition never enjoyed taking us on.

'I spent 12 good years with Hearts and saw the team and the stadium change. I was signed by Tommy Walker, a quiet man who did a great job. When he started, the game was more about individual talent than team tactics and, to be truthful, when tactics and the need for a team unit came to the fore, he struggled a bit. After I signed in 1964, I played amateur for two years to allow me time to sit my chartered accountancy exams.

'Like many fans, one of my favourite memories of Tynecastle is the goal I scored which knocked Rangers out of the Scottish Cup back on 13 May 1968. For a while I used to ask myself why so many people remembered that goal in particular. I think, looking back, the reason was the win that night summed up everything that is good about Hearts and Tynecastle.

'We had drawn the first game at Ibrox on 9 May and 44,000 people had packed the ground for the replay. I remember running out and noticing that they were still helping kids over the wall and because there were so many of them they were sitting around the track. I remember there was only a couple of minutes left when I got past Dave McKinnon, the Rangers defender, and slotted the ball into the net. The place erupted and everyone who was there remembers the game vividly.

'Scottish Cup matches have always been special for Hearts and the supporters always followed us wherever we used to go. I remember we played Partick Thistle in the 1973–74 season and 12,000 people watched us draw 1–1 at Tynecastle on 16 February 1974. It was the time of the power strikes and because of that the replay started in the afternoon at Firhill rather than in the evening. We all thought not many Hearts supporters would get away from work. Somehow, however, they did and there were thousands of them at the game, which we won 4–1 and which was made even more special for me as I scored a hat-trick.

'The other match I remember that maybe not many other people do is when I scored a hat-trick against Kilmarnock in a friendly game with a difference. At the end of the 1964–65 season Hearts lost the league in the last game of the season to Kilmarnock when they beat us 2–0 at Tynecastle. In the summer after that, we went on a pre-season tour of Norway and because Willie Wallace had been left behind as he had refused to sign a new contract, I was given my chance for a regular first-team place.

'Our first game after that tour was against Kilmarnock at Tynecastle in a friendly organised by the SFA, which around 12,000 people attended, a turn-out which stunned me. It was an experimental match in that they extended the 18-yard line to run all the way to the touchline and players couldn't be offside unless they crossed that line. That meant there was all that extra space in the opposition half where you could run about and not worry about offside unless you were ahead of the last defender in the 18-yard area.

'I loved all that extra space. I scored five goals and we won 8–2. I thought it was an experiment that worked but we heard nothing about it afterwards. Looking back, because the SFA didn't take the experiment of changing the offside rule any further, it was a bit of a waste of time and my five goals at Tynecastle were forgotten.

'My favourite time as a player was during the 1973–74 season, when I scored 29 goals, 18 of them in 29 league games. My life was made easier because I had such great players beside me. Rab Prentice was an outside-left who was a magnificent crosser of the ball, while big Drew Busby just barged past players and made my life very easy.

'We have had some great players in the past, going way back to Alfie Conn, Jimmy Wardhaugh, Alex Young and Willie Bauld. For me, though, the best player I took the field with at Tynecastle has to be Willie Hamilton. He was an inside-forward who was a football genius. It's a tragedy there isn't any video footage available, as the things he did with a football would inspire. Willie died aged just 38 and football lost a real star.

'I still go to Tynecastle with my son Alistair, who is a season-ticket holder, and I hope the club enjoys good times, as the supporters deserve real success.'

Cammy Fraser (midfielder, 1973–80)

'Hearts signed me just when I thought I wasn't going to be good enough to play for anyone. Dundee United had freed me at the age of 15 because Jim McLean thought I was too wee. That was that as far as I was concerned. He was the top man at the time and if he thought I was too small to make it, then I reckoned I was finished.

'Within about six weeks, though, I had signed on at Tynecastle and never looked back. I had scored a hat-trick in my first Junior game for Lochee United in a derby against Lochee Harp at Thomson Park in Dundee when someone from Hearts who had been at the game asked me if I would be prepared to go to Tynecastle on the Monday for signing talks.

'I'd never even been to Edinburgh before but I didn't have a job, having just left school, and decided to give it a go. I think my first wage on the ground staff was about £13 a week. The groundsman at that time was Willie Montgomery. He was a real character who did a great job looking after the pitch. He was a bit of a friendly ogre, if you like, and if he wanted us to sweep the terraces or replace divots instead of going training, the manager had to let us go otherwise nothing would get done.

'I have a lot of memories of the old Tynecastle, especially the enclosure opposite the Main Stand, which used to be rocking when the team was doing well. One incident I recall was during a home game against Falkirk when Bobby Prentice got the ball from Jim Cruickshank in the left-back position and ran the length of the park, beating what seemed like everyone before he got into the box. He then turned around and came back the other way, beating them all again. He might even have passed it back to Cruicks.

'Another funny moment was when Eamonn Bannon hit a penalty right into the school during one match. He came up to take the kick and sent the ball sailing over the terracings into the playground at the School End!

'John Cumming used to take us on training runs up the

Pentlands. He was a great man but these runs used to last as long as he could – which was always longer than us. I'll never forget the day when Jim Cruickshank stopped for a cigarette behind a bush and then waited to catch up with us as we came back down the hill.

'Having been signed by Bobby Seith I made my first-team debut at the age of 16 and it was great to play in a side with guys like Alan Anderson, Dave Clunie, Jim Cruickshank and Donald Ford. It was also an honour to be a teammate of Drew Busby. He'd been with Third Lanark before they went defunct and used to tell us all sorts of stories about himself and Drew Jarvie up front.

'I always remember Bobby Moncur booted me out of Hearts without even a phone call, which was quite strange after nearly eight years at Tynecastle. The Dundee boss at the time, Donald Mackay, who had been the coach of my school team in Dundee, called me on the Thursday and asked if I'd come up to Dens Park the following day for signing talks. I asked what the situation was with Hearts and he said things had been sorted out at that end. So that was it. I called Willie Gibson – my wife is his cousin – to bring my boots over on the Friday morning – and headed to Dundee without having the chance to say goodbye to all the lads.

'The transfer was rushed through and I made my debut at home to Meadowbank Thistle on the Saturday. The move also took me back home and it proved to be the right decision. Although things ended on something of a sour note, I'll always be grateful to Hearts for giving me the career I had.

'I went back to Tynecastle on a number of occasions with both Dundee and Rangers, with a fair degree of success, it must be said. I've also visited Tynecastle a few times but, to be honest, the ground isn't the same with the seats having been put in and I think it's lost a lot with the new look.

'One of my trips back was to make a Hearts Supporters' Club's player of the year award to Scott Severin. It was the silver anniversary of the award and as I had won it 25 years previously, I was asked to do the presentation. It was hard for me to believe that here I was handing over a trophy with my name engraved on it to someone who wasn't even born when I won it. I didn't consider myself too old at the time, being 47, but it certainly got me thinking.'

Stevie Fulton (midfielder, 1995–2002)

'There is no doubt in my mind that Tynecastle played a significant role in our Scottish Cup win in 1998. We were drawn at home in every round, which was a major advantage and certainly made things easier for us. As well as the benefit of playing so many ties at home, we also avoided Premier League opposition until the final. We got on something of a roll and even in the league that year not many teams left Tynecastle with full points.

'I think what we achieved in the cup that season best sums up the advantage Tynecastle gave us. We could tell that the crowd believed that we could do something that year and we picked up that optimism as a team. The better we did, the bigger the crowds and the better the atmosphere, so the whole thing had a real knock-on effect.

'The celebrations the day after the Scottish Cup win will live on for ever in the minds of the people who were there. What got me was the number of people on the streets outside Tynecastle, only for us to be then told the stadium was full as well. A lot of the supporters had been waiting for hours for the team to arrive and it was quite a sight.

'The gaffer had told us beforehand what it would mean for Hearts to win the Scottish Cup but none of us could have imagined just how many folk would come out to celebrate. I am sure we would have filled Parkhead a few times over that day, as there were thousands of people out on the streets. I remember my kids running about on the park kicking a ball, having a great time, and probably thinking that winning a cup was quite normal.

'I always found the Hearts crowds great and the year after the cup win was a prime example, as, even though things weren't going so well for us on the park, they really stood by us.

'Under Craig Levein, the team seemed to move on to a different level, finishing third two seasons in a row and doing well in Europe. But I am sure most Hearts supporters would have swapped all that for another cup win.

'I didn't have to think twice about signing for Hearts when I was given the chance and my first game for the club at Tynecastle was against Raith Rovers on 14 October 1995. I had played there for Celtic before the stadium was redeveloped and for me the new stands gave it a better atmosphere. It was always good with the big terracings but even better when it became less open and more enclosed with all the seats.

'To be honest, I felt the old ground was a bit scary when playing for the opposition. I can always remember having to take corner kicks with Celtic and just wanting to put the ball down and take it as quickly as possible, as there would be all sorts of things flying at me. I certainly didn't want to hang around any longer than was necessary. Having said that, I enjoyed a few good results for Celtic at Tynecastle and it was always a ground where I felt comfortable playing – Pittodrie was another one I liked.

'The stadium obviously wasn't as big as most grounds in the Premiership in England but it was still able to produce a brilliant atmosphere. I am sure the Old Firm players enjoyed going there because even though they were used to playing in front of far bigger crowds, Tynecastle could generate a fair amount of noise with 12–14,000 fans inside.

'One other highlight of my time there that sticks out was scoring twice against Hibs at Tynecastle in the year we won the cup. Although we didn't win that particular game, as it finished 2–2, it still gave me great satisfaction, as I always took a fair a bit of stick from the Hibs fans.

'There is no doubt that Tynecastle has a special place in Scottish football history and the demonstrations against the board when Murrayfield came onto the agenda showed that a lot of people didn't want to move. It's the club's spiritual home and the protests underlined just how much the ground meant to people. After all, Celtic and Rangers fans wouldn't want to leave Parkhead or Ibrox, so why should Hearts fans be any different?

'I had a thoroughly enjoyable time with Hearts and didn't want to leave. I felt I had another two good seasons left in me when I had to go. But these things happen in football and life goes on. I moved to Kilmarnock under Jim Jefferies again and have to admit it felt weird going back to Tynecastle for the first time with Killie. Kilmarnock lost the match that day but the reception I received from the supporters was brilliant and made me appreciate my time there even more. Don't get me wrong, I was trying my hardest to beat Hearts and I'm sure everybody understood that had to be the case. But I never got any stick from the fans and I think that must be the first time in years I had been to an away ground and not taken abuse from the home support. Mind you, I am not sure it would have been the same had Killie won!'

Freddie Glidden (centre-half, 1946–59)

'Hearts signed me in 1946, having seen me play for Murrayfield Rovers, and the story surrounding that is actually quite funny. I was working in St Andrew's House and got a phone call asking me to come to the reception, as there was a Mr Fraser wanting to talk to me. That was the name of my local minister in Stoneyburn and I couldn't think for the life of me what he would be wanting with me.

'I went along and there was Mr Fraser, except this person happened to be the Hearts scout who wanted me to go to Tynecastle to meet Davie McLean, the manager at the time. All sorts of things had been racing through my mind but what I thought was going to be a meeting with a man of the cloth was actually the start of my Hearts career.

'I was actually half a season at Whitburn Juniors before Hearts took me and sent me to Newtongrange Star, which was the normal custom in those days for lads signed provisionally. They were basically a nursery team for Hearts in those days and we got a good apprenticeship, as we would play against old miners who were slow but good at bringing the young ones down to their speed! I was there a couple of years and Willie Bauld was actually there in my second season, so we played in the same junior team for a while.

'Eventually I went to Tynecastle and at that time Hearts had three teams running: there was a team in the East of Scotland league, a reserve team, which played in the North Eastern League, and also the first team. Virtually all of the boys were local from Edinburgh and district, so we all got to know each other pretty quickly. There was no foreign influence at all in those days and that helped newcomers to settle in. There were a certain number who were full time but many more who were part time, including myself, as I was working with the West Lothian water department.

'I used to train on a Tuesday and a Thursday night, and was lucky if I got a game with the third team on the Saturday. The most a player would get in the second team was about £6 a week, which I suppose was quite a bit of money if you had another job to go to. One of my favourite stories is when we played in the final of the Scottish Cup in 1956. We got £100 a man but by the time I had tax taken off, I had £66 3s 4d for winning the Scottish Cup in front of something like 134,000 fans at Hampden.

'My debut for Hearts came at Tynecastle against Queen of the South in November 1951 and I remember it being a bit of a baptism of fire, as it was one of the few occasions I was at right-back and that day I was up against a fellow called Jackie Oakes, who was a flying machine. I thoroughly enjoyed it, as I was a fit young fellow back then.

'I started off playing at inside-right and then gradually moved to right-half. That's where I basically played at Tynecastle until Bobby Dougan got injured and I was moved to centre-half, where I stayed for quite a long time after that.

'The proudest moment of my time with Hearts has to be the 1956 Scottish Cup final when I captained the side to victory at Hampden. We had a wonderful side and it was a great day. I regret that television was just in its infancy back then, as I have to rely on newspaper cuttings and my own memories. Actually my father-in-law was an avid fan and he started collecting all the little cuttings from the *Evening News* and the *Dispatch* from the late 1940s and put them in a book, which he called 'This Is Your Life, Freddie Glidden'. I have a lot of stuff that I would never have had if it had not been for his foresight.

'After the win at Hampden, the team bus took us back from Glasgow via Whitburn and Blackburn, where I stayed, and my mother and father were standing at the gate of my house waiting for us to come along the road. We passed right through, allowing them to congratulate us, and then carried on into Livingston Station, where Tommy Walker was brought up. It was a bit of a circuitous route back to Edinburgh but we eventually arrived at the Maybury to pick up an open-top bus. From then on it was an absolute sea of people all the way in along Princes Street to the North British Hotel, with me, of course, at the front with the cup! It was sheer euphoria. We had our tea there, were congratulated by all sorts of people and then made our way home and that was it.

'I had actually driven to Tynecastle that morning in my own car but had to get somebody to pick it up for me and take it home. We had a great set of boys and everyone got on well with each other, which is quite difficult in a football team. None of us really drank at all and if we had the odd glass of sherry that was considered big time.

'I was fortunate enough to win all the domestic honours with Hearts but the 1956 Scottish Cup win was the sweetest as the club hadn't won it for something like the previous 50 years. We were the first team to bring it back to Tynecastle after that run and it is something I'll never forget.

'Things have certainly changed over the years but one thing which sticks in my mind is that in all the time I played, I don't remember having my jersey pulled once, as that just wasn't part of the game. I think I'd get very annoyed if I was playing in the modern era – I just have to look at the penalty box in a game when a corner is being taken and it looks like there is a war breaking out with everyone shoving and pulling each other.

'The ball, of course, was much heavier in the old days. People use to talk about the Terrible Trio, and say that when they were on their day Willie Bauld would run down the wing and cross the ball over with the lace facing away for Alfie Conn to head it.

'It sounds funny but the only seats at Tynecastle when I played were in the stand – the other three sides were terracings. In the 1950s, before there was any trouble at matches, a lot of Hearts fans used to stand behind the opposition keeper's goal for the first half and then walk round for the same thing for the second half.

'Tommy McKenzie was one of the real characters who used to play a lot of practical jokes on guys and we all used to fall for them. One I remember actually happened in South Africa. We were out buying fruit for ourselves and a lot of us had bought pineapples. Well, Tommy got hold of one of them, nipped the top off it and spooned out all the insides. He then put an apple inside it to give it a bit of weight before pinning the top back on. It goes without saying that the lad who went to have his pineapple got the surprise of his life!

'That's the sort of thing which used to happen with us but it was really just part of the tremendous camaraderie in the team and kept everyone together well. Another like that was John Cumming. He was super fit and always on the go, and I remember a funny tale from a trip to Canada with Hearts. We were actually mates sharing the same room and I wanted to lie in my bed one day while he wanted to go out somewhere. He kept telling me to get up but I wasn't interested and before I knew it he had taken the bed, the kind that folded up into the wall, and shut me up in the wall. He just put it back up with me inside it, which was a bit of a laugh.

'Leaving Tynecastle in 1959 was the saddest part of my career and it was a very emotional day when I walked out of the ground for the last time. I had hurt my back halfway through the season before and it was one of those niggling things that wouldn't go away. It meant I was never at my very best, although I was also getting on a bit by then. I was sorry to leave. I went on to play for Dumbarton for a couple of years after that but I never considered them as being my team. When anyone asks me about football, I always talk about Hearts.

'There was not enough security for me to go into management when I left football and after I finished up altogether I became a sub-postmaster in Grove Street in Edinburgh, which was actually quite handy for getting to games at Tynecastle.'

Craig Gordon (goalkeeper 1999–present day)

'I remember quite clearly the UEFA Cup tie against Stuttgart at Tynecastle. I was in the crowd in the Main Stand that evening for the second leg and what a night it was. It was just a shame we went out on the away goals rule.

'Tynecastle is a great stadium for atmosphere and I particularly relish games against the Old Firm and Hibs. Best save there? The one I made in stoppage time against Motherwell in August 2005 from David Clarkson's shot has to be up there, as it helped us win 2–1, which was our fifth victory on the trot at the start of the season.'

John Hagart (manager, 1973–77)

'When I took over the job from Bobby Seith, my first game was a 5–1 defeat away to Dundee United, which wasn't the best of starts. But then we went on a sixteen-match unbeaten run, which saw us clinch a place in the top ten and took us into the new Premier Division. The following season we got to the cup final but lost 3–1 to Rangers. While we weren't the best team in the land, we had a good bunch of lads who worked very hard for each other.

'There were a lot of good characters, such as Davie Clunie, Roy Kay, Alan Anderson, Donald Ford, Drew Busby, Willie Gibson and Donald Park, who was a great wee young lad. Jim Jefferies was a youngish lad in the team at that time and was a real winner.

'Personally, I was delighted it was him who brought the Scottish Cup back to Tynecastle in '98. I thoroughly enjoyed the European adventures and the night we faced Lokomotiv Leipzig was a memorable occasion. That would prove the first European victory in the club's history. We won 5–1 at Tynecastle and it was a very proud moment.

'That is just one of the games I cherished at Tynecastle but my abiding memory is a police chief inspector coming into the dressing-room and telling me to take the team out again as the crowd wasn't going to leave until they saw the players again!

'There was a lot of good banter in the game in those days but one thing which didn't get a lot of publicity back then was the fact that money was always very tight. I vividly remember trying to hang on to Ralph Callachan in the face of interest from Newcastle United. I tried to explain to the board that we had to keep Ralph for another year as we had a guy called Eamonn Bannon coming through. He wasn't quite ready at that stage but I knew he'd be OK in another season. But they had to get the money in, as the bank was putting them under great pressure. The Newcastle chairman and his manager Joe Harvey came to the game at Tynecastle on the Saturday and they desperately wanted Ralph. I took him to meet them on the Monday at a pub just outside Berwick and he signed for Newcastle there.

'We were due to meet Celtic in a rearranged league game on the Tuesday night and I wanted to leave Ralph's move for another week in order to have him in my team for the trip to Parkhead. But the board were having none of it and one director said, "John, you have to sell him, as we need the money. He could be knocked down by a bus on Tuesday."

'We ended up being relegated and a big part of that was Ralph leaving and Jim Cruickshank having a bad injury. That was the first time the club had been relegated and it was a real dent to my pride. The club wanted me to go and that was a complete and utter surprise for me; Willie Ormond was brought in as my replacement.'

Johnny Hamilton (winger, 1955–67)

'We were an exceptional side and most of the guys were superb footballers who had the chance to go elsewhere but decided to stay at Tynecastle as they enjoyed it so much. That benefited everybody, as it meant we kept playing together and understood each other's games really well. I could get around the park a bit and I think it was a compliment when I was nicknamed the "Pigalle Wonder" after a top greyhound of the time.

'I can recall scoring for Hearts against a Scotland XI in a World Cup trial game at Tynecastle. It was the full Scottish side and we won 3–2, and I don't think they played another club side after that.

'Back then, we had massive crowds for every home match and it was a successful period for the team. I was fortunate enough to pick up every domestic medal but, to be honest, each one was as special as the other, as we had worked so hard as a team to get the victories. It didn't matter who we were playing, we trained just as hard for every match and didn't take anything for granted. The club did us well by giving us each of the medals on a heart-shaped plaque. The names of the players were on one side and the particular match was on the other. It was a nice wee touch and when I'm no longer here my sons Gary and Ross, who are both season ticket holders, will no doubt share them with each other.

'I eventually came back to Hearts on the coaching side with the youngsters but I had to pack it in as I had a newsagent's business on the go, which meant I was doing too much. I had to fold one of them and the reason it was the football was because if I'd packed the business in and gone full time at Tynecastle, a new manager might have come in and that could have been it for me. I had to be careful, as I had just taken the business over and gone part time with Berwick under big Jock Wallace to keep playing and stay fit. The shop was actually just up the road from Tynecastle at the top of Robertson Avenue. I still kept in touch with the fans and used to go along to matches when I could. I would like to have kept on the coaching side of things but there just wasn't the security I needed.

'I was fortunate enough to play alongside some real characters like Bobby Parker, who was captain and very good with the young lads. John Cumming was just a magnificent example to everybody and Willie Bauld and Jimmy Wardhaugh were also teammates. The club couldn't go wrong with players like that and they basically stayed there all their days.

'I am glad the Lithuanian guy Mr Romanov has done something about Tynecastle, as the situation was getting ridiculous. Having said that, I much preferred the old-style ground. Being a winger and with the fans so close to the pitch I sometimes thought they were playing alongside me as well! I remember one game we played against Celtic some time in the 1960s and both sets of fans spilled onto the park because there were so many supporters inside the ground.

'I could see them trying to keep off the pitch, as they knew they weren't allowed on the field of play, but they couldn't help themselves in the end. The referee had to stop the game to allow them to get back onto the terracings. Could you imagine that happening nowadays?'

Paul Hartley (midfielder, 2003–present day)

'I think everyone was delighted when the decision was made to stay at Tynecastle. It's a great arena for football and when it's packed to capacity, those are the games you really want to play in. I wasn't sure what the future was going to hold for me in the summer of 2005, but the arrival of George Burley as manager was a big factor in me signing a new deal.'

Davie Holt (left-back, 1960–69)

'While an amateur with Queen's Park, I was fortunate to be selected to play in the Olympics in Rome in 1960 and lost my job because of it as I was unable to work overtime. When I came back from the Games, I had to turn professional and grasped the opportunity when Hearts asked me to sign. I had given them my word before going to Rome that I would sign when I got back, as I had no job. When I came back, though, I received a call from a Hibs scout asking if I could come through to Edinburgh to talk terms with Mr Shaw, the manager.

'I told him he would be wasting his time, as I had already given my word to Hearts. He insisted that I come through, though, explaining it would look good on his record that he had persuaded me to come through to talk to the club.

'I duly talked to Hugh Shaw and told him that I could not go back on my word to Hearts. During the discussions, the chairman, Harry Swan, came into the room and asked Dave if he had managed to get me to sign. He said he hadn't, as I wouldn't change my mind about going to Tynecastle.

'The chairman then put his hand in an inside pocket and produced a pen. He then went to the other inside pocket, pulled out a cheque book and asked me to write down my figure. He basically asked me to name my price for signing. I was never money orientated and explained again that I couldn't go back on my word to Hearts, and I think that surprised them.

'Hibs actually came back for me later on in my Hearts career and met the price the club was looking for. However, Hearts then said they were actually looking for a player as well as the sum of money, which was quite considerable in those days, and the deal never happened.

'I spent nine tremendous years at Tynecastle and I wouldn't have swapped them for the world, although I did leave under something of a cloud. When I signed for Tommy Walker, I was promised a job for life and was told that even once they had decided they had no further use for me, I would be kept on for another year to allow me time to look for employment. That fell by the wayside, though, which was a big disappointment. That soured it for me and I turned my back on football for a long, long time after that.

'Hearts invited me back to Tynecastle in 2003 for an SPL match and that was the first time I had been back at the club since I left in 1969. I have to admit there were tears in my eyes when I walked into the ground again. It was just unbelievable, as the memories came flooding back at an alarming rate.

'I enjoyed a very happy time at Tynecastle and feel very fortunate to have been there.'

Darren Jackson (midfielder/forward, 1999–2001)

'One of the things I will always remember about Tynecastle is being a mascot there for Hearts in 1978 against Alloa Athletic. I can't remember how it all came about but I probably asked to do it having been brought up a Hearts fan. My dad had taken me to the match and it completed a dream double for me, as I had just captained the Leith Walk school team that morning to the league title – and Dad was the manager.

'It is funny how things work out but Jim Jefferies was captain of Hearts that day against Alloa and he then signed me all those years later when he became manager.

'Just seeing me playing professional football made Dad, a lifelong Jambo, proud. Watching me standing in the Scotland line-up at the World Cup finals must have been unbelievable for him as well, but seeing me run out in a maroon strip for my debut against Kilmarnock probably crowned everything for him.

'I was nearly 33 when I played my first game for Hearts. We

came back from 2–0 down against Killie to get a draw, with Gary McSwegan scoring his first goals for Hearts.

'Out of choice, I don't think anyone would leave Tynecastle, as there is no doubt it is a great venue for football. There is no doubt the stadium helped the team as well, because the atmosphere created by the fans was great. I remember playing there with Celtic and it was a game Celtic dominated but the fans just kept the Hearts team going. Sometimes I don't think the supporters realised just what a big role they could play during matches at Tynecastle.

'The stadium could be intimidating for visiting teams but the away dressing-room was intimidating for players as well, as they would be sitting pretty much on top of each other and it could be quite frustrating.

'Personally, I think it's fantastic when a stadium has fans right down on top of the players, especially when the ground isn't that big. As a Hibs player I hardly ever won there, but for any footballer Tynecastle was a great place to go and play.

'After joining Hearts, the fans were superb, but I have to say that as a Hearts player I enjoyed going to Easter Road, which is another great venue in my mind.

'Even though the grounds in Scotland are not the biggest – apart from Parkhead and Ibrox, where players get a buzz from playing anyway – there is something special about having the crowds on top of you at places like Pittodrie, Tannadice and Tynecastle.'

Iain Jardine (midfielder, 1985–89)

'I never managed that many goals in my career and so I remember quite vividly the free-kick I scored against Hibs at Tynecastle in the 1986 New Year's Day derby, which we won 3–1. January 1st is the best day of the year to play a game, particularly a derby, and to score as I did at the Gorgie Road end in a win over Hibs just doesn't get much better. Alan Rough was the Hibees keeper that day, with John Robertson and Sandy Clark getting the other Hearts goals, in what has to be one of the highlights of my career.

'I recall it being a really wet day, with the players slipping all over the place, and that just added to the whole drama. It may be a long time ago but I could probably still tell you every move in the 3–1 game. I had some truly great times there and actually remember, funnily enough, also scoring against Hibs in a victory at Easter Road.

'During my time with Hearts, we had the Indian sign over Hibs. We always used to say it was easy money playing Hibs, an easy win bonus for the players. Wallace Mercer always looked after us because he wanted to win the game so much as well and we knew there was always extra money involved. We always thought it was good to play Hibs back then, as we knew we would win!

'Playing for Hearts was such an honour and I know there were times during that great season when players would continue with injuries, as they thought they'd never get back in the side. Often we would strap up injuries we'd normally rest, as we were too frightened to lose our place.

'Tynecastle was a fantastic theatre in which to play football and, to be honest, it took me a long time to get over leaving. When I went back, I used to sit in the stand and kick every ball, wishing I were still out there.

'Ask any professional footballer which ground he would like to play in when it's full, and I'd bet the majority would say Tynecastle. It all stems from the passion of the fans. The supporters were always superb there. We always thought we were 1–0 up before we went out onto the park thanks to the support and the fact the team was full of winners such as Gary, Robbo, Walter, Kenny Black, John Colquhoun, Neil Berry and Brian Whittaker. We went into matches knowing we would win, and any time we drew a game it felt like a morgue – but that was just the special effect Tynecastle had on us.'

Sandy Jardine
(full-back/assistant manager, 1982–86; co-manager, 1986–88)

'I was the old man of Hearts compared with some of the young players who were coming through the ranks. I stopped playing when I was 39 years old and it was about the time when the teenage dream team of John Robertson and Gary Mackay were making their mark.

HOME DRESSING-ROOM

'I joined Hearts as a player/assistant manager in July 1982. They got me at the second attempt, as the then manager Tony Ford tried to sign me the season before but Rangers wouldn't let me go.

'I must admit when I first arrived at the club it was a bit of a culture shock in many ways. For instance, at Rangers if I needed a new pair of football boots I just asked for them and they would be delivered to the club. When I turned up at Hearts and asked for new boots, I had to get a chitty for £20 and buy them myself. Also, the training gear wasn't great and the training facilities were even worse.

'Luckily, the players and the spirit in the team were a lot better. I know Hearts fans won't want to be reminded of the year we finished second in the league and lost in the Scottish Cup final but up until those last few weeks we played some great football. It was a dreadful feeling when we lost both but look back at the team we had that year. Craig Levein, John Robertson, Gary Mackay, Sandy Clark, John Colquhoun – all great players.

'I was proud to make my 1,000th first-class appearance as a Hearts player in a match against Rangers in 1986 and was enjoying my football even as I got older. Aberdeen had asked me to take the top coaching job at Pittodrie but Hearts were desperate for me to stay. To keep me at the club they appointed me co-manager with Alex in May 1986. I hear that Wallace Mercer didn't think that the co-manager idea worked but I totally disagree.

'Before I was appointed, Alex and I went to see the Hearts board and said the team was getting older and needed new faces and restructuring. We warned them we had to blood new players and because of that we wouldn't be finishing second in the league and would slip a bit during the time when the reorganisation took place. That's what happened, but we warned them and expected we would get time to make our long-term plans bear fruit.

'Unfortunately, the board were having none of it and I was sacked in 1988. Alex would have gone, too, but he wouldn't have got any compensation, so he stuck it out.

'I enjoyed the years I spent at Tynecastle. Hearts are a great team and it was a privilege to play for them.'

Allan Johnston (winger, 1990–96)

'Everyone looks forward to playing at Tynecastle, as a good atmosphere is guaranteed. It's a special stadium and has to be one of the best in Scotland for its size and with the fans so close to you on the park.

'Alex MacDonald was the manager who signed me but I don't think I had been there very long when he was sacked and Joe Jordan took over. I was on the bench under him but never managed to get into the team that often. After he left, Sandy Clark came in for a season. Tommy McLean then took over and a few of the young ones got bumped. Once again I found myself on the bench a lot of the time but not playing very much.

'It wasn't until Sandy got the job that things started to change. Joe had agreed that me and Gary Locke would fly to New Zealand to play over the summer in a bid to toughen us up but just before we were due to set off he left the club and Sandy arrived. He cancelled the New Zealand trip and gave us our debuts, having known us from the reserve team. Jim Jefferies then got the job and we enjoyed a good run in the cup and got to the final. It was good to be there – I scored in the semi-final – but disappointing to lose. The team obviously learned, as they went on to lift the trophy in 1998.

'One of my best moments with Hearts actually came at Ibrox when I scored a hat-trick against Rangers. It was a great team performance that day and I was just lucky enough to be in the right positions at the right times to score the goals.

'One of the games I remember from Tynecastle itself was a match I didn't actually play in. It was the European tie against Atletico Madrid and while I was gutted not to even get on the bench, it was an incredible occasion.

'I always seemed to get a bit of stick from the fans when I played there after leaving but I suppose that's normal for former players at their old club. I have still got many fond memories of my time there, although I eventually left as I was being messed about with a new contract. I wasn't looking for a lot of money and it was a shame things worked out as they did.'

David Johnston (winger, 1977–78)

'I went to George Watson's College in Edinburgh and we didn't play football there at that time, although things later changed. I enjoyed the game, though, and was playing for the school's scout troop when Dougie Allan, who ran Hutcheson Vale Boys Club, saw me play. He thought I had potential and I joined his club.

'I actually signed for Hibs first on schoolboy forms but the registration was ruled invalid, as George Watson's wasn't affiliated to the SFA, although the school is now. It meant I was a free agent and during that time I signed for Hearts. It was actually Bert Paton who signed me from juvenile football, as Willie Ormond had not yet been brought in as manager and Bert was standing in until he did.

'I may have played only one competitive first-team game for Hearts but it is one I will never forget. My direct opponent that day was a superstar of the Scottish game. I remember running out and lining up against Jimmy Johnstone, who had left Celtic and joined Dundee. It was 20 August 1977 and we won 2–1, thanks to goals from Graham Shaw and Drew Busby. I played pretty well in the match and felt I got the better of Jinky that day. Not many footballers could ever even think that.

'In the last minute, I injured my foot when I ran through and saw a chance to score. I hit my shot, followed through and ended up kicking my opponent's studs, which left me with a stress injury to my foot. I couldn't kick a ball for six weeks, which was a big blow.

'The other difficulty I had back then was with a certain Rab Prentice. He was my direct rival for the left-wing position in the Hearts team and he was well established in the side. The foot injury put me back a bit and I was set to go to university to study law. That meant I would be a part-time footballer in a full-time team and that wouldn't have been much fun.

'Trying to get Rab Prentice out of the team while just training part time would have been a tall order. I did go and train with Stirling Albion for a while and remember being very impressed by their coach Alex Smith, but I knew deep down I was going to give up the game and switch to rugby, which I had played a lot of at school.

'The fact that I wasn't going to give up my law course for sport of any description meant whatever I took up had to be fun and playing part-time football would not have been as much fun as continuing to play rugby. The decision to switch sports is one I don't regret, as I went on to win 27 Scottish caps, which was a great honour.

'I don't watch much professional football nowadays but getting a game for Hearts and playing against Jimmy Johnstone made my one first-team appearance a very special occasion.'

Willie Johnston (winger, 1982–85)

'When I first went to Tynecastle, I was a smoker. I didn't drink but I smoked all the time. I used to have a wee room to myself and I'd go along there in the mornings before training and have a couple of fags and a cup of tea. Some of the young boys used to come along and we would just sit and talk football, about what happened at the weekend or the next game coming up. It was just like a wee boot room for us. The management team of wee Doddie and Sandy Jardine knew about it, as they were aware that I smoked when I signed.

'It was a great park to play on and even when I was with Rangers we always looked forward to going to Tynecastle because of the big crowds and the atmosphere. I remember scoring a glorious 30-yarder against Celtic at Tynecastle. I had come on as a substitute and Roy Aitken had had a go at me about being too old. Peter Latchford was in goal but I knew him from our time at West Brom and was confident I could beat him from distance. The ball flew into the back of the net and needless to say I had a few choice words for Mr Aitken after that.

'I was only there for a couple of seasons and was coming towards the end of my career. It was good because wee Doddie and Sandy knew I couldn't last the 90 minutes. If I started a game, they'd said, "Give us a good 45 minutes and we'll take you off," or if I was on the bench I'd get the last half-hour maybe. Gary

Mackay, John Robertson, Craig Levein and Davie Bowman were all just laddies when I was there and it was a great time to be at Hearts.

'I was happy I made the move to Tynecastle and it was a brilliant time for me late in my career. I was getting too old for football, though, and it soon dawned on me. I think I had a season to go with Hearts when we were heavily beaten in the reserves at Tynecastle in the spring of 1985. That's when I knew I'd had enough. I went out that night and got pissed, then went in to the club the next morning to see wee Doddie and tell him that was it, I'd had enough.

'That reserve game against Celtic was my last one for Hearts. I knew my time was up and that it was time to go. I was 38 years old at that stage and wasn't going to play on much longer. It was getting harder and harder, and I had to make a decision.'

Joe Jordan (manager, 1990–93)

'The stadium had a reputation, and rightly so, as a difficult place for opponents to win. It was always associated with the support and Hearts always commanded a great following at Tynecastle.

'It was a typical British stadium with the fans close to the field of play. Tynecastle retained the atmosphere well and made it difficult for opponents, whether in a league game, a midweek match or a big European night.

'It had yet to be developed when I was there and the old terracings were still in use, but there were no complaints from me about it. When you're a manager in the dugout, you are basically doing what is necessary to get through the 90 minutes. I was always aware of the supporters being so close behind the dugout but never had a problem with that. It was good and I enjoyed it. You want the punters close to the pitch and on top of teams, as it is intimidating in the right manner and works to your advantage.

'As a player, you can savour the moment coming onto the pitch, especially on a big European evening under the floodlights. But as a manager I was always focused on the game and didn't pay much attention to what was going on off the park. It was the same when

I was a player. It really didn't bother me if I was playing at Anfield, Elland Road or wherever. I just went onto the pitch and played the game. The fact that it may have been Hampden Park or Wembley didn't faze me. I am not being flippant but I was just focused on the game and that applied even more so as a manager.

'The European nights there were always special for players and I can recall one or two special moments. The game against Slavia Prague sticks in my memory. Glynn Snodin scored late on and it was a real turnaround in the match. I seem to remember the players asked for videos of the game, as it had looked like being a lost cause, only for Hearts to win the match.

'Tynecastle is the history and tradition of the club, and is basically Hearts' roots. I'm a bit of a traditionalist and can understand the fans who have supported the club for many years, if not their entire lives, having been peeved at what happened over Murrayfield.'

Walter Kidd (right-back, 1977–91)

'The supporters always called me "Zico" and I actually met the chap who claimed to have christened me that in a pub. He said he was at the World Cup in 1982 and saw Zico make a great run up the wing for Brazil. He saw me do one at Tynecastle and started shouting, "Zico, Zico!" The rest of the Gorgie Road end joined in, the nickname was born and it stuck with me forever. With my hairstyles, they could never mistake me for the real Zico. I had a perm like Henry Smith, which was a sight to behold, then I cut it all off and got called "Bald Eagle".

'I was born in Edinburgh but didn't go to Tynecastle much as a boy because I was always playing football. I had a great time at the club and was captain in the 1985–86 season, when we just missed out on the Premier League and the Scottish Cup. People keep saying that was a dreadful season. I say to them, "No, it wasn't, it was just the last couple of weeks which were rubbish."

'Looking on the positive side, we had a great team and we played some great football. John Robertson, Craig Levein, Sandy Clark, John Colquhoun. All great players but Robbo was the best. You can look far and wide but you won't find a better striker than him.

'What a lot of people maybe didn't realise back then was that we were all on the same wage plus bonus money. It created a family atmosphere at the club and we all worked for each other. Nowadays, some players get more money than others and the camaraderie we had is difficult to emulate.

'When I started playing at Tynecastle, people stood on the terraces, but when I finished, the stands had been built and it was a good stadium. The fact the crowd is so close to the pitch made it the most atmospheric stadium I have ever played in. The only one which came close is in Valencia. We played there on a pre-season tour and it reminded me of Tynecastle.'

Bobby Kirk (full-back, 1955–63)

'I really enjoyed my career at Hearts and there are so many good memories. We had a great season in 1955–56 and the Scottish Cup win has to be the highlight for me.

'I was a decent kicker of a football and my teammates had voted me onto the penalties. There was a game against Hibs at Tynecastle when we were awarded three penalties in the one match. I scored with the first one, hit the post with the second and scored with the third. I could have kicked myself over the penalty I missed. I usually put my penalties to the goalkeeper's right but on that occasion changed my mind and put it to the left. It beat their keeper Jackie Wren but came off the woodwork.

'I left Hearts in 1963 to go to Gala Fairydean as player/manager. I was at home in Dalkeith that April when I read in the early edition of the *Evening News* that I was being released. I expected to be shown a bit more respect after spending eight years at the club but that seemed to be the way they worked in those days. I was devastated. I wasn't expecting it and couldn't believe what I was reading after winning so much with them. That was Hearts' style at the time and I blame Tommy Walker. He had a great reputation as a player but he wasn't respected as a manager, certainly not by me anyway.

'I took my boots home after being told I was leaving and to be honest I kept waiting for them to ask me for the money for them. That's the way they were. I remember wee Willie Bauld asking if I'd had to pay for them.

'I ended up back at Tynecastle coaching the youngsters in 1967 but the only reason I went back there was because Tommy Walker had left. I couldn't have faced him again, that's for sure. I have only been back a few times since, mainly because my son Gary got me tickets while he was working for Craig Levein on the coaching staff. I have to say Easter Road is a palace compared to Tynecastle. I couldn't believe what the ground looked like when I saw it; it's just a dump.'

Davie Laing (wing-half, 1942–54)

'The 12-year period I spent with Hearts was a wonderful part of my life and undoubtedly the highlight of my career. We didn't win much in terms of silverware but that didn't bother us too much as we just tried our best and everywhere we went we had a full house watching us, as Hearts were such a marvellous team in those days.

'We were regarded as one of the top clubs in Scotland. There was the likes of Alfie Conn, Willie Bauld, Jimmy Wardhaugh, Jimmy Brown and Charlie Cox, all super players and wonderful characters. I remember the first game Conn, Bauld and Wardhaugh played in together and it was quite an occasion with Hearts beating East Fife 6–1 at Tynecastle. They were a worthy side themselves at that time but Willie got a hat-trick, Alfie scored two and I also got one from the penalty spot. I was the regular penalty-taker for Hearts for quite a while and was pretty accurate. I wouldn't have let anyone else take it for anything – not even one of them. They had their job to do and that was it.

'We knew as soon as we saw the three of them together that they were going to be something special and that League Cup match against East Fife was certainly the start of something very special in the history of Hearts. The great thing about them was they were all so different. Willie did very little running but was always in the right position and his ball control and heading ability were superb. Alongside him was Alfie, who could run up and down the park and put in the tackles, and you knew what you were going to get from him every time. Jimmy, on the other hand, didn't know what he was going to do sometimes but it all came so naturally for him. The three of them were so different as players but as a trio they were simply superb.

'Few teams will ever have a combination like them again. I was at left-half and Charlie Cox was at right-half; we were the providers of the service for the guys and they did the rest. They scored a lot of goals between them and as the players behind them we tended to get overshadowed a bit. Having said that, they did appreciate the service but the guys who put the ball in the net always get looked upon differently.

'Those days were indeed very special and one thing which sticks in my memory is walking to matches with the fans. When I lived in Kirkcaldy, I used to jump on the train, get off at Haymarket and then walk to Tynecastle. After the game, there would be hordes of supporters, particularly those from Fife – including the opposition – waiting outside the entrance to the ground and we would all then walk back to the station along Gorgie Road, which used to be chock-a-block with people before and after the match. You couldn't see that happening in the modern era.

'I also recall feeling how Hearts were such a "family" club as soon as I signed. There was a social club built close to the ground and all the players' wives and friends used to go there and mingle with the supporters, and that helped the tremendous connection between the fans and us – and of course there was a wonderful man in charge of the team in Dave McLean.

'As if to underline the "family" feel of the club, my late wife Betty and Jimmy Wardhaugh's wife Anne helped in the canteen on match days. They would take the food in and we would walk into the ground to play. It was a special kind of tearoom, a sort of modern-day players' lounge if you like, next door to Tynecastle where the tennis courts used to be. We also often went there for a cup of tea during the week to chat with the supporters. Our families became lifelong friends thanks to Hearts and it was a terrible blow when I learned that Jimmy had passed away.

'Golf was an important part of life at Hearts as well and Jimmy, Alfie and Willie as well as Tom McKenzie, Ken Currie and Jimmy Brown were all regulars. It was a key part of the club in those days and we even used to meet up in the close season for an outing or two.

'Tynecastle back then was a tidy, well-kept place and although the dressing-rooms were a fair size, I remember having to stand on the bench to reach my jersey on the peg. In my day, not many people had cars and they took the bus or train to the game, so there wasn't the pressure as there is today to find spaces to park the car at Tynecastle. In fact, when we went to play Aberdeen in Pittodrie, it was regarded as a real adventure and we used to travel up the night before the game as it was regarded as so far away. The roads were not the best and it could take a while but we loved going up there.

'I was fortunate that I didn't miss many games for Hearts and was one of the more regular players for the team over that period. I'm not sure why but, although I was quite a strong tackler, I never got hurt that often.

'I played for Hibs after leaving Tynecastle and the feeling of suddenly finding myself playing alongside the likes of Lawrie Reilly and Gordon Smith after all those years at Hearts was very hard to explain. The great thing about the derby matches, though, is that they were all lock-outs no matter where the teams met and the atmosphere was tremendous. Such was the attraction of Hearts that even games against East Fife and Raith Rovers would attract decent crowds.

'I eventually moved into journalism with my involvement on the sports desk of the *Edinburgh Dispatch*, which was ironic as Jimmy Wardhaugh also went into papers when he joined the *Edinburgh Evening News*. I really enjoyed that time, as it kept me involved in the game; although reporting on Hearts was a bit strange and awkward, as I had to make sure I wasn't too biased towards them and also ensure I didn't go too far the other way.'

Craig Levein
(centre-half, 1983–97; manager, 2000–04)

'The Bayern Munich tie in 1989 was a big occasion for us and will always be one of my favourite memories of Tynecastle. It was a full house plus a few more, as no doubt more tickets were printed than should have been. It was a terrific occasion and to actually win the game was beyond everybody's expectations.

'As for the goals I scored, for some reason I always remember a header against Aberdeen in the 1985–86 season. If I'm not mistaken, I scored the last goal in front of the Shed before they tore it down and put up the Wheatfield Stand. At the end of the season before that, Shaggy [Stephen Frail] crossed the ball and I scored with a shot at the near post, and I always remember thinking afterwards that nobody would ever score in front of the Hearts fans at that particular end again.

'There was a big bath for the players at that time and there used to be nothing better than after we got hammered at training on a Tuesday having a bit of a laugh in a Radox-filled bath. There was also a wee tearoom, where the likes of Jimmy Bone, George Cowie and Willie Johnston would come in early and have a cup of tea and a blether before training. We used to play head tennis on a Friday in the brown gymnasium and that was a big thing for the likes of myself, Kenny Black, John Colquhoun, wee Robbo and Sandy Clark. Wee Alex was keen on that and I think I've still got some signed pound notes from him! Friday actually almost became the hardest day of the week for us, as the games became so competitive that they would sometimes last up to an hour and half before training.

'I remember one day before a match when Davie Bowman got his cheekbone broken by Jimmy Bone when they clashed. That's how competitive the games were. We used to get hammered at first, as Alex MacDonald, Sandy and Jimmy would play against the younger ones such as myself, Blacky and John. It took us a long time to gain the upper hand but we did eventually.

'The Dunfermline game in 1995, when I injured myself in what proved to be my last game for Hearts, is a sad memory for me. I remember the evening clearly and it was a League Cup tie very early in the season. As soon as I made the tackle, I knew I had done something serious. I knew I was in trouble as it was the same knee that I had hurt the last time. I had operations and did the rehabilitation but the knee never got back to being solid and stable enough to play on.

'After playing in so many matches and enjoying so many highs at the stadium, it was sad for that to be my parting performance. But you can't pick and choose these things. I spent two years of gut-wrenching hard work trying to get myself back into a situation where I could play again, as I felt that other than my knee I was fit. I was desperate to get back but the emotion which came out on the day I announced my retirement from playing was a culmination of the gradual acceptance of the fact I was finished – that part of my life was over and I had to move on to something else.

'Anybody who has played football will tell you that is a sad occasion, as we'd all love to play until we're 60. It was unfortunate the way things worked out but I might not have achieved what I did as a manager had it not happened.

'I stopped playing in 1995, left Tynecastle in 1997 and then came back in December 2000 as manager. The biggest difference I noticed was the salaries – but not mine, unfortunately. The wages were up by around 700 per cent. It was a different culture but I almost fell off my seat when I saw the wage bill.

'I will never forget the 5–1 win over Hibs at Tynecastle in August 2002 or the incredible 4–4 draw against them when we scored twice in injury time on 2 January 2003. They are two of the most wonderful experiences for me.

'Beating Celtic, thanks to Austin McCann's late winner, was also a special moment, as, although I had beaten the Old Firm as a player, that was my first win as a manager. People judge you on how you do against Celtic and Rangers and to finally get that breakthrough in such a spectacular manner was a great occasion. There was also my first European game as manager against NK Zeljeznicar at Tynecastle. We won 2–0 and that was a special evening for me, too.

'I worked with a lot of good people at Tynecastle and met a lot of good folk and had some great times with the supporters. I was lucky enough as a player to be well respected and I am quite proud of the fact that during my time there as manager I managed to keep things going in the right direction despite everything that was going on each year.'

Gary Locke (midfielder, 1990–2001)

'I had a season ticket from the age of about four or five and used to sit in the wing stand with my dad. As I got a wee bit older, I got a season ticket for the terracings and was lucky enough to see some cracking Hearts teams, particularly the one which came so close to the Double in 1986. I hardly missed a game that season but wished I hadn't been at the one at Dens Park when Hearts lost out on the league on the last day of the season.

'I left school when I was 16 and went straight to Hearts, where I spent two years on the YTS [Youth Training Scheme]. Looking back, it's funny to see how I got my chance in the first team. Myself and Allan Johnston were actually supposed to be going to New Zealand to play during the summer as, with just a couple of games left to play, Joe Jordan thought it would be good for our football education.

'It had reached the stage where we had sorted out bank accounts over there and then the day before we were due to leave, Joe Jordan was sacked and Sandy Clark took over. He told us both that we'd be involved in the first team before the end of the season and that was a massive turning point in our careers. The following week I was on the bench at home to Airdrie but didn't get on; the next weekend, though, I replaced Derek Ferguson against St Johnstone at McDiarmid Park late in the first half.

'I was a nervous wreck before my first start at Tynecastle, which was a pre-season friendly against Everton. That was absolutely brilliant but a bit strange, to be honest, as I could see all my mates who I used to stand with on the terracings, except now they were standing there giving me abuse all the time.

'My first season as a young player at Hearts was brilliant but after that, though, it all went pear-shaped. It seemed to me that Tommy McLean didn't really like me and I didn't play many first-team games. The season after that it was all change again when Jim Jefferies came in and we were back in favour. He was great for my career and I'd like to think I have repaid him with my performances. It's good when a manager has a lot of faith in you as a player and I think that's where I was quite fortunate. He's the sort of gaffer who will give you another chance to prove yourself after a couple of bad games rather than just throw you out of the team.

'My European debut at Tynecastle was a superb night for me personally, as I set up both goals in a 2–1 win over Atletico Madrid and was voted the man of the match. That was my first taste of European football and it was really special as the ground was full and that was the first time I had experienced the ground like that. It was pleasing as the return leg wasn't so great, with us getting hammered over in Spain.

'It was a wrench to eventually leave Hearts but I got a chance to play in the English Premiership after Jim Jefferies went to Bradford and that was an opportunity I couldn't turn down. Although I'd have been quite happy to stay on, I think I had maybe been at Tynecastle too long and needed a wee change. I thoroughly enjoyed my time in England but it wasn't long before I found myself back in Scotland with the gaffer at Kilmarnock and that obviously meant me going back to Tynecastle as an opposition player, which was quite strange at the time. It was a 1–1 draw after Killie had gone down to ten men in the first half but I had a nightmare, according to my dad, who was always very honest with me. In my defence, I had to play in a number of different positions after Sean Hessey had been sent off.

'I think the problem was I was pretty nervous and desperate to impress the club I'd left. Every time I went back there as a player I always got the same team talk about keeping my head and not getting carried away. I have never had a problem there, though, and I don't know where people got the idea I was a hothead.

'It was very strange sitting in the away dressing-room, where you can hardly swing a cat. Hearts always seem to turn the heating up in there! They did that when I played there and it was always roasting when I was there with Killie. The players were just glad to get out onto the park.

'I think the biggest asset which the Scottish Cup-winning squad of 1998 had was that everyone got on great together both on and off the park. We just seemed to click that season and were very unlucky not to go all the way in the league.

'If we ever had a social night out, there would always be over 20 of us there, despite it being difficult for guys who were married or had kids. Sometimes we'd head into Bonnyrigg and my local, where we'd just all be treated as one of the locals. Davie Weir also helped out as he had a mate in Falkirk who owned a pub just outside the town. We used to go there as there wasn't the hassle we'd get if we went out in Edinburgh. It was a place where nobody bothered us and we could all just have a good laugh, mostly at the expense of Stevie Fulton, who would fall asleep anywhere.

'He also used to be the star of the show on the club holiday to Majorca, as he was prone to doing stupid things all the time. He was the character in the dressing-room at the time and was always up for a laugh. Stevie didn't mind prancing around in his birthday suit on occasions and there was one time when he came flying out of a toilet covered head to toe in loo paper and proceeded to run about the pub pretending to be a mummy! There were a few of us who enjoyed a laugh but Stevie was always up for anything. That was absolutely hilarious – and summed up the spirit in the camp, which definitely helped us out on the pitch.'

David McCreery (midfielder, 1989–91)

'I had a lovely time at Hearts in the two years I spent at Tynecastle. The whole place was fantastic and the people there deserved success, as they worked so hard. As a footballing arena it was superb and the people all made me feel very welcome. Wee Doddie was tremendous and Wallace Mercer was great also. What Alex MacDonald had was everybody fighting for each other – the team spirit was superb – and there were also jokers like Scott Crabbe and Robbo.

'By the time I came to Edinburgh, I suppose you could say I was approaching veteran status and I have to admit they took it easy on me in training. Doddie used to allow me some less-intensive sessions. He played on to a fair age himself and knew how to get the best out of players my age at that time. I had a thoroughly good time there and one thing that struck me most was the level of fitness of the players; George McNeill and Bert Logan were the guys mostly responsible and their fitness regime was superb.

'Tynecastle may have been towards the end of my career but it was still a special period for me personally. I was surprised how much I enjoyed my time at the club and looking back I often think it is something I should have tried much earlier. It was wee Alex who had made it special. He was superb and a very charismatic figure. The thing about him, though, was that he knew when to joke and when to be serious. His man management was fantastic and I think the results he got were evidence of that. It's just a pity he never managed to win anything there.'

Alex MacDonald
(midfielder, 1980–81; player/manager, 1981–85; manager, 1985–90)

'The joke back then was that Sandy Clark and I would keep playing forever, as he stopped when he was 40 and I kept going until I was 37. I used to tell him I would always get more games than him, as, after all, I picked the team!

'When I arrived at Hearts, I wasn't impressed at what I saw. The training methods were poor and not enough emphasis was placed on fitness. I had come from Rangers, where Jock Wallace had concentrated on stamina. I remember running up and down the sand dunes at Gullane under his regime. I wanted that type of commitment at Hearts and we slowly got it. The older players I brought in, like Willie Johnston, Jimmy Bone and Roddy MacDonald, made a big difference and taught all the young players. I remember Jimmy in particular was great with them all. The Tynecastle tearoom was the place he used to pass on his advice.

'People talk about how good a team we had in 1986, the year we nearly won the Double, but, to be honest, I just have bad memories about that time. Yes, we had great young players like John Colquhoun, Gary Mackay, John Robertson, Craig Levein and Sandy Clark, but we still finished second best. That isn't good enough for Hearts. I remember vividly after a game against Dunfermline I said Alan McLaren would one day play for Scotland. I can remember people laughing at me but he proved me right. He was a great player and it was a great shame that injury cut short his career.

'We finished second in the league in the 1987–88 season and two years later in the 1989–90 season finished third behind Aberdeen on goal difference, so I was pretty pleased by the level of consistency we had as a team.

'As a player I felt I gave total commitment to the club. I played 181 times for Hearts as a player, scored 21 goals and really enjoyed it. I took over the captaincy from Jim Jefferies and always found Tynecastle a great place to play football. The feeling when you ran out onto the pitch was magnificent. The place always gave the players a lift and made the opposition feel uneasy.'

Roddy MacDonald (centre-half, 1981–87)

'Scoring an own goal at Tynecastle against Hibs was a moment I won't forget. I tried a pass back to Henry Smith, mistimed it badly, lobbed him and the ball fell into the net.

'But apart from that, Tynecastle was always a great place to play football and had an atmosphere all of its own. I used to go there when I was a Celtic player and knew we would always get a hard time. As a Hearts player, the supporters were great to me even after that error against Hibs.'

Frank Mackay (left-half, 1955–56)

'I signed provisionally for Hearts when I was playing for Slateford Athletic and they sent me to Edinburgh City at the same time as George Thomson. We played one season there as the club folded. That forced Hearts' hand and they signed me in the summer of

1955 and I was there until 1956. It was a great experience. My older brother Tommy had been a provisional signing but was freed without being called up to play at Tynecastle. David, on the other hand, was always going to be there as he'd been a stick-out. It was weird going into a club straight from the juniors with my brother already established in the first team. The first team tended to be a bit "cliquish" – I was a newcomer and didn't I know it! We all trained together but I knew I was a second-class citizen.

'Willie Bauld, though, was a gentleman. Some of the first-team players didn't want to lower themselves to speak to a reserve player like me but Willie was great and was always willing to chat. When you consider the level he attained and how much the fans loved him, it was fantastic for me that he was happy to talk to me. In fact, he was the kind of guy who would walk along Gorgie Road and talk to anyone prepared to listen.

'Having David as my brother didn't work in my favour at all, as the expectation levels were very high. I remember the very first game I played for Hearts was in a reserve game against Partick Thistle at Firhill. I admit I didn't have the best of games and did virtually nothing, as the ball seemed to pass me by during the whole game, but it was my first match out of the juniors. We got slaughtered that day and lost heavily, I think about 6–1, so it wasn't just me playing badly.

'We travelled back to Edinburgh by train and I was sitting in the same carriage as the trainer Donald McLeod and one of the directors. I was unlucky enough to find myself sitting next to the director, who had clearly had too much to drink and seemed to have a fixation about how badly I had played. I heard everything he was saying and I have to admit it was shocking for me. Despite it having been my first game, he kept making comparisons along the lines of, "He'll never be the player his brother is." That was horrific to hear and really crushed my confidence. It was a rude awakening for me and I began to wonder what I had let myself in for. I wasn't the most confident of guys in any case and that was the last thing I needed. To be fair to Donald McLeod, he was horrified as well and reported him to Tommy Walker.

'Although it definitely didn't help being the brother of David, I loved being at Tynecastle. The highlight had to be being part of the official party at the 1956 Scottish Cup final. The reserve bus followed the team bus back from Hampden to Edinburgh. There was then the open-top parade and it was a fantastic experience for someone whose family had all been Hearts daft. My dad was a lifelong supporter and all the boys went along to games as laddies.

'I was never jealous of David, as he was always at a higher level than me; in fact, he was a notch above most players. We never played in the same team together, as I could never get in to the first team and he was never out of it. I might have not enjoyed the experience anyway, as I remember talking to Alex Young one day and him telling me that David used to scare the life out of him on the pitch with all his shouting.'

Tosh McKinlay (left-back, 1988–94)

'I have obviously played at Tynecastle for Hearts as well as for the opposition and there was always a great atmosphere inside the ground. Ibrox and Parkhead generate their own atmospheres but there is no doubting that Tynecastle, particularly for European matches, was very special.

'When I was there, Hearts defeated the likes of Bayern Munich, Atletico Madrid and Bologna and for me the Bayern game is the one that sticks out. It was the old terracings at the time and the place was packed. Something was lost from football grounds when the seats were put in but luckily for me I played there in the era when fans stood at matches and that night the stadium was filled to the rafters.

'There is no doubt in my mind that European sides found Tynecastle a difficult place to play, as they never really experienced anything like it on the Continent. When they saw the name Hearts come out of the hat in a draw, they probably didn't know much, if anything, about the club, but after they had been turned over at Tynecastle they certainly knew all about it when they left.

'As well as Bayern Munich, I have fond memories of the night Hearts played against Slavia Prague. That was another terrific occasion. Prague were another good team but Hearts' home record in Europe was generally pretty good when I was there.

'It doesn't matter how experienced you are, atmospheres can get to you as a player and that is what happened a lot at Tynecastle. In terms of where it was situated it was a special wee stadium, tight and enclosed, and proved intimidating for visiting teams. It was a typical old ground situated in amongst houses and very much part of the community.

'Clubs have got to retain their identity and should never be moved out of the area in which they have their roots. That is my opinion and I would imagine if you asked the punters, 100 per cent of them would have wanted to remain at Tynecastle.

'When I left in 1994, there were just the three stands up, so going back with Celtic was a wee bit different with everybody sitting, but for me it was still one of the best all-seater grounds for atmosphere. The Wheatfield Stand is a huge structure, which virtually hangs over the pitch, not set back with a running track like the more modern grounds.

'I made my debut in December 1988 against Rangers at Tynecastle in Robbo's first game back after his short spell at Newcastle. The win kicked off my Hearts career in the best possible fashion and the move to Tynecastle ultimately proved a great stepping-stone in my career. I had maybe spent a wee bit too long with Dundee but I moved to Celtic after Hearts and then won Scotland caps, which was great. I am very grateful to Hearts for giving me the platform.'

Dave McPherson (defender, 1987–92 and 1994–98)

'I certainly saw many changes at Tynecastle, having first joined in 1987 when the Shed was still there. That's where all the diehard Hearts fans congregated and where all the singing started. I remember there was uproar when there was talk about that stand being demolished to make way for a new one but time moves on and the fans had to move with it.

'My first league match for Hearts at Tynecastle was against Falkirk in 1987 and that sticks out for me, as we won 4–2. I had come to Tynecastle after winning the league with Rangers the previous year and it did take me a couple of games to settle into my new surroundings but the Hearts fans made it really easy for me.

'The dressing-rooms have always been very traditional and there's still the smell, if you like, of the bygone days, which is nice for the players. Some dressing-rooms, like those at Hampden Park, are ultra modern, too sanitised and feel more like a medical centre. There's a hot pipe which runs through the away dressing-room [at Tynecastle] and I think a few players have seen misplaced legs or arms burnt on it! But all that adds to the character and you just don't get that sort of thing at other clubs.

'There has always been a strong bond between the players and the fans, and that's what made Tynecastle so difficult for the opposition.

'One of my favourite stories involves big Gilles Rousset and one incident in particular which took place during a club holiday in Majorca. He'd never played golf before and wasn't too clued up on the etiquette involved. Both of us are of a similar height but I had extended clubs to play with and he didn't, so you can imagine what he looked like. He stepped up onto the first tee and smacked his drive into one of the tee boxes, the ball shooting about 30 yards behind him with Gilles shouting: "I don't believe it! I don't believe it!"

'Towards the end of the round he then drove one of the buggies straight onto a green, plonked himself down and began examining his feet. He had never worn golf shoes before and was having quite a problem. He was just sitting there on the green saying: "My bleesters, my bleesters!"'

Gordon Marshall (goalkeeper, 1956–63)

'I remember we had suffered a terrible result in the first leg against Standard Liège in Belgium in the European Cup when we lost 5–1 and I actually think I was responsible for three of the goals. The whole experience was new to us, as it was the club's first time in a European competition.

'We didn't cope well with things over there, particularly training in new tracksuits when the temperature was 90 degrees in the afternoon and the team hotel and food were terrible.

'However, we had them back at Tynecastle for the return leg on 9 September 1958 and played them off the park. Willie Bauld was just brilliant that night and scored both of our goals in a 2–1 win, which was our first victory in Europe. I think one of their players kicked Willie in the first five minutes of the game and you just didn't do that to him! That woke Willie up and he just went to town and made them pay. It was such a shame he finished up on the losing side that night but we hadn't really given ourselves much of a chance after the first leg.

'Another special memory for me was obviously my debut for Hearts at Tynecastle as a 17 year old, when we defeated Kilmarnock 3–2 on 17 November 1956. I had been a Hearts supporter as a boy and gone along to games with my dad, so to actually play for the team at Tynecastle was a dream come true for me. I remember seeing a photograph of me surrounded by the likes of Bobby Parker, Tom McKenzie, Freddie Glidden, Jimmy Milne and Johnny Cumming and thinking to myself that was some protection for a young goalkeeper. They were great players and it was a super club to play with at that time.

'With players like Jimmy Wardhaugh, Willie Bauld, Alex Young, Johnny Cumming and Dave Mackay we never worried about the Old Firm at all. It was nothing but a great privilege for a youngster to come into an environment like that.

'Along with the European nights, the derby matches against Hibs were always great occasions. One I particularly recall, though, is a game which will hold fond memories for Hibees. I was in goal when Joe Baker scored four against Hearts in the Scottish Cup at Tynecastle in a 4–3 win – and we missed a penalty that day. We had been going really well and everyone expected us to win but it is amazing how derbies invariably never work out like that. The funny thing is, Ian Crawford used to take our spot-kicks and in the build-up to the cup tie he spoke about spending a lot of time working on the penalties, as Ronnie Simpson, the Hibs keeper at that time, had a great reputation for saving them. We spoke about practising them

A record crowd of 53,396 crammed into Tynecastle to see Hearts take on Rangers in the third round of the Scottish Cup on 13 February 1932. (Photo courtesy of John Kerr)

Alfie Conn (left) looks on as Willie Bauld feels the full force of this challenge from Partick Thistle's goalkeeper during a 5–0 triumph in August 1953.

Aug 1953 - Hearts v Hamilton. Bauld challenges the Hamilton keeper Ritchie, whilst Conn of Hearts and Waddle of Hamilton look on. Hearts won the day 5-0.

Willie Bauld nets for Hearts against Rangers in March 1956.

Hearts V Rangers at Tynecastle, March 1956. Willie Bauld scores.

Delighted fans get a close up of the 1956 Scottish Cup as Matthie Chalmers takes it around the ground.

Tommy Walker introduces Willie Bauld to the Duke of Gloucester before a 5–1 victory over Aberdeen in December 1958.

It's ten of Hearts as (from left to right) Bobby Flavell, Tommy Sloan, Tommy Darling, Willie Bauld, Ken Currie, Jimmy Wardhaugh, Jimmy Brown, Bobby Buchan, Colin Liddell and Bobby Parker pose for a photograph.

It's derby delight as Alfie Conn is congratulated by manager Tommy Walker (right) and Willie Bauld and Jimmy Wardhaugh after scoring the winner against Hibs.

Chairman Nicol Kilgour proudly displays the 1957–58 League Championship trophy with the triumphant squad.

Bobby Blackwood is all smiles as Gordon Smith scores for Hearts in a 5–3 victory over Ayr United on 3 October 1959.

The legendary Willie Bauld kicks off his testimonial match against Sheffield United in November 1962. The match finished 2–2.

Willie Bauld (left) watches his testimonial game against Sheffield United from the sidelines alongside trainer Donald McLeod.

Groundsmen Willie Montgomery and Matthie Chalmers are left frustrated as fog forces the postponement of a league clash with Rangers.

Jim Fotheringham, the former Arsenal player, and Andy Bowman lead the way in training.

These supporters found the ideal vantage point at the School End to watch the action unfold at a packed Tynecastle.

Hearts stars Donald Ford (left) and Tommy Murray with 'Miss Hearts', Gloria Donaldson, at the club's centenary rally which was held at Edinburgh's Usher Hall in September 1974.

Drew Busby heads for goal in Hearts' epic 5–1 victory over Lokomotiv
Leipzig in September 1976.

A champagne moment for
Hearts after clinching the
First Division championship
in 1980 with victory over
Airdrie. Jim Jefferies,
Malcolm Robertson, Frank
Lidell and John Brough are
at the forefront of the
celebrations in the
Tynecastle bath.

Craig Levein (left) and John Robertson with chairman Wallace Mercer
and manager Alex MacDonald.

Gary Mackay (left), Ian Westwater and David Bowman shortly after signing for the club in the summer of 1980.

John Robertson leaves Clyde's John McVeigh in his wake as he shows his predatory instincts in his first season with Hearts.

John Robertson and Neil Berry turn away in delight
after Sandy Clark (out of picture) scores in a 3–0 victory over Rangers
at Tynecastle in November 1985.

Lithuanian millionaire Vladimir Romanov and his close associate
Sergejus Fedotovas take their seats at the extraordinary
general meeting which voted to halt the sale of Tynecastle.

Vladimir Romanov with his son Roman, who was appointed
to the board as a non-executive director in 2005.

throughout the week so we knew what we had to do during the game and made sure we had prepared as best we could. Of course, we never did get round to it and what happened at Tynecastle? Yes, we were awarded a penalty and Ronnie duly saved it! Needless to say, we were left wondering what might have been.

'I was proud to follow in the footsteps of guys like Jimmy Brown, Jimmy Watters and Willie Duff. In my opinion, Jimmy Brown was the daddy of the goalkeepers, a real father figure. I used to go and watch him, and certain things always stick in my mind, such as seeing him walk between the two posts and kick the base of them. He was always immaculate during games – and never seemed to get dirty even when he dived in the goalmouth. He also wore the latest line in sweaters and appeared to be ahead of his time. He was a class act, someone of pure quality.

'Looking at the modern Tynecastle, I wonder how we ever managed to get 49,000 fans inside the ground and have to look at old photographs to remind myself of the size of the crowds. Internally, it has never really changed that much apart from the corridors having been moved about a bit and the players coming out at a different place.

'I spent seven years at Hearts and it was a special period in my career. I actually went back there as a Hibs player when Hibs had a better team than Hearts. I never really thought about going back there with Hearts as rivals as I was brought up in an era when you went to Easter Road one week and Tynecastle the other to watch your football. You basically went where the good football was being played.

'I have happy memories of Tynecastle, and I have also got the medals to go with them.'

Jimmy Murray (inside-right, 1950–61)

'I came to Hearts as a 17 year old and scored on my debut against Stirling Albion two years later in 1952. I didn't play another game for two years, because at that time Conn, Bauld and Wardhaugh were the main men and, thanks to their form, no one could get in. I suppose it was a tough period to try to break into the side, although

I did guest for Reading for a wee while during my National Service.

'When I did get into the team, it was to basically replace Alfie after he had been transferred to Raith Rovers. Willie and Jimmy were still there, as was Alex Young, and I was fortunate to get help from the players already in the team. When you think of the likes of Dave Mackay, Johnny Cumming and Freddie Glidden as well, there were an awful lot of good players back then. They did all the work and I just had to put the ball in the back of the net.

'Season 1957–58 saw us hit the top of our form. We scored a lot of goals and won the League Championship and League Cup. It was a great time to be there with superb crowds and everybody lapped it all up.

'I played in the World Cup trial match at Tynecastle and was lucky enough to get on the plane to Sweden in '58 – playing there has to be the highlight of my career. It transpired that I scored Scotland's first goal in the World Cup finals, although to be honest I didn't realise the significance of it at the time. A lot was made about it later but I was just doing my job. I remember Eddie Turnbull sending in a free-kick against Yugoslavia, I met it with my head and the ball was in the back of the net before you could say "John Robertson"! There have been a lot better goals scored by Scotland since then but I suppose I can't get away from the fact it was the first one for us in a World Cup finals.

'Everybody who played in Sweden was given a special bag with two pairs of Adidas boots to take home. Adidas was just starting to catch on at that stage and the boots had screw-in studs with special soles. When I returned to Tynecastle, the lads saw them and said they'd never catch on but in hindsight I wish I'd have taken out some Adidas shares back then.

'Returning to club life after the international scene took a bit of readjusting but the great thing about the squad at that time was the team spirit and terrific camaraderie. I have so many memories of the place but two in particular stick in my mind. The first was when we were playing Rangers and we had wanted to try the new white football. It hadn't been officially given the green light but we had been training with it and wanted to use it on this occasion. I remember Rangers refused to play with it and this ball came flying out of the away dressing-room. They didn't want to use the lighter one but I don't think it mattered, as I think we still beat them.

'The other memory I have is of Alfie Conn being a real joker. There was one time when I was getting treatment on an injured knee and was using a new idea that involved discs to apply deep heat to the affected area. As the other players came in to have a look, I explained what was happening and tried to tell them the reason they couldn't feel the heat was because it was supposed to go deep and took a while to warm up. It took me some time to realise that Alfie had pulled the plug out of the socket and there was no power getting through to the discs.

'Another incident happened when we were taken on a training stint for a few days to Crieff Hydro. We used to enjoy going there as the facilities were excellent, although once it appeared to be a place where ministers got special rates as we walked in to find a bunch of them there and we realised we would have to be on our best behaviour. Golf was also a favourite when we were at Crieff and on one occasion Alfie and Willie Bauld got up to no good by filling one of the training staff's golf bags with coal so it was too heavy to be lifted onto the bus. Once they were found out, I think it was two or three weeks before they played again.

'We also used to train at Gullane quite a bit and Kilspindie was also a great golfing haunt for Hearts back then. Going to Gullane we used to get the bus to Aberlady and then run over the tank traps and goodness knows what else to arrive there. I had to laugh when I heard Jock Wallace saying it was the place to go when he was Rangers manager. If I had been given £1 for every time I had been there, I'd be a millionaire. We had been there long before him, running up and down the sand dunes with Johnny Harvey, as he used to be a physical training instructor and knew the score. Jim Fotheringham had come to Hearts from Arsenal and had never experienced anything like that in his life before. The first time he saw it he didn't want to do it and eventually came in three-quarters of an hour behind us.

'Johnny Harvey was a great motivator for the team. We never really saw Tommy Walker and it was Johnny who made us what we were. The two of them maybe selected the team for a Saturday but it was Johnny who motivated us during the week and made things happen. Tommy was always in the stand during games but Johnny was there in the dugout and was always on hand with the "magic" sponge as well.'

Antti Niemi (goalkeeper, 1999–2002)

'Although I didn't have too many appearances for Rangers, I actually played at Tynecastle two or three times while I was at Ibrox, so I was well aware of the stadium when I moved to Edinburgh. The first occasion I experienced the ground I was warming up with Andy Goram at the Rangers end. I was pretty nervous, as the atmosphere was good with people so close to the pitch.

'I think it is a special place and unique among modern stadiums. It is difficult to fault the atmosphere, as there is always a noise generated irrespective of the size of the crowd – it often felt full with 12,000 people inside it and you would sometimes wonder where the extra 6,000 could go!

'My first game there as a Hearts player in December 1999 didn't go too well, as we lost the derby to Hibs 3–0. I had only just completed my move from Rangers and hardly knew any of my new teammates' names. I think the only name I knew that day was Mixu Paatelainen – and he was playing for Hibs! That was a bad memory but fortunately I went on to enjoy much better times there. The games against the Old Firm were always special, while the European nights were memorable. The UEFA Cup clash with Stuttgart was one such evening and I remember that occasion well and what might have happened had Gordan Petric scored with a late chance.

'Another of my favourite highlights was my last game for the club before signing for Southampton when we beat the Hibees 5–1; Mark de Vries scored four goals on his full debut. Considering I had been in the team that had lost 6–2 at Easter Road, it was nice to get a bit of my own back on them.

'The move to Tynecastle was a good decision and really helped my career. I wasn't playing for Rangers and needed to get out of there. I had a great time at Tynecastle but when the chance came to play in the English Premiership just after the start of the 2002–03 season, it was too good an opportunity to turn down. I had been in Scotland for five years, two and a half of which were spent playing regularly for Hearts.

'Although I had just signed a new long-term contract at Tynecastle, the football was enjoyable and Edinburgh was a beautiful city, it was basically an easy decision to leave and I have no regrets about moving.'

Derek O'Connor (striker, 1978–85)

'I was always a Hearts man, having lived in Wheatfield Place until I was about 19 years old. I watched the team as a wee laddie and I always remember Hearts losing 7–1 to Dundee. That was a real shock for me at my age.

'My career got off to the best possible start with a goal against Aberdeen at Pittodrie with my first touch of the ball on my debut. It was a bad time to have come into the team, though, as the club had made a lot of promises to bring in new faces but didn't do so, as the money wasn't there.

'I was seven years at the club and had my ups and downs with the various managers. Bobby Moncur tried to sell me to Partick Thistle, as he had a couple of players lined up, but I refused to go. I was disappointed to say the least and there was a lot of trouble and bad feeling within the club at that point.

'He had brought in his own players, such as Alfie Conn, Willie McVie and people like that, and the club was virtually split down the middle. The ill feeling didn't do anybody any good. With his signings, there was a feeling of them and us and, to be honest, a lot of guys moved on because of the bad feeling at the club. When Bobby Moncur left, I think he realised he had made mistakes and when Alex MacDonald came in he helped steady the ship. He brought me back full time as I had gone part time and returned to my old job of surveying for an electrical contracting firm. Alex had me back training morning, noon and night and got me back into things, and despite everything I have to say I thoroughly enjoyed my time at Tynecastle.'

Donald Park
(midfielder, 1972–78 and 1983–85; assistant manager, 2004–05)

'I first came to Tynecastle in 1972 and spent six years with Hearts. Although we got to a Scottish Cup final in the mid-'70s, it was actually a hard time for the club with the new Premier Division coming into existence. It was a bit of a struggle but we made it into the top flight before eventually being relegated.

'The night when we played Lokomotiv Leipzig, 29 September 1976, in Europe was definitely the most memorable occasion I was ever involved in as a player or otherwise in football. I remember it being a typically damp Scottish night in Edinburgh with the mist swirling around and the ball zipping across the surface. That certainly added to the special atmosphere and it turned out to be a wonderful evening for Hearts. What made it so special was the fact we came through a really tough tie against a top East German side. To win the match comfortably 5–1 was superb and has to rank as the outstanding highlight of my time with Hearts.

'When it came for me to leave Hearts in 1978, I was amused by how things transpired. I received a phone call from Willie Ormond, who was the manager at the time, to say that Partick Thistle had come in for me. I thought about it briefly and told him I wasn't sure, as they were a part-time team. Wee Willie replied, "We would like you to go." I knew then my Tynecastle days were numbered and that I'd better go and speak to them. Willie wanted to sign John Craig for the left-hand side of midfield and, as it turned out, Denis McQuade was also part of the deal. They both came to Tynecastle, with me going in the opposite direction.

'In 1983, I came back to the club as a part-time player for two years under Alex MacDonald and Sandy Jardine. The stadium hadn't changed that much but the team had certainly moved on and Hearts were a really good side. There was a good mix of older players and kids, although not much middle ground. I think I was 32 at the time and decided not to go full time as I had a decent job, but, to be honest, I found it very difficult. Having said that, I think we won the first five or six games in my first season back and that gave us the springboard to qualify for Europe again that year.

'I left in 1985 but strangely enough found myself back at Tynecastle a number of years later as part of the Hibs set-up.

'I obviously coached a lot of the youngsters at Easter Road but didn't have to think twice about returning to Tynecastle again when Robbo asked me to be his assistant after Craig Levein left to go to Leicester City. I enjoyed my time at Inverness with him and we seemed to dovetail well. The position gave me the chance to get back to Hearts and Edinburgh, so there was no hesitation about saying yes.

'The developed ground is a magnificent place to play football and that has a lot to do with the crowd being so close to the pitch. In my opinion, the stadium is conducive to exciting football.

'After accepting the job, I would bump into some of the Hibs guys now and again, and, in fact, I got a New Year text from Ian Murray and Derek Riordan wishing me a happy 2005 – with a number of expletives thrown in as well, which wasn't surprising! On one occasion, I met Riordan in town and he said he thought me being at Tynecastle was quite strange. And this was the guy who used to call me a Jambo twat when I was at Easter Road, so I don't think I could ever win.

'It was great when I was appointed assistant manager to John Robertson but I was very sad when it ended after only a few months. In saying that, I have great memories of Tynecastle and Heart of Midlothian Football Club.'

Willie Pettigrew (striker, 1981–84)

'Tony Ford was the manager at the time I came to Hearts but it was actually Wallace Mercer who signed me. I used to travel through to Edinburgh from the west with Roddy MacDonald, Peter Shields and Stewart MacLaren.

'At the time, Hearts were trying to get out of the old First Division and had brought in a few experienced professionals. We just missed out on promotion that year on the last day of the season. We had to go to Kilmarnock and win but didn't do so. We had a lot of young guys in the team and were a bit unlucky but we did manage to go up the following year.

'Funds were tight back then and the club was really watching the pennies. After training, if you wanted a warm bath you had to get back inside quickly, as the boiler would be turned off after heating just so much hot water. They apparently couldn't afford to keep it going. They also only washed the training gear once a week, so you had to be in early in the morning to get a decent piece of kit.

'I have fond memories of Hearts. Jim Jefferies was still at Tynecastle as a player when I arrived, although he left that season. Willie Johnston and Peter Marinello were also teammates and those two would bet against two snails crawling up a wall if they could! There was always a great atmosphere and it was a terrific place to play your football.

'I remember scoring four goals against Clydebank and also Clyde, which were highlights. There was also a game against St Johnstone on New Year's Day 1982, which we won when both teams were going for promotion. I was in the Premier League with Hearts but never really played for the club at that level before moving to Morton. Wee John Robertson had emerged and he actually did to me what I had done to other strikers and pushed me out the door. What goes around comes around, I guess! I was never bitter, though, as John was a great guy. Jimmy Bone was also brought in and the pair of them up front meant games for me were few and far between.

'Hearts are a big club and something of a sleeping giant, and I think that was half the problem, as they chased a dream which just got further and further away.'

Neil Pointon (left-back, 1995–98)

'I joined the club just as the stadium was being transformed with the new stands going up. I think the School End had just been finished but there was still the old terracings at the Gorgie Road end. I had played there previously when the Shed was up, when Everton played in Gary Mackay's testimonial, so I had seen it change quite a bit. I thought it was an excellent ground for atmosphere and I have a lot of great memories from my two and a half years there.

'I left in the summer of 1998 and although I didn't play in the

Scottish Cup final victory, taking the trophy back to Tynecastle to celebrate with the fans was a brilliant experience. Sadly, the whole experience was soured a bit because of the hassle we had trying to get onto the pitch at Parkhead after the win. The euphoria had died down a little bit but we didn't actually get to see the lads lift the cup.

'I left that summer, the same as Robbo, but I think it hit him a lot harder than it did me, as I'm sure he thought he was going to get into the coaching side of things at Hearts.'

Willie Polland (full-back/centre-half, 1961–67)

'Although I started my career at Raith Rovers, I had always supported Hearts and when I got the chance to go to Tynecastle in 1961 I thought to myself, "Somebody up there likes me", as it was something I never thought would happen.

'I actually came to Hearts from Raith at the same time as Willie Wallace, who went on to great things with Celtic. My years there were undoubtedly the high point of my football career and Tynecastle still holds some special memories of the good football and special people I met.

'There were quite a few characters in the dressing-room when I was at the club and the one person who springs to mind immediately is Willie Hamilton. He was just as good as Jim Baxter and in my opinion it would have been difficult to split the two of them. Willie was such a laid-back sort of person but so talented as well. He didn't train well and couldn't run far without gasping for breath. But out on the park he was a different person. He could beat opponents for fun and was capable of hitting the net from almost anywhere. We would be thinking, "He'll never score from there", and then all of a sudden he'd smash the ball home from around 30 yards out.

'I was playing the day Willie made his debut for Hearts. He scored one of the two goals in a 2–0 win over Dundee at Tynecastle. I remember the match well because Bertie Auld gave me a bad kick on the front of my leg. After I'd gone out of football, I used to meet up with Bertie now and again, as we were both involved in the pub trade. I always had a laugh with him about the number of marks he left on players – and he'd always reply, "I could say the same about you, Willie."

'On that note, I recall being at a function one night when this guy from Motherwell came up to me and started to roll up the leg of his trousers. I said to myself, "What's going on here?" and then he explained he was showing a scar I'd left on him.

'Willie Hamilton was a class apart. When you looked at him, you thought he was about to fall asleep, as he always seemed to have a tired look about him. Once out on the pitch, though, he came alive and was just so clever on the ball.

'I remember travelling back from Norway with Hearts after we had been invited to play during British Week over there. We had flown over but made the return journey by boat and I think one director and myself were the only members of the Hearts party not to be seasick! Johnny Harvey asked me to try to find Willie, as he couldn't see him anywhere, and I came across him sitting outside at the back of the boat sheltering from the wind. He was in a bad way, was throwing up and looked really ill. I eventually persuaded him to go back inside and I thought then that there was no way he'd be able to play on the Saturday. But he was absolutely brilliant that day at Tynecastle. I played that afternoon and can remember saying at half-time in the dressing-room that the pitch felt like it was rocking and rolling from side to side. The crossing had been so rough that I was still feeling the effects.

'Willie certainly made his mark at Hearts but I'd actually met him before I went to Tynecastle. When I was at Raith, I used to train at Airdrie once a week on a Tuesday. Willie was originally from Airdrie and came up from Sheffield United on his holidays to see his mum, and that's when I got to know him. When Hearts were thinking about signing Willie, Johnny Harvey asked me about him one day when we were having a chat. I said I knew him, that he was a poor trainer but brilliant during a match. The next thing I knew he had joined Hearts. Willie soon asked me how I got from Armadale to Tynecastle and asked for a lift when I told him I drove there. He then arranged to get a bus from Airdrie to Armadale and we'd go in together. I think he did that for about a week before he got himself a wee van. The way he played football he deserved a Rolls-Royce.'

Bobby Prentice (outside-left, 1973–79)

'Although I spent six years at Tynecastle, it is fair to say the first two or three were my best. A few new players had come in around about the same time, with the likes of myself, Kenny Aird and Drew Busby, and it was basically a new forward line. Donald Ford was still there at that time, of course.

'There was a lot of turmoil at the club between 1976 and 1979 as my Hearts career drew to a close, and there were a lot of changes on the managerial and coaching side which made things difficult for the players. When Willie Ormond came to the club, it was the beginning of the end for me. Different managers bring different ideas and I think the game had also become a bit more defensive in the late '70s. Things tightened up a bit, which didn't help wingers like myself and maybe I struggled to get into the team because of that.

'If teams are doing well and winning games, it is easier for wingers to get a game, but when sides go on the slide they tend to suffer. By the time 1979 came, I had been there six years and, to be honest, I was ready for a change. I had been a Hearts supporter since I was a young lad and it was a dream come true to play for the club but I needed a fresh challenge and signed for Toronto Blizzard. That was a good move for me and helped me to see a bit of the world as well. I spent two years there before joining an indoor league in Baltimore for a couple of years and then finished up in Buffalo, still in the indoor game, in 1983–84. It was after that I came back home to Scotland and now and again I'd pop along to Tynecastle to watch some games.

'I still have one or two decent memories from my spell there. Obviously playing in the 1976 Scottish Cup final was a highlight, as was my first derby match against Hibs in 1973 when we beat them 4–1 at Tynecastle. That came after we had lost 7–0 at Easter Road and it was sweet revenge. We had gone into the game determined to rectify what had happened in the previous match and bring some pride back to the club. It was a special day for everybody but particularly memorable for me with it being my first game against Hibs for Hearts.

'Another great night was the Leipzig European tie at Tynecastle when we won 5–1 on 29 September 1976. We had a great celebration after that victory! Actually, we had been going well during the first part of that season – we beat Rangers 3–0 at Ibrox when I scored my first goal for Hearts – but then injuries eventually got the better of the squad, which wasn't the biggest to start with.'

Steven Pressley (centre-half, 1998–present day)

'In terms of the size of support which Hearts attract, I believe that Tynecastle is an ideal stadium. The crowd is very much on top of you and 17,702 is an ideal capacity.

'There have been great European nights, with the game against Stuttgart in September 2000 in particular sticking in my mind. There was a roller-coaster of emotions, which spilled down from the stands. The fans made it a night to remember, although we were to be knocked out by the narrowest of margins.

'The thing about Tynecastle is that the fans are so close to the players. It's a well-designed stadium, which creates a great atmosphere. I played there for Dundee United before joining Hearts and was one of those who always enjoyed coming to Tynecastle. My first game there for Hearts was a League Cup tie against Raith Rovers at the start of the 1998–99 season and the stadium made an immediate impression on me.

'In my time away with Scotland when talking to the Old Firm players I got the impression that Tynecastle was the one stadium outwith their own which they looked forward to playing in. I think that was because it had a similar sort of atmosphere to what they were used to. It was one of the games of the season they looked forward to, which is testimony in itself to Tynecastle.

'But I also remember their complaints about the size of the away dressing-room. It is tiny and there is a hot pipe running through it, which makes it quite a stuffy place before a game.

'As far as I'm concerned it's a fantastic stadium in which to play football. Considering how many fans it holds, it's one of the best atmosphere–capacity ratios in the game. When we first heard the ground was going to be sold, it was a sad day for everyone associated with the club. It wasn't just the current fans who were disappointed. We are talking about generations of supporters who had gone along to the ground every week to watch their team. I'm sure Tynecastle became a second home for a lot of them and it must have been very difficult for them to hear that the stadium would have to go.

'After all that, they must have all been delighted when Mr Romanov came in and said he wanted Hearts to stay in Gorgie.'

John Robertson
(striker, 1981–April 1988 and December 1988–98; manager, 2004–05)

'My first game at Tynecastle was actually a reserve match against Hibs, believe it or not, early in the new year of 1981. We won 2–1 in front of a crowd of around 2,000 people and I remember being absolutely knackered as it was the first time I had been on such a big pitch in such a high-tempo game. I'd left school that Christmas and that was the start of it all.

'My competitive debut for the club was at home to Queen of the South on 17 February 1982, when I came on as a subsitute. It was quite funny as I had played in a 0–0 draw against East Fife reserves the night before, did quite well and was named in the squad for the following day's match. Alex MacDonald told me before the start of the game that I was on the bench but if Hearts went three goals ahead, I would get on.

'My big brother Chris put us ahead early on and I got quite excited when we went 2–0 up. Queen of the South pulled one back right on half-time and I thought to myself that was that. But Chris scored again early in the second half and then we went 4–1 ahead with half an hour left to play. I was champing at the bit and I think it had escaped Alex's mind what he had said.

'He actually turned round with 17 minutes left and asked us what the score was. Somebody said, "It's 4–1, gaffer", at which point he looked at me and said, "Why didn't you tell me? Get yourself stripped!" He took Gerry McCoy off and I played up front alongside Chris, the only time we played together in the first team for Hearts.

'There's also a funny story surrounding the first goal I scored for the club. I had done the usual work on the Friday and had come in on the Saturday morning to get the boots ready and lay out all the kit. Myself and a couple of the other ground staff lads were then told to go and have our lunch and being prime young athletes at the time we nipped up to the chippie and got some fish suppers.

'After finishing them, we came back to the ground and went about our normal duties when the manager asked to see me. I immediately thought I was in trouble for some reason but was then told that Willie Pettigrew had failed a fitness test and that I'd be on the bench. I was put on at half-time and managed to get our third goal against Alloa Athletic when Paddy Byrne laid the ball on a plate for me with five minutes to go. That was the first of 214 league goals I would score for Hearts.

'In the early days, my job was to help clean the stadium and that included painting the stadium or even sand blasting the referee's room. We always used to get up to some real fun and games at the ground. Whoever the physio Andy Stevenson saw first in the morning would get the worst job to do, which included cleaning out the home toilets with a toothbrush. Everybody used to hide from him and make sure he knew we were hiding. The prime position was the toilet in the away dressing-room, as we could always hear him coming along the corridor and it gave us enough time to scarper. If you got to the back toilet, you were safe, as there were baths and cupboards and such like where guys would hide. One day Gordon Marr was caught. He had jumped onto the parapet above the door and was watching Andy tell people in no uncertain terms that the first person he caught would get the worst job ever. He took two steps forward and the whole parapet came crashing down with a startled Gordon landing behind him. I think he spent the next fortnight doing the worst jobs imaginable!

'Me and Davie Bowman lived a couple of streets apart and used to get the old No. 45 bus up to Tynecastle every day. We went to the same primary school and secondary school, and it was a blow when he was sold to Coventry. But that was a reflection of the state the club was in at the time and they had to accept the offer for him.

'In 1988, I spent eight months at Newcastle United after Sandy Jardine had decided it was time to cash in on me. I didn't really settle down there and came back up the road and thankfully picked up where I left off. Some players are meant for some clubs and it appears I was meant for Hearts.

'My rapid return to Gorgie would not have been possible without the involvement of Edinburgh businessman Ramez Daher, who sponsored me for the first three seasons of my second spell at Tynecastle.'

'The club was struggling a bit and Wallace Mercer wanted to bring John back to Tynecastle from Newcastle,' remembers Daher. 'We had sold him for £625,000 in the April of 1988 but they wanted £750,000 eight months later and Hearts were reluctant to take on that responsibility. I said I would take care of his wages, so when Hearts brought him back I sponsored him for the first three years of his contract. He took a pay cut to come back but I think he was earning something like £400 per week and was the top earner at Tynecastle.

'The very first game I saw at Tynecastle, John scored a couple of goals, and I was impressed by him immediately. I have followed the team ever since then and when I was in a position to help, thanks to my fruit and vegetable business, I did so. It was a good deal for me as well, though, as everyone knew about my company after that.

'I was at Tynecastle when Robbo broke Jimmy Wardhaugh's goals record and, to be honest, I felt part of the process, as I felt I had contributed something to John and done something for the club.

'He's a great guy and when he came back as manager I was delighted. He talks too much, though. Once he starts he never stops.'

'It was good to get back to Tynecastle, and the Scottish Cup win in 1998 was fantastic and could never be beaten as a player,' remembers Robbo. 'People keep asking me if I have any regrets about not getting on during the final but I absolutely don't. It was all about Hearts winning the trophy. I wasn't caring by that stage.

If I had gone on to do a certain job, then fine, but just to go on for the sake of it might not have worked. The team were hanging on, defending well, and sometimes substitutions can upset the rhythm. I just wanted the final whistle to go. Even if I had got on for 30 seconds, what difference would it have made? Not a bit of difference to me. I have a winner's medal and that's good enough.

'The celebrations the day after in Edinburgh are etched on my mind. To go round the city in an open-top bus is one of the things you'll never forget in your life. It just does not get any better than having 400,000 people out on a glorious sunny day to cheer you on. We then came back to a packed Tynecastle and I know I didn't get home for a couple of days. It was just mad, as things kept going on and on. Sunday was the parade and the Monday was a Bank Holiday – it was just party time.

'Beating Jimmy Wardhaugh's goalscoring record with a penalty against Rangers at Tynecastle on 10 May 1997 in the final game of the season was very special. Time was running out with four minutes to go and I wondered if I was going to get there. Then Gordan Petric brought me down in the box. I told myself, "Just concentrate and hit it down the middle." That was the plan but then all the Rangers players were telling Andy Dibble to stand still, so Plan A went out the window and in came Plan B. I managed to keep my nerve and the relief after scoring was fantastic.

'My father was a great Hearts man who loved the likes of Freddie Glidden and Conn, Bauld and Wardhaugh, so for him to think about his little boy beating Jimmy Wardhaugh's record must have been fantastic.

'There had been a lot of publicity about the situation and the fact it could have been my last game, as at the time Jim Jefferies didn't know if he was going to offer me a new contract or not. It had been billed as possibly my last chance to do it and I managed to get two late in the game to break the record – and I got another year's deal afterwards as well.

'My last game against Dunfermline at Tynecastle was also special. Jim brought me off with 20 minutes to go and the ovation I got was fantastic. A week after the cup final, I had a meeting with Jim and

Billy Brown and they made it clear they were considering a new one-year deal for myself but thought it was the right time for me to move on and start afresh on the back of winning the Scottish Cup.

'It was a very emotional time. I walked across from the offices into the stadium. The ground was empty and I just picked up my boots and walked out. It was tearful, but football can be like that and before you knew it I was along the M8 to join Livingston.

'Inverness Caledonian Thistle gave me my first chance as a manager and it was very difficult to leave the club as they were great people up there. I felt I was maybe too young to take the Hearts job but I didn't know when it was going to be offered again. I never thought Hearts would come calling so soon and when I went into the manager's office for the first time I let out this great roar as it all seemed so surreal. I had dedicated myself to giving everything I had to keeping Caley in the SPL but then found myself catapulted straight from there into the group stages of the UEFA Cup.

'It was suddenly all quite different and, to be honest, it was a much bigger job than I had ever imagined. I was very sad when I left after just under seven months in charge but what happened will never diminish my love for the club.'

Gilles Rousset (goalkeeper, 1995–2001)

'The time I spent at Tynecastle was fantastic and I met so many good people during my period with the club. I remember coming over for the first time thinking that my English was reasonably good only to discover that my Scottish was very poor. I found Gary Locke's accent impossible. He was from Bonnyrigg and a lot of what he said in the early stages passed me by.

'The Scottish Cup win was a huge occasion for everyone involved and the celebrations the day after were just incredible. I don't think it was until a wee while afterwards that I really began to appreciate what we had achieved. We had suffered a few disappointments in finals before that but I don't think we would have won in '98 had we not gone through all that.

'I was desperate to see Hearts play Bordeaux in France in the

UEFA Cup in 2003 but I got stuck in traffic and missed my flight. I had to go back to my house and watched the match on television. That was a nightmare for me but I was so happy and felt so proud when I heard all the Hearts supporters chanting my name during the match, which the lads won 1–0. I have always had a great relationship with the fans and that was so special for me. I made sure I came back to Edinburgh for the second leg and, although the result was a disappointment as Bordeaux won, it was great to be there.

'Tynecastle and the club will always have a special place in my heart and I will always consider myself a Jambo.'

Stefano Salvatori (1996–2000)
'The first game I played at Tynecastle was in the Scottish Cup against Celtic and that was a memorable time for me. It was a superb stadium to play football in and the fans were very passionate, which made it special for the players. I also enjoyed the city of Edinburgh and its people, who were very friendly towards me. I stayed for three years in the Caledonian Hotel and during my time in the city I got to know the owner of Bar Roma and also enjoyed Indigo Yard at the West End. I even bought a nice flat in the city centre. I enjoyed my years at Tynecastle and the club still has a special place in my heart.'

Rudi Skacel
(midfielder, 2005 on loan from Marseille)
'The crowds at Tynecastle have been great and I don't think I've played in a stadium quite like it, with the supporters so close to the pitch. I was very pleased to score so many goals early in my first season but personal success means nothing to me. It's the team which counts.'

Andy Thorn (centre-half, September 1996)
'Dave Bassett was supposed to be going to Manchester City as manager and I was going to go with him from Wimbledon. Then Jim Jefferies got in touch with me the night before the Celtic League Cup quarter-final on 17 September 1996 as he had a lot of experienced

guys missing. Although I was having problems at the time with Wimbledon over a new deal, I had kept my fitness levels up. I spoke to Dave and he said I should play and get a game under my belt. Jim then got back in touch on the morning of the game and again asked me to come up and play. The only flight I could get at that stage, though, was about three o'clock in the afternoon from Heathrow.

'I was picked up at the airport and then went to the team hotel for a pre-match meal. It was basically over a slice of toast that I met the guys for the first time – and Robbo ate the lot! I had to get in quick, as he was going to have everything.

'I didn't have a great knowledge of Scottish football but I knew all about Hearts, as, after playing with him at Newcastle, I had followed Robbo's career. I didn't realise, though, that there were quite so many players out until I arrived for the game. It was a very young team out on the park; in fact, when I glanced along our back line, the kids looked like they should have been still doing their homework. It was an unbelievable night, however, and one of the best I have ever had in football.

'I loved my time there and the Celtic match was just unbelievable. The support was fantastic and I am sure the atmosphere was one of the main reasons we beat them. With such a stadium and the fans right on top of the players, Tynecastle was a real weapon for Hearts.

'It was a brilliant occasion and I've never soaked up so much pressure in a football match in all my life. We just had to defend well and hope to get something at the other end of the pitch. Thankfully, Robbo came up with a good finish during the second half of extra time. It goes without saying, though, that I was knackered at the end.

'Another thing I remember is that Gary Naysmith made his debut that night. It was a fantastic evening – but we had an even better night afterwards!

'It transpired Dave didn't actually go to Manchester City and I ended up signing for Tranmere after my brief spell at Hearts. I played in a 1–1 draw against Motherwell a few days after the Celtic match, as the team was still having problems with injuries and suspensions. It came as a bit of a surprise – I had a few drinks the night before but got through the game! Looking back it would have been good if we could have got something sorted out but it wasn't to be. But I'm pleased I was able to help out in some way.'

Mark de Vries (striker, 2002–05)

'There is something magical about Tynecastle and my first game there on 11 August 2002 will live with me forever. I signed from FC Dordrecht in Holland and had heard a lot about the Hearts games against Hibs, but to score four goals against our arch rivals on my first start for the club was just a dream.

'I will never forget the build-up to the match and the game itself, and I was still talking about the 5–1 victory years after it happened. During the first part of the match, I couldn't hear what my teammates were saying due to the noise of the crowd but after the first goal from Andy Kirk went in, I seemed to come out of a trance and all of a sudden was aware of them and what the gaffer was shouting from the touchline. I remember vividly when the referee blew the final whistle I said to myself, "Thank God that's over", as I was absolutely knackered and had been relying on pure adrenalin to get me through the last five or ten minutes.

'People kept coming up to me in the streets in Edinburgh to speak to me about what it felt like. It was just incredible and something I doubt I will ever better in my career. I was very proud to have been part of the team which put five past Hibs. We had lost a couple of players and there were a few new faces with the manager trying to build something. But scoring four goals on my full debut against Hibs didn't make life easy for me. The expectations were there from all the supporters from day one.

'I thoroughly enjoyed my time at Tynecastle and the way the stadium is built must be a delight for every professional footballer. The public is so close to the pitch that you can just about speak to the fans and I would think every footballer loves to play there. I don't have a bad word to say about the club and I have to admit the decision to go to Leicester City was the hardest I have ever had to make in my career.'

Graham Weir (striker, 2000–present day)

The Tynecastle highlight for me has to be the two goals I scored in injury time against Hibs on 2 January 2003. We escaped with a 4–4 draw. It was an unbelievable ending to a match that I'll never forget.

My other memory is not so pleasant, though. When he was manager, Craig Levein found out that I had been playing golf with teammate Neil Janczyk the day before we were due to take on Hibs in the Festival Cup in September 2004. I was dropped for the game and after the match we were ordered to run up and down the entire length of the Gorgie Road Stand with our golf clubs on our backs. My legs were killing me at the end of it. I don't think I'll be making that mistake again.

Alex Young (striker, 1955–60)

'I was playing junior football for Newtongrange Star when Tommy Walker signed me after his scout, Duncan McClure, who used to play for Hearts, recommended me. Just three weeks after playing junior football, I was in the first team at Hearts.

'My first game was against Partick Thistle, when I was in the side in place of Willie Bauld, and we won 2–1 on 27 August 1955. I scored 23 goals in my first season and was part of the team that won the Scottish Cup in 1956, beating Celtic, which was a great feeling. I also scored the winner when we beat Third Lanark 2–1 in the League Cup final on 24 October 1959.

'I loved my time at Tynecastle and I was sad to move along with George Thomson for a figure of I think around £42,000 to Everton, but they were an equally great club. In saying that, winning two league titles in three years, a Scottish Cup and a League Cup all in five years was fantastic for me at Hearts.'

BACKROOM STAFF

Norrie Gray (kit man, 1995–present day)

'There are four guys in football for whom I have total respect: Gilles Rousset, Antti Niemi, David Weir and Steven Pressley. They are all quality guys. Gilles was unbelievable. Every Thursday, if the weather was lousy for training, he would shout through, "Norrie, could you run me a bath?" Once in, the next thing I'd hear is, "Norrie, an espresso, please!" quickly followed by, "Norrie, a paper, please." So there he was, sitting in his bath with his newspaper and cup of coffee looking like the cat that had got the cream.

'Having said that, once the laughing and joking had finished, everything for him in terms of his football had to be spot-on. Whether he was training or playing, he was totally focused when he set his mind to it. After games, it was back to the joker.

'We couldn't find him after a pre-season friendly against Tottenham one summer as he was in the away dressing-room sitting drinking a Budweiser with David Ginola. On another occasion, I got a phone call from him at the ground asking for the use of a screwdriver. He was doing some sort of job in the house and didn't want to buy one so came over from the West End to Tynecastle to borrow it. Needless to say, we never got it back.

'Nothing fazed the big man, although he did stutter a bit when he got excited. One summer, he was going off on holiday to California and wanted to buy tickets for the baseball in Anaheim. He didn't want to get embarrassed over the phone, so I ended up going to his house and doing it for him. He was an absolute gentleman but I'm told when it came to parting with pennies he wasn't the most forthcoming.

'Antti was another laid-back guy, another gentleman and someone who would never ask you to do anything for nothing. One Sunday morning, he was supposed to come into Tynecastle to pick up his gear as he was flying from Edinburgh to Amsterdam on international duty with Finland the next day. As luck would have it, there had been a power cut on the Sunday and the phones had all gone down. Antti had eventually got in touch with Peter Houston in a bit of a panic and Housty had left a message with me to phone him. "I can't come to collect the kit as it was my wife's birthday yesterday," said Antti. He had had a drink and couldn't drive over from Dalgety Bay, so he asked me to put the gear in a taxi and send it over the bridge.

'It was a lovely sunny day, so I decided to take it over myself. His wife answered the door and I told her it was a parcel for Antti

Niemi. Thinking it was the taxi, Antti came to the door with his wallet to pay for the delivery. He invited me in for a drink but I was driving and in any case had to get back. He reported back to Tynecastle the following Thursday with Jari Litmanen's strip and a big bottle of Finlandia vodka for me!

'Another funny thing about Antti is his favourite blue thermal vest he wears under his keeper's top. It's a long-sleeved polo neck thing and there are more holes in it than anything you could imagine. He's had it since his Rangers days and after every game he'd take it home and his wife would check it and sew it for him. He took it with him to Southampton when he left Hearts and refused to allow me to replace it. I think he even has it to this day.

'David Weir had a fetish about socks and always asked for a new pair at every home game. He never made a big issue out of it but always enquired if it was possible.

'I've enjoyed some great times in the Tynecastle kit room and the scenes after the Scottish Cup win were just incredible. But what people maybe don't know is that all the spare jerseys from the game were stolen. I had driven the kit through to Celtic Park, came back to watch the game in Edinburgh and then met the bus on its return to Tynecastle that night. The hampers were put away and the kit was placed in a corner of the dressing-room. But a lot of people had been let into the stadium on the Saturday night when the bus came back and I returned on the Sunday morning to find the whole lot had been nicked! The hampers hadn't been touched but there wasn't a cup final jersey left. Also, Billy Brown had kept the Rangers team sheet signed by Walter Smith as a souvenir as it was his last game in charge. That got pinched as well!'

George McNeill (fitness coach, 1983–95)

'I became involved at Hearts through Pilmar Smith, who had sponsored me as an athlete when I went to Australia. I had retired from running and he asked me to come in and help out at Tynecastle. I went along and met Alex MacDonald and Sandy Jardine, and the pair of them were quite keen on fitness. Soon after that, I was in two days a week and introduced the speedball as part of the players' gym work. It was like a miniature punch bag and was used to help build their upper-body strength and improve their reflexes. That was 1983 and the club then went on a great wee run when we were regular competitors in Europe.

'The players used to play a lot of head tennis, which Alex was keen on. It was supposed to help the touch, and they also did a lot of the gym circuits. I think the increased gym work they had to do was initially a shock to the system for some of the players, although there was a group of youngsters coming through such as Gary Mackay, John Robertson and Davie Bowman who were all keen to further themselves. It was something which footballers had never really tried to do and they quite enjoyed it.

'What I also did was take them through the close season and that was unheard of. We'd spend a concentrated five- or six-week period at Meadowbank when we would do stuff almost every day. That's where a lot of them showed real improvement. Instead of going on their holidays, they would come in to start their pre-season training with gym and speed work.

'Gary Mackay was a terrific worker. He was very weak physically in his upper body when we first started and couldn't even do one pull-up on the bar but he made a great improvement the more we worked together. Craig Levein was a natural athlete and could have run for Scotland, whereas wee John Colquhoun was a natural moaner. He would do it but loved a moan. I probably saw the greatest difference in a player in Scott Crabbe. He wasn't blessed with natural pace but we made him stronger and a wee bit faster with a six-week period at Meadowbank and he went on to have a really good season that year.

'There was a lot of friendly banter between everyone; the guys couldn't really shout at Alex or Sandy as they were the managers and I was the person between them and the players. I could give it as well as take it, though!

'While I had been on Hibs' books, I didn't regard that as a big problem – just look at wee Robbo, his allegiances were initially at Easter Road. Once the fans recognised you as a member of the backroom team, you were pretty much accepted.

'I spent 12 years working at Tynecastle and never took a penny from Hearts. But the way it worked out was that I'd be invited to the directors' boxes home and away, and got to go on all the European trips as well as the players' end-of-season tour.

'One story I smile about is when Sandy Clark was in charge at a derby clash at Easter Road. He was banned from the touchline and had these walky-talky things that weren't very reliable. He told me to sit beside him in the stand and ferry the messages to the dugout. He told me to go down and tell Tosh McKinlay to tuck in, as well as three or four other instructions that I didn't understand. I went down the back stairs to the tunnel but by the time I'd got to the bottom I didn't have a clue what I was supposed to say. I decided I'd better go through with it anyway and I stood alongside wee David McCreery, who was all excited as the game was raging on.

'I couldn't get a word in and as I was standing there the ball went out to John Robertson, who put in John Colquhoun and he stuck it in the net. Everybody went wild on the bench and once things had calmed down, Dave asked me what the instructions were. I just told him, "Sandy says to keep it going," and then turned round and made my way back up the stairs. I was hopeless with all those complicated things.

'I also remember Hearts used to have great Christmas nights out when the players would all have on fancy dress. Tosh McKinlay used to hate these events as he didn't drink and found himself out with guys like Mike Galloway. When they got drunk, they'd take Tosh's car keys off him and throw them down a drain. These nights were an absolute nightmare for Tosh, walking along the streets of Edinburgh dressed up as Humpty Dumpty and hating every minute of it. They were a really good bunch, though, and I think that's what got them through so much at the time.'

Dr W. Dewar Melvin
(club doctor, 1980–to present day)

'I became Hearts club doctor in 1980 and it's only since our move to the youth academy at Riccarton in 2004 that the medical and physio facilities have improved. In the past, there was just the one room we shared at Tynecastle to treat the players and it was on the way to the tearoom, so it became a glorified corridor.

'Space and money were always a problem in the past at Tynecastle. We even struggled to get filing cabinets but things have changed since we moved our training base to Riccarton. We can get scans carried out very quickly, which means we can rapidly evaluate the injuries. This is good for the manager, the player and the team.

'I'm there on match days, both home and away, liaising with our physio. I will come down to the touchline if the injury looks serious or if I can help.'

Tom Purdie (head of security, 2000–05)

'As the person in charge of Hearts' security at the time, I was over with the team on the pre-season tour to Northern Ireland in the summer of 2003 when the side was scheduled to play a friendly at the showgrounds in Ballymena.

'Craig Levein had the players all primed for the agreed 7.45 p.m. kick-off and they were coming off the pitch after the warm-up when the announcer welcomed the club and its fans to the match. He said the game was due to kick off at 7.30 p.m., despite the referee believing it was 7.45 p.m. as well. There were a lot of hurried discussions behind the scenes and we thought the guy on the Tannoy had caved in when he started to announce there had been "a slight misunderstanding between ourselves and Heart of Midlothian. We thought it was a 7.30 p.m. start, they thought it was a 7.45 p.m. start," before adding, "so we have come to a compromise and the match will kick off at 7.37 p.m.!" He just wouldn't give in and refused to back down. It was priceless and even made Craig laugh.

'It's funny how these things work out but when I took on the Hearts job I renewed a family link stretching back to 1875 when my great-grandfather's cousin, Tom Purdie, was the first player to captain Hearts.

'I was disappointed to have to leave Hearts in early January 2005. I got back into football eight months later, when I became head of Livingston's security at Almondvale. Ironically, my first game was against Hearts on 11 September 2005.'

Alan Rae (physio, 1982–2005)

'I first joined Hearts on an ad-hoc basis in 1982. I wanted to finish off in 1990, as combining my full-time job with what I was doing at Hearts was getting too much to handle. However, Wallace Mercer offered me a contract at that stage, which I signed, but sadly the manager, Alex MacDonald, was sacked about six months later.

'It was a difficult time for the club as Joe Jordan came in and there was a huge turnaround in attitudes and training techniques. To be honest, the expectations of me by someone who had come from clubs like AC Milan and Leeds United outstripped what I could provide. Although we did manage a working relationship over a two-and-a-half-year period, it was quite a difficult time and I don't think I was the only one who felt that. I think he found it tough as well, as he was maybe promised things which didn't materialise.

'In fairness to Joe, he developed a team which was very hard to beat and which was very unlucky at times. He also started off a youth initiative scheme that went from strength to strength, so credit where credit is due.

'The most serious injury I have had to treat was an abdominal injury suffered by Roddy McKenzie when he was about 17 years old and a great young goalkeeper at Hearts. He got the injury after an opposition striker late-tackled him during a game at the Civil Service ground at Granton one afternoon. He suffered badly from the challenge and it was a difficult injury for him to get over. I knew he wasn't well but sadly the problem was initially dismissed by two NHS hospitals. I realised it was a serious injury and should not be ignored, so I fought and fought to ensure that he received more hospital treatment. It was only after more treatment that the injury improved and he went on to have a successful career. It taught me a lesson that physios sometimes have to stand up on their two legs and be obnoxious to get things done.

'The player whose career arguably suffered most through injury was Craig Levein. He was on the crest of a wave in 1987 but sustained an injury to his knee ligaments. Nothing was more satisfying for me than seeing Craig come back from that injury in style and play for his country in the World Cup in Italy in 1990, although I don't think he was necessarily Andy Roxburgh's flavour of the month at the tournament.

'Sadly, Craig picked up more knee injuries later in his career and had to retire early. For me, that was a crying shame, as he could have gone on to even greater things in football.

'I made my mind up to leave Hearts at the end of August 2005 and informed the club of my intentions in April. I didn't retire – I just felt it was a good time to leave. I was 61 and had enjoyed 23 years with the club. I just felt it was time to do something else.'

John Harvey (international scout, 1995–2004)

'When I was eight years old, my father was Hearts' trainer and I used to clean all the boots of players like Alfie Conn and put them in the drying room. Every time I'd go into the dressing-room, Alfie would ask me, "Are you still rubbing your knees with green cheese?" I often tried to find out what he meant without any luck. I still don't know.

'It was fantastic to be around the club with the likes of Tommy Walker as manager and the old, old directors such as Wilson Strachan. They were characters.

'When my dad took over as manager, I was always OK for tickets but even when my mother was alive and we'd go to games at Tynecastle, we always used to get stuck behind the big pillar in the Main Stand. One of Dad's first signings was Jim Jefferies and in a twist of fate I went on to work with Jim at Berwick Rangers, Falkirk, Hearts and then Kilmarnock.

'I must have been connected with Hearts for around 30 years since those boot-cleaning days and having my dad, John senior, as Hearts manager was great. It was a sad day when Craig Levein told me towards the end of 2004 that I no longer had a job at the club. It was just like getting stabbed in the heart.'

CHAPTER FIVE

THE REAL MACKAYS

Dave Mackay (right-half, 1953–59)

'I played for Scotland in vital matches and won trophies with Spurs but the greatest thrill of my professional career was unveiling the league flag at Tynecastle. We won it in the 1957–58 season and more than 30,000 people were there for the final match of the season against Rangers, which we won 2–1. It was a great occasion and it eclipsed everything else I ever did in my career. I remember I was lifted up on someone's shoulders and the Tynecastle crowd roared. Rangers finished runners-up that year but they were 13 points behind us. We had a great team. I don't think I ever played in a better side at any level.

'Willie Bauld, Alfie Conn and Jimmy Wardhaugh: what players. For me, though, John Cumming was the top man. He was a wing-half, just like me, and what a brave player. I remember he had a clash of heads with Willie Fernie against Celtic in the Scottish Cup final of 1956, which we won 3–1. It didn't put him off and he came back onto the pitch after getting the blood cleaned up. I remember saying to him that I would do all the headers in the midfield. Did he listen? He may have had a serious head wound but he still kept heading the ball. He had to have 11 stitches put in the wound after the game but the fact he carried on playing that day showed what his attitude was like. He was a real Lionheart.

'People always saw me as the hard man of Hearts. In fact, there is a famous picture of me playing for Spurs, grabbing Billy Bremner of Leeds United by the neck, which is on display in the office of Sir Alex Ferguson at Manchester United. I think that picture just showed my will to win and why I had so much success during my football career.

'You may not believe this but I never got sent off. I got booked a few times but never sent off. I was always hard but fair, and I was great at slide tackling. My timing was magnificent when it came to tackling.

'I was part of the team which won the Scottish League Cup in the 1954–55 season and again in 1958–59, the Scottish Cup in 1955–56 and the league title of 1957–58 but had first played at Tynecastle for Saughton Secondary School Under-15 team alongside my brother Tommy and it was a magnificent feeling. All of my family were Jambos and they were so proud. More than 5,000 people turned up for the match against King's Park School from Glasgow in the final of the Scottish Schools Cup, which we won 2–1 after drawing 0–0 with them in the first match at Hampden. Tommy scored the winner and I supplied the cross.

'After the game, the team was marched down Gorgie Road back to our school with a piper in front of us – it was a day I would never forget. To be playing at Tynecastle a few years later for the full Hearts team was a dream come true.

'I was 17 when I signed for Hearts and I had a spell with Newtongrange Star before that. Tommy Walker was the manager and he offered me £10 a week and £8 during the summer break, plus a £20 signing-on fee. I first played at Tynecastle for the reserves against East Fife and a week before my 19th birthday made my debut against Clyde in front of 16,000 people on 7 November 1953. We lost 2–1, which was a disappointment, and I remember Jimmy Wardhaugh scored our goal. It was my first real experience of the unique atmosphere at Tynecastle and I was hooked.

'One of my best memories was when 30,000 people turned up to see us play Falkirk at home just after we had won the League Cup back in the 1954–55 season. We beat Motherwell 4–2 at Hampden then beat Stirling Albion 5–0 away before taking on Falkirk. It was a great occasion, as the whole club was on a high after our League Cup win and this was our first home league game since. I'll always remember the noise the supporters made when we ran out of the tunnel that day. They always gave you a great reception but this time it seemed to be even louder than usual.

'I played all round the world, managed in the Middle East, played in great European stadia but none compare with Tynecastle. It is and always will be part of the Gorgie community.

'I remember as a kid I sneaked into Tynecastle with my brother, Tommy, and we stood on the terracings just marvelling at our surroundings. When I was older, I used to watch Willie Bauld play and he was magnificent. I never dreamed I would one day play alongside him. It's funny because out on the pitch I used to shout and scream at him if he wasn't doing what I wanted. Off it, such was his presence that I could hardly bring myself to speak to him. I just got carried away with myself on the pitch but off the park I was quiet. Especially when I was put in front of one of my heroes like Willie Bauld.

'I still go back to Tynecastle when I can and the ground is part of the fabric of Edinburgh. When I sneaked into it as a boy, I thought nothing of it, as I felt it belonged to me, my family and everybody in Gorgie, every Hearts fan in the world. We had our local public park as boys where we used to kick a ball about but we also had Tynecastle Stadium. It was ours, too. It was a crying shame Hearts considered moving from there. They may have had debts, but some things in life are more important than money and keeping the club at Tynecastle is one of them. It gave me many happy memories that I have carried with me throughout my life.'

Gary Mackay (midfielder, 1980–97)

'There is no stadium like Tynecastle anywhere in the world and don't let anybody tell you otherwise. It's a place that even the opposition love coming to because of the great atmosphere the place generates. The stands are so close to the pitch you can hear the shouts. It is a citadel for football, one that I will never forget and one that belongs to the people who support Heart of Midlothian.

'I first walked through its front door on the day I signed, when Bobby Moncur was manager. Hearts didn't have much of a youth policy when I joined but I came to the club around the same time as Ian Westwater and Dave Bowman. With that pair on the books, the youth policy improved overnight.

'I was immediately taken in by the grandeur of Tynecastle and when I first ran out there as a 16 year old in a Scottish Cup replay against Morton on 28 January 1981, it was a dream come true.

'I had many great matches at Tynecastle but the league match I remember most was a game against Motherwell on the final day of the 1994–95 season, which we won 2–0. We were in a three-way fight with Aberdeen and Partick Thistle to avoid the play-off relegation spot and had to win the match to make sure we stayed up. There were over 11,000 people at that game and they made a hell of a noise, which helped us to win. I think that was probably my best league match in a Hearts jersey. I remember Brian Hamilton scored for us but Motherwell came back with a vengeance. I thought they might get an equaliser, then I won a penalty that Robbo scored from.

'After the game, we realised the significance of the win. Dundee United were already down but our win took us above Aberdeen, who finished up in the play-off spot, and ahead of Partick Thistle and Kilmarnock on goal difference. That was such an important match, as the club just couldn't face relegation again. If we had gone down to the lower division, it would have been a long way back for us. Staying in the top division meant we could improve, and the next season Jim Jefferies was appointed and a whole new exciting era began. That wouldn't have happened if we had lost that day against Motherwell. That is why it was such an important match.

'The other game I remember was one which I started on the

bench, but the atmosphere that night summed up the allure of Tynecastle. It was the UEFA Cup quarter-final against Bayern Munich back on 28 February 1989, which we won 1–0. For anyone who was there that evening, it was a special occasion. Hearts had been a bit of a yo-yo club up until then and even I couldn't quite believe we were playing a great side like Bayern Munich in a UEFA Cup quarter-final.

'We had beaten St Pat's of Ireland, Austria Vienna and Velez Mostar to get there and it was a great occasion for us all. I remember to this day the wall of sound the fans made. Iain Ferguson scored the winner for us and although we lost the second leg in the Olympic Stadium 2–0, it was a turning point for the club. For me, it showed that Hearts were back in the big time and could compete with the best of them at that time.

'What do I remember of Tynecastle? Well, I was there 17 years and, looking back, things changed a lot over that time. I remember that the dressing-room had a big bath that we all used to jump into at the end of the game. Hygiene-wise you would never even consider doing such a thing nowadays. Back then, though, we used to sit in it for hours, listening to people like Jimmy Bone telling us all his football stories. In saying that, it was a pleasant surprise when they finally put in showers.

'The more established I got in the team, the more rituals I had at Tynecastle. For instance, I had to have the same peg in the dressing-room: the one right in the corner. I also had to have two towels after a match: one for my body, the other for my hair, which was my pride and joy – I was the most delighted man at Tynecastle when I was allowed to bring in my own hairdryer. Training-wise there was no gym at all and all we had was a medicine ball we used to throw around and a weights bar to use. Apart from that, there was nothing.

'When I see what all the players eat nowadays and the fact they are all on balanced diets, it makes me laugh. When I started out, we didn't bother too much about what we ate. I used to have the same lunch every day: two banana rolls and a German biscuit, which was usually fetched by Paul Ritchie, who was on the ground staff at the time. Yup, the same Paul Ritchie who went on to win the Scottish Cup with Hearts. It was only later on that the club, and everyone else in Scottish football for that matter, realised how important diet was. When eating properly became important, I remember menus being pored over and a special room being set aside in which the players could have their lunch together. Les Porteous, the former club secretary, realised we had to eat better and set aside the sponsors' lounge for us to eat in. It was a great idea, although you had to get there before Stevie Fulton or else all the best stuff would have gone.

'I still get a great buzz every time I walk into Tynecastle. I just have so many good memories. In saying that, I'm no different to the fans, many of whom have been going there much longer than me. It's a stadium that lives long in the memory and the fact they planned to sell it to a housing company and move away from Tynecastle for good was an utter disgrace.

'Mismanagement forced the club into serious financial difficulty and to have debts of more than £19 million was a joke. Heads should have rolled because of it. The fans led the protests against the sale and against Chris Robinson, and they should be proud of themselves. They were magnificent and the fact that the move to Murrayfield was halted was down to them. They should all be congratulated.'

CHAPTER SIX

A WINNING TEAM:
JEFFERIES AND BROWN

Jim Jefferies
(defender, 1967–81; manager, 1995–2000)

'I made my debut when I was 21 and just loved the place from the start. Tynecastle is the ground where Heart of Midlothian belongs. I still love going back, as the atmosphere is second to none – although as Kilmarnock manager I've had my fair share of defeats. It is a place that is perfect for football, a place where the supporters' backing gives Hearts a goal start. I never had to get my players fired up for a home game. All they had to do was walk out onto the pitch, look around them, hear the noise and take it all in. That was enough and far more important than any words of encouragement I could ever give them.

'There are lots of games I remember well. I think our 5–1 win against Lokomotiv Leipzig was a fantastic night. We had lost the first leg 2–0 and 18,000 people were in Tynecastle for the second leg on 29 September 1976. I remember Willie Gibson scored a couple of goals and Drew Busby, Jim Brown and Roy Kay all got one. The place was going mad.

'In the league, I remember a game against Aberdeen, if only because I scored two goals and that didn't happen very often.

However, the game that I remember as a player more than anything is one which has been lost in time. Among the current generation of Hearts supporters, not many will know that after being beaten 7–0 in the infamous derby game of 1973, the players who were beaten that day made a pact to turn over Hibs the next time they came to Tynecastle. We were determined to really stuff them. We had to wait until the first Edinburgh derby of the 1973–74 season to do it but we fulfilled our promise to each other.

'Now that was a game we all enjoyed! Everybody kept talking about the 7–0 game and all the players got sick of it. We said we would destroy them and that's what we did. We won 4–1 that day but it could have been 8–1 we were so much on top. I remember Eric Schaedler scored an own goal then Kenny Aird, Donald Ford and Drew Busby put us way out in front. God, that was a great feeling. I had never felt as low in my career as after the 7–0 game but the 4–1 win helped redress the balance a bit.

'As a manager, three European ties stick out for me, despite the fact that Hearts lost them all. We went out on the away goals rule against Red Star Belgrade, with whom we drew 0–0 away and then 1–1 at home. We got a 1–1 draw against Real Mallorca after being beaten 1–0 away but maybe the best European night in terms of atmosphere was when we played Stuttgart on 28 September 2000 in the UEFA Cup.

'We had lost 1–0 over there and the return match was fantastic. The match was at 2–2 then Colin Cameron scored with a penalty after 83 minutes, but despite a valiant last seven minutes we just couldn't get the fourth goal. The crowd was in great voice and Stuttgart were living on their nerves by the end, as they had two men sent off in that last hectic seven minutes. God, we were unlucky that night.

'As a ground, Tynecastle is fantastic because the crowd is on top of the players and it is a difficult place for the opposition to win. I also remember the scenes there when we returned from that famous day at Parkhead when we won the Scottish Cup after beating Rangers 2–1 in 1998. That was the best weekend of my life. The scenes were just unbelievable and it took us an hour to get through the last wee bit at Gorgie to the stadium. The floor of the bus we were in was swimming in champagne. The atmosphere was electric and the joy on people's faces was great to see. We went into the reception in the Gorgie suite and the place was jumping. I remember when we went in the door, "Celebration" by Kool and the Gang was on the Tannoy system. The disc jockey's choice of music that night was magnificent and the minute we walked in you could sense the happy atmosphere.

'It was such a great night that some of the boys never went home and went straight to the civic reception in the City Chambers in Edinburgh the next day in their tracksuits. I stayed in the Caledonian Hotel that Saturday evening along with a group of friends and got up early the next morning to get ready for the open-top bus parade and the civic reception.

'Believe it or not but I didn't think I had been too drunk. Maybe it was impossible as I was so drunk on adrenalin. In saying that, I went to the wee shop at the Caledonian Hotel to try to get some headache tablets but they didn't have any and told me to go to a chemist in Shandwick Place. I walked into Shandwick Place and saw this chap with a Hearts top on, clearly still the worse for wear, heading home after an all-nighter. I said to him in passing, as it was quiet in the street, "Did you enjoy your day?" He was half-asleep and looked up and said, "God bless that Jim Jefferies," and walked away! I walked on and then turned round after about 50 yards and stopped. Looking back, I saw him standing there looking bemused and thinking, "Oh no, it couldn't be him."

'When I got served, I still had my tracksuit on and I told the girl behind the counter I needed a headache tablet. The assistant looked at me, gave me the pills and said, "Oh, you aren't paying for that," and gave them to me for free. The attitude of the fans that weekend showed what Hearts means to Edinburgh and Gorgie, and what Gorgie and Edinburgh means to Hearts.

'Nobody wants to see the club leaving Tynecastle, nobody at all. OK, a lot of the stadium is outdated but it could be improved and I always thought that could happen. I never lost faith and never will. Tynecastle attracted characters both on and off the pitch. Even the foreign players like Pasquale Bruno and Stefano Salvatori were taken in by the atmosphere. When you are doing well and the crowd gets behind you, it's great, but the other side is that when you are behind and not playing well there is no hiding place. The supporters want you to win but to do it in style. Hearts supporters have been brought up with a tradition of great players playing at a great stadium. Long may it remain.'

Billy Brown (assistant manager, 1995–2000)

'One of the games that sticks in my mind was, like Jim, the European night against Stuttgart on 28 September 2000. We had played the likes of Red Star Belgrade and Real Mallorca, who were top clubs at the time, but the most memorable match was Stuttgart at Tynecastle. We had lost 1–0 in Germany in the first leg and I remember having a chat with Antti Niemi the day before that game about how to defend free-kicks, as they were very dangerous from those positions. I'd suggested Antti have someone on one of his posts, so we agreed that Thomas Flogel would be that person. Antti didn't want him there but I told him to do it and believe it or not that is where their winner came from, the Bulgarian star Balakov chipping the ball between Thomas and Antti. If Flogel hadn't been there, Antti would probably have saved it! We therefore came back to Edinburgh with a 1–0 deficit and knew we would have to have a real go.

'We changed things that night, brought in Kevin James and went route one with Andy Kirk wide left. Stuttgart were a top side, as the following seasons proved, and it turned into a great game. The players gave their all, the fans were unbelievable and the special atmosphere Tynecastle produces on European nights almost helped us to pull it off.

'At that stage it was coming towards the end of our reign, as Chris Robinson was getting impatient, to be honest, and it wasn't really an ideal environment. A couple of months after that game, Jim [Jefferies] and I left Tynecastle. Jim had wanted to resign for a couple of weeks. Our last game was a convincing home win over Aberdeen on a Saturday and I think it was the Monday night when Jim had a meeting with Doug Smith, who was the club chairman at the time, and it was all over. I was then pulled across and unceremoniously sacked. I felt I was very, very harshly dealt with, and very unfairly, but I suppose that's football and, in fact, it was never totally resolved to my satisfaction.

'It was a sad way to leave, as we had enjoyed such a good time there and such a successful time, with so many players having been brought through who went onto the international stage. To leave on the note I did didn't reflect the time I'd had at Hearts. I thought we still had some shelf life left but it wasn't to be.

'The Scottish Cup win in 1998 was obviously the highlight but it was a culmination of a lot of hard work by a lot of people. When Jim and I went to Hearts, they had escaped relegation on the last day of the two previous seasons. The team we took over had been there a long time and the players were getting old together. We had to turn things around and so we chopped and changed as we went along. We brought people in for a short time to do jobs we needed done while we were building up the team which won the cup and which, quite frankly, should have won the league as well that season. We brought guys through the system like Paul Ritchie, Gary Naysmith and Scott Severin, who hadn't been in the first team before.

'We arrived at Tynecastle in 1995; that was our third cup final and we had built up to that team of '98. The first final in 1996 when we lost 5–1 was heartbreaking. Rangers played exceptionally well but we lost Gary Locke after about seven minutes and that upset the rhythm of the team. I remember coming home that night through Gorgie past Tynecastle to the George Hotel. All the supporters were crying – I was crying as well! However, it made the same journey two years later all the more special. We realised in '96 what it meant to the fans and I don't think you can really enjoy success until you have tasted a bit of failure.

'We came back to celebrate in the Gorgie Suite after the win in Glasgow but the next day was just fantastic. Even talking about it now makes the hairs on the back of my neck stand on end! The open-top bus made its way through the streets of Edinburgh to Tynecastle and it was an experience that I will never forget. As the bus turned off Gorgie Road into Tynecastle, some of the players who were on the roof actually nearly fell off. The scenes were fantastic. It was what Hearts deserved and, to be honest, what Jim and I deserved as well after what we had built there.

'One of the biggest pleasures looking back is seeing the players we brought through play for Scotland. Just consider someone like David Weir. We had him for a trial at Falkirk when we were at Brockville and he ended up playing at the World Cup finals and captaining an English Premiership side. Naysmith is another one. We gave Gary his debut when he was on the ground staff in a League Cup tie against Celtic at Tynecastle. We'd had four players sent off the previous Saturday at Ibrox and were really struggling for numbers. We even brought up a trialist from England called Andy Thorn, who just played that night and the first half of our next game at Motherwell. I'll always remember asking Andy how he was feeling during extra time in that cup tie. "Don't even think about taking me off," came his reply, "because everything that comes into our box I'll either head or kick." And he did.

'There were also a lot of people behind the scenes at the club who were unsung heroes: Norrie Gray, the kit man; Alan Rae, the physio; and John Harvey, who did all the match reports, were vital. The club couldn't have functioned without them. People may not know this about Norrie but he used to take all the gear through to the game wherever Hearts were playing about 11 a.m. and then come back. He did the same for the cup final – he dropped off all the stuff at Parkhead but didn't stay to watch. He turned the van round and came back to Edinburgh.

'Alan Rae had a big, big influence on everything that happened to Hearts for more than 20 years. All these lads who came through the ground staff had to come through the Alan Rae years and they all had to be disciplined boys. If you asked the likes of Gary Locke, Paul Ritchie or Allan Johnston to carry the hamper, they'd do it, as that was the way they were brought up. The Hearts guys were traditionally well behaved and well mannered, and Alan had a lot to do with that, as well as Walter Kidd and Sandy Clark, of course.

'One other thing that sticks in my mind and it happened when we were training one Sunday morning along at Roseburn in 2000.

A WINNING TEAM: JEFFERIES AND BROWN

It was a lovely day and I was playing in one of the wee games we used to set up. Juanjo hit a shot that struck the tips of my fingers and broke three bones in the back of my hand! I had to get two plates inserted and they are still there to this day, along with a big scar. I wasn't even in goal. I had gone to try to close him down and he battered the ball against my fingers. I've never played since.'

CHAPTER SEVEN

AWAY DUGOUT

Terry Butcher
(centre-half: Ipswich Town, Rangers, England; coach:
Dundee United; manager: Coventry, Motherwell)
'I always enjoyed going to Tynecastle with Rangers as I invariably
won. I think I only lost there once as a player but only chalked up
my first win as a manager with Motherwell at Tynecastle in the
latter half of 2004.

'The fact that the crowd is so close to the pitch makes it a classic
British stadium as far as I'm concerned. You don't notice it that
much as a player in terms of individual comments and voices and
obscenities, as you're so concentrated on what you're doing. The
noise factor, though, is tremendous and while you sometimes don't
understand what they are shouting, it all adds to the atmosphere.

'My first memory of the ground wasn't a particularly good one,
as there were a lot of racist chants directed towards Mark Walters
on his debut on 16 January 1988. I remember bananas coming on
the pitch and down in one corner there was virtually a
greengrocer's stall! It wasn't just Hearts, though, that sort of thing
was common at most of the grounds.

'Mark, however, won everybody over with a sublime piece of
skill. Our keeper Nicky Walker half-volleyed the ball out to the left

wing, where Mark was standing. Former Rangers player Hugh Burns was the right-back for Hearts and challenged Mark as though he was really going to crunch him but Mark flicked the ball through his legs and went round the other side of him in the one movement. It was an unbelievable piece of skill and you could hear the whole crowd gasp. After that, everybody just applauded the ability of the man.

'The Tynecastle crowd has always been very intense, vociferous and very pro-Hearts, which is everything you'd want a home crowd to be. I enjoyed playing there and enjoy watching matches there. You are always treated well and with respect but at the same time you understand that the Hearts fans and the team want to beat you.

'It is important for the team to enjoy the feeling of having a 12th man in the supporters. What you don't want is a stadium like Murrayfield, for example, where the crowd is so far away. As a manager or a coach, I would want the fans to be intimidating by being close and on top of the players. That's what's great about Tynecastle.'

Kevin Gallacher
(winger: Dundee United, Coventry, Blackburn
Rovers, Newcastle United, Scotland)

'I played at Tynecastle for Dundee United and then representing my country against Estonia there in a European Championship match was something I was looking forward to. Unfortunately, things didn't turn out as I had hoped. I remember their centre-half pulling my jersey and I brought my arm up to push him away. The pain was immense when I made contact and I knew straight away I had broken my arm. I tried to play on for a while but it was hopeless, as my arm went limp.

'After only 17 minutes, I had to go off, which was a huge disappointment, and I remember watching the rest of the game at the Edinburgh Royal Infirmary. All of Scotland has Billy Dodds to thank for helping us win that match. He came on as a substitute for Ally McCoist with 20 minutes left and scored with his first touch, pressurised their defender to score an own goal and then got the winner to make it 3–2. And I watched it all from my hospital bed.'

John Greig
(centre-half: Rangers, Scotland; manager: Rangers)

'I was brought up in a Hearts-supporting family and was keen to sign for my boyhood heroes. My brothers were a lot older than me but they were all Hearts fans and I used to get taken along to games.

'This was back in the 1950s when Hearts had a team of real stars. They were magnificent and a joy to watch. I went to Princes Street to see them come back with the League Cup trophy in 1954.

'Willie Bauld was a great favourite of mine and it was a privilege to watch Dave Mackay. As a boy, I didn't appreciate how good he really was but years later I realised the quality he showed, how important he was to Hearts and to every team he played for. Alex Young was another Hearts player I thought was magnificent and when he went to Everton he was even more successful, as he won the English league championship with them in 1962–63 and then the FA Cup in 1965–66.

'Unfortunately, I missed a lot of games as I was always playing football as a boy. However, when I had a match at Saughton Park with a two o'clock kick-off, I used to run down to the stadium after I was finished and try to get in to one of the top-floor flats overlooking Tynecastle so I could see the rest of the game. It was something a lot of Hearts fans tried back then.

'Although I supported Hearts as a boy, I stopped when I signed for Rangers at the age of 16. I got fed up waiting for Hearts to sign me and really felt that they had let me down. Tommy Walker came three times to see me but told me I was too small to be a footballer. That really hurt and, to be honest, every time I ran out for Rangers at Tynecastle I used to try extra hard to show them they were wrong not to sign me. In saying that, I tried even harder to beat Hibs every time I went to Easter Road, for obvious reasons.

'The minute I signed for Rangers I gave them 100 per cent, although as a schoolboy supporter of Hearts, I obviously always had a soft spot for them. In my loft just now, among my most prized possessions, is a Hearts top that their former player Malcolm Robertson gave me. I kept it, as it was the closest I ever got to wearing the strip of my boyhood heroes.'

Alex Kiddie
(winger: Celtic, Aberdeen, Falkirk)

'I played for Aberdeen at Tynecastle in the late 1940s but even as a winger I wasn't aware of the crowd being so close to the pitch. However, I was back in January 2005 for a game for the first time in nearly 60 years, as my son Paul was reporting on it for the *Edinburgh Evening News*. The proximity of the fans to the players was very noticeable. I was amazed I could hear what instructions Steven Pressley was shouting to his teammates, for example. It was a great atmosphere.'

Ally McCoist
(striker: St Johnstone, Sunderland, Rangers, Scotland)

'I scored probably the most important goal of my Rangers career at Tynecastle. The date was Wednesday, 4 September 1991 and it was a Skol Cup quarter-final tie. Mark Hateley nodded the ball on to me and I scored to make it 1–0. It sparked off a series of events which saw me signing a deal to stay at Rangers for the rest of my career. Because of that, the goal I scored at Tynecastle will always be a good memory for me.

'That season had been pretty dreadful up until then, as I was stuck on the bench as Mark Hateley and Mo Johnston were banging in the goals. However, Walter Smith, who had taken over from Graeme Souness as manager, said he would give me a chance and he was as good as his word. My opportunity came that night at Tynecastle. He put me into his starting line-up and I played well. That goal got me back in the first team on a regular basis at a time when my future at Ibrox was in the balance.

'After that match at Tynecastle, Walter called me in and I signed a contract that kept me at the club to the end of my career. What if I hadn't scored that night and the ball had hit the post or been cleared? Maybe I would have had to leave Ibrox, as I was 29 years old and wanted to keep playing first-team football. As it turned out, fate and a goal at Tynecastle resurrected my Rangers career.

'Five months later, on 1 February 1992, I scored the winning goal at Tynecastle, which was a real achievement as Hearts had a great defence at the time. Craig Levein, Dave McPherson and Alan McLaren were hard opponents and among the most difficult I have ever faced. It was the year we won the championship and Hearts had a great side, so to win there was a big thing.

'When I scored, I headed for the crowd and gave a big cheesy grin as my mate Dave McPherson had said that the Hearts players were sick of seeing my grinning face in the papers. They had to endure it once again!

'I have always loved playing at Tynecastle and the atmosphere there is terrific. Maybe Hearts supporters will remember an Edinburgh derby there on 16 November 1996, which I attended. I was watching the match and decided to dress up as Hearty Harry, the Hearts mascot, at half-time. There I was, prancing about the pitch, waving to the crowd and then just before I went up the tunnel I whipped off my outfit and both sets of supporters realised it was me. It was great fun.'

Ralf Rangnick (manager: Stuttgart, Schalke 04)

'When I was in charge of Stuttgart, we had a very good UEFA Cup game against Hearts at Tynecastle. It was a close match played in a great atmosphere and I remember Hearts fielding a centre-half, who didn't normally play in the team, in attack. He was this huge guy, the tallest footballer I think I have ever seen in my life! Later I was told his name was Kevin James. We nicknamed him "Jaws", as he reminded us of the character from the James Bond movie. One of my defenders was Marcelo Bordon and he kept saying to me, "Coach, what I am supposed to do with this guy? How do I defend against him? He is so tall." I believe the player maybe joined a basketball team after leaving Hearts!'

Eddie Turnbull
(player and manager: Hibs; manager: Aberdeen)

'I had many great tussles with the Hearts at Tynecastle. There were lots of wins and lots of defeats but of course some were more notable than others. I can recall captaining Hibs in a Scottish Cup third-round tie on 1 March 1958, the day when Joe Baker scored four goals. That was a great day and I also enjoyed the 7–0 victory at Tynecastle in January 1973 when I was manager. That was quite an astonishing day but I had a lot of sympathy for the Hearts manager at the time, Bobby Seith, with whom I was very friendly.

'I was also quite friendly with Willie Bauld, Alfie Conn and Jimmy Wardhaugh. We had some great tussles in that era. Even before that, big Bobby Parker was a real character, a bit of a hard nut but a good player nonetheless. A young Dave Mackay came into the Hearts side just as I was finishing my playing career and he was another hard player, as was John Cumming. They were hard but fair.

'I actually went to the derby at Tynecastle in December 2004 when Hearts won 2–1 and it still looked a good stadium. I could never understand why anyone would want to leave there. It just lends itself to a great atmosphere. I have always thought, though, there was a better atmosphere with people standing.'

CHAPTER EIGHT

WHISTLE WHILE YOU WORK

Hugh Dallas
(Grade One referee from 1990; FIFA from 1992; retired 2005)

'I have officiated at the Maracana, the San Siro and the Nou Camp, and although I have been impressed by their grandeur they don't hold a candle to refereeing at Tynecastle in terms of atmosphere.

'The crowd is so on top of you that you can hear what they think of every decision you make. I remember in the early days I went to what used to be called the Shed End corner and got pelters from the supporters just for going near them. I remember making a mental note in that game not to go back down there for a while.

'It is just a magnificent place to referee. If you get to do a match against either of the Old Firm or Hibs at Tynecastle, you soon find out that it is a very intimidating place to do your job. They talk about foreign crowds being partisan but the Hearts supporters, when their team are pressing forward, are among the most partisan I've ever seen. The best way to describe it is as a proper traditional football stadium. I reckon when they say Brockville was worth so many points to Falkirk per season before they moved, Tynecastle was worth more to Hearts.

'The referee's room is small and compact with no lockers. It was one of the last changing-rooms in Scotland that still had a communal bath for refs but we didn't use it for health and safety reasons. Thankfully, they had showers put in but you still had to step into the bath to have a shower. In all the years I have been going to Tynecastle, it is the only dressing-room I can think of in the SPL that never changed. It is only a few paces from the ref's room to the tunnel and then out onto the pitch.

'The one good thing I felt through all my time at Tynecastle, regardless of the hostile atmosphere I had to endure when I made a decision the fans weren't happy with, was the strong feeling of protection. There could be flashpoints but the security is well organised and I always felt protected. In saying that, in the early days I remember some punters coming from the Main Stand on to the top of the tunnel, and I'm talking about guys in collars and ties. They were all removed quickly, but those days are long gone.

'Refereeing at Tynecastle was always the biggest challenge for me in Scotland outside taking games at Ibrox or Parkhead. When you referee the Old Firm at Tynecastle, you can expect a game and you know you are going to be working. The opposing players sometimes get wound up and with the tackles flying in, their momentum occasionally takes them off the field and they end up in with the spectators. You won't see that happening in many grounds around the world, as there is usually a running track which separates the pitch and the fans.

'Despite what happened in the game against Rangers back in March 2005, when I awarded a late penalty and Hearts called for an SFA inquiry into the decision, my love of taking charge of matches at Tynecastle hasn't diminished. It's a ground I always enjoyed refereeing at.'

Stuart Dougal
(Grade One referee from 1993; FIFA since 1996)

'I don't think I have ever been involved in a more sensational finish to a game than the 4–4 derby at Tynecastle in January 2003. Nothing compares to it in all my career and I genuinely feel lucky to have been part of what happened that day.

'Graham Weir scored for Hearts in stoppage time to make it 4–3 and then Hibs gave away possession almost straight from the kick-off by launching the ball upfield. I remember looking at my watch and there were ten seconds left as Hearts headed back up the park. Mark de Vries set up Weir and he equalised with literally the last kick of the game. We just sat in the referee's room afterwards with a look of amazement on our faces as if to say, "What the hell just happened there?"

'I was hoping that after such an ending any mistakes I may have made would have been forgotten but the then Hibs manager, Bobby Williamson, called me that night on my way home from the game to ask where I had got four minutes of stoppage time from. I said that there had been a number of stoppages, including one when an empty bottle of vodka had been thrown onto the pitch. I was quite comfortable with the time added on and told Bobby his team had actually scored in stoppage time as well to make it 4–2. You never know if Bobby accepts anything but we were still talking after it.

'I have been fortunate to referee many big games abroad but the atmosphere Tynecastle can generate is up there with the best and really crackles at times, particularly in games involving the Old Firm or Hibs.

'The referee's room at Tynecastle is one of the worst in the SPL. It's so small that we tend to become a bit friendly with each other. They still have the old big bath there and the trend nowadays after matches is to have an ice bath to get rid of the lactic acid. It was done by a lot of the players and the refs tried it. I've had a couple but they don't have a plug for the bath and I had to use one of the apples left for us as a water stop. Having said that, Hearts always helped make up for the lack of facilities by providing juice, water, fruit, tea and coffee.

'Going to Tynecastle is always a great experience for a referee. It is a real challenge and the atmosphere there is always incredible.'

CHAPTER NINE

TERRACE TALK*

Bob Aitchison

'Following Hearts has always been a family affair for me. I was first taken to a game by my dad, John, while my mum, Grace, was also a great supporter and was secretary of the Musselburgh branch of the Hearts Supporters' Club. I remember when I first started watching them in the early 1950s we used to get the tram up to games. My son Craig continued the tradition when he became a ball boy.'

Frank Aitken (Ayrshire)

'It is a bit of trek from Ayrshire for every home game but it's worth all the effort. I was a member of Glasgow Hearts Supporters' Club but am now involved in Mallorca Hearts SC as one of the founder members. I have some Spanish friends who really enjoy coming over and it shows the attraction of the club that people are prepared to spend their time and money travelling over for matches. It works

---

* Supporters on match days and through emails inundated the authors with their very own special Tynecastle tales. Unfortunately, not all could be included in the book but here are a selection of some of the stories which make the famous ground so special to so many. Where possible, we have included information about the contributors.

in reverse as well, with the Scottish branch of the Real Mallorca Supporters' Club. Most of the Mallorca fans, although they don't support Hearts, have a soft spot for the club following the European tie we played over in Spain. With the club already up and running, it goes without saying that the draw was a dream come true.'

Davy Allan
(leading member of the London Hearts Supporters' Club)

'My earliest memories are of standing right behind the goals that Hearts were attacking, then running round at half-time to be at the opposite goal for the second half. In these days of all-seated stadiums, and segregation, it's strange to think that a good third of the crowd would previously have swapped ends in every match.

'The first season I was allowed to travel unaccompanied as an 11 year old from Musselburgh for midweek games was during the Texaco Cup games of season 1970–71. I remember the anticipation generated by seeing the bright lights of the floodlights as you approached the ground and the smell from the brewery always seemed that much stronger in the dark. A particularly memorable game was the first-round 4–1 comeback victory against Burnley after being 3–1 down from the first leg.

'Moving to London in 1984 restricted my attendance at games to four or five a season until 1997 when I got a season ticket. I now travel up to about 15 games a season from Tonbridge in Kent. When you're standing at the platform in the driving rain at 6.30 a.m. on a Saturday you sometimes wonder if it's worth it; walking along Gorgie Road at 2.45 p.m., you know it is.

'I've spent the last six years working on the London Hearts website (www.londonhearts.com) and we have the biggest online archive of Hearts statistics and images. Through that work, I have begun to discover the breadth and depth of the history of Heart of Midlothian.'

Steven Anderson

'My dad used to lift me over the turnstile and sit me on the wall with a bag of sweets to watch the Jam Tarts play. At half-time, I used to get a drink of water from the fountain out of the metal cup behind the Gorgie End. Later on, I remember standing at the refreshment kiosk in the Shed End, singing my heart out. Now I sit on my bum, still singing my heart out, but with my son. In 50 years' time, I hope it's his turn to talk about his Tynecastle memories.'

Rob Aynsley (Newcastle)

'Although I'm a season-ticket holder at St James' Park, studying in Edinburgh gave me the chance to watch a couple of games at Tynecastle. Some of my mates would come up from Newcastle for a bit of banter and we'd go along to the games. I watched Aberdeen at the end of January 2005 from the Main Stand and couldn't believe that's where the directors are entertained as well. It's just a crumbling wreck and I can see why they wanted to do something with it. It brought home to me the huge gulf between the teams like Newcastle and teams in Scotland. Having said that, it was a good vantage point to see the action and there was real character about the place.'

John Baillie

'The first game I went to at Tynecastle was between Hearts and Rangers on 5 March 1960. To be honest, I had a soft spot for Rangers back then, but please forgive me. I was only six years old.

'Hearts won that day 2–0 with goals from John Cumming and Alex Young. I left a big Jambo and the fact we won the league that year just cemented my love for the club. My wife June follows Hearts as well and got into them when we first started going out together. She was from Kilbarchan in the west and it was good to get a convert to the Tynecastle cause.'

Colin Bickerton (Edinburgh)

'I supported Hearts as a boy and used to go to all the games as my granddad John Bickerton was the commissionaire at the main entrance and he always used to put tickets aside for me. Quite handy, I suppose, and he came to the rescue on a number of occasions.

'I was actually a mascot for some years at Tynecastle when Walter Kidd was the captain. In those days, mascots would normally get to keep the coin which the referee had tossed up at the start but David Syme decided to keep his one and I got absolutely nothing. That really bugged me!

'Any victory over the Old Firm at Tynecastle is special and one in particular I can recall is when John Robertson scored the winner against Celtic in extra time. That was a great result as we had a few players out suspended that night and it was also the match a pretty much unknown Andy Thorn played his first game for Hearts.'

Andrew Boa (Essex)

'I hadn't been to a match at Tynecastle for around 35 years until my wife and I got tickets from our daughters for a game against Aberdeen in January 2005. They were part of a special treat for our 40th wedding anniversary and, having initially been taken by my dad to games involving Conn, Bauld and Wardhaugh, it was a great idea.

'When I was younger, I used to stand and watch matches from opposite the Main Stand but I was quite impressed by the rebuilt stadium. It's a great place to watch a game of football and my wife, who had never been to a game before, even enjoyed it.'

Bill Brotherstone (Lauder)

'My first Hearts game was way back in 1936. There used to be a local cup called the Wilson Cup and Hearts played Second Division St Bernard's in it. We won 3–1. It was on a cold winter's day and I remember the groundsmen had to move the snow off the pitch to allow the game to go ahead. It was the first time I saw Tommy Walker in action. He was magnificent. Only John Robertson came close to matching him. The Conn, Bauld and Wardhaugh era was also a special time to be following Hearts.

'The only thing I would say through all my years following them is that I never thought we had a continued stream of good wingers.

For me, the best I ever saw were Eddie Rutherford in the 1950s and Freddie Warren, who was a Welsh wizard on the wing.

'I am a member of the Lauderdale Hearts Supporters' Club, which is based in St Bothwell's and picks up people in Earlston, Lauder, where I live, and other villages on the way up to Edinburgh. I got my first season ticket when I was 66 years old, when my wife Jean and daughter Gwen clubbed together to buy me one. I've renewed it ever since.'

David Brown

'There are a couple of games which stand out in particular since I attended my first game back in 1969 at the age of nine. The first one is a Scottish Cup quarter-final replay with Celtic in 1972. Hearts had drawn 1–1 in the first game at Celtic Park thanks to a Derek Renton equaliser. The replay was on the Monday in front of over 40,000 fans. The tickets had cost 30p and a programme was 5p.

'My overriding memory of the night was the game being held up due to severe crushing on the terraces not long after Celtic scored what turned out to be the winner. A young Celtic fan helped me escape being injured as the fans pushed forward. He lifted me onto the trackside, where hundreds of other supporters had also sought refuge. A policeman assisted my father in the same way. The game was stopped by the referee as more fans spilled onto the pitch. Thankfully, the game was restarted shortly after and I survived what was a nightmare experience for someone who had not long since turned 12.

'The other match which sticks out in my mind is the European Cup-Winners' Cup clash with Lokomotiv Leipzig in September 1976 when we won 5–1 after losing the first leg 2–0. For me, this was probably Hearts' finest hour in a European match.'

Douglas Cairns (Jedburgh)

'My first-ever game came in 1962, Hearts against Third Lanark, and I'll never forget it for one reason – I got smacked in the face by the ball. I was 13 years old and was in the front of the Gorgie Road End, standing looking over the wall, when this ball came flying over and hit me full on. Thankfully, there was no damage done but it was some introduction to football for me!

'The European highlight for me is the 5–1 thrashing of Lokomotiv Leipzig, while I also remember watching the second leg of the Texaco Cup final against Wolves at Tynecastle.

'One of my favourite managers has to be Joe Jordan. I know he wasn't too successful at Hearts and a lot of people didn't like him, but I used to go to all the Scotland internationals and he was something of a hero of mine.'

Steven Colquhoun (Edinburgh)

'A game against Celtic on 20 November 1976 was an occasion to remember, as it was the first game attended by my mum and a pal's mum. Looking from the Gorgie Road End to the Shed, I used to say to myself, "When I'm older, I'll get to stand over there with the big guys." The Shed rocked but it was not for a wee boy like me.

'During the game, apart from the seven goals on show, the ladies witnessed the proverbial "pee where you stood" phenomenon, the amazing self-propelling Bovril, the native language of the "urban terraces" and the friendliness of complete strangers when a half bottle was thrust into your hand to celebrate or console depending how things were going. Being only 14 at the time, I sadly declined the offer.

'A hat-trick by Willie Gibson was a highlight before our 3–2 lead was blown apart by two late stunners from Celtic. The game ended 4–3, but what a game to remember.'

Ron Connolly (Edinburgh)

'My first visit to Tynecastle was in 1941 at the age of five, when my dad, who had played as a professional in the 1930s with Dundee United and Leith Athletic, took me to a match against Motherwell. In the intervening years, I've had many memorable visits but the greatest one of all was in 1956 when we were drawn against Rangers in the quarter-final of the Scottish Cup. At that time, I was on leave from National Service in the Royal Scots, having just returned from serving in Egypt and Cyprus. The match, of course, was all-ticket but in those days there was no ticket office, superstore or reception area. Nor could you buy tickets by e-mail, telephone or post; the only access to the club was a hatch in the wall located a few yards from the players' entrance towards the School End.

'This hatch was about two feet square, just big enough to poke your head in, and had an ancient brass bell push at the side. On pushing this, a wooden shutter was slid open so that you could state your business. From this hatch, nearly 40,000 tickets were about to be sold.

'When I arrived, the queue stretched from the hatch, along to the School End exit gates, into the ground, along the bottom of the terracings, behind the goals, out the Wheatfield exit gates, along Wheatfield Place to the top of Wheatfield Road at the junction with Gorgie Road and up to Robertson Avenue, where I joined it. Eventually, I got a ticket and the wait was worthwhile as I don't think any team in the world would have lived with Hearts as they raced into a 4–0 lead against a Rangers team which included Young, Woodburn, Thornton and Waddell.

'After disposing of Rangers, we beat Raith Rovers in the semi after a replay and, as everyone knows, went on to beat Celtic in the final.'

Neill Cooper (Edinburgh)

'The events at Parkhead when we won the Scottish Cup back in 1998 seemed like a dream. Tears and mixed emotions followed by lots of screaming and singing. It was odd because, as we got on the buses back home, there was a strange silence and reluctance to talk. Had we been conditioned to expect to be the bridesmaid again? Had it sunk in? Was it a cruel dream? The hour it took to get back from Celtic Park seemed longer with the lack of chanting.

'Hermiston Gait junction was awash with maroon, with every woman, man and child wearing something in support of the team. The initial parts of the A71 leading to Gorgie Road had almost everyone out of their windows. At that point I started to cry again and realised we had done it! The evening and day that followed will remain clear to me for ever and the fact that everyone headed to Tynecastle showed the importance of the ground to the supporters.'

Keith Devlin

'The derby when Husref Musemic scored the winner has a special place in my memory as I lost a shoe in the Shed celebrations. It was my first experience of the Shed at a Hibs game – what about those dreadful toilets? We made our way up towards the back, where there was a bit of space and a great view, and held our breaths as the game kicked off.

'It seemed that no sooner had play started than Hearts' new signing Musemic had headed home what proved to be the winner. The place went wild but, unprepared for the Shed sway and with treacherous conditions underfoot, I battled to stay upright and slipped on the small terrace. Thankfully, and immediately, those fellow Hearts fans around me grabbed me by the arms and hauled me back on my feet, with a friendly pat or two on the head.

'Glad to be back on my feet, it took a moment or two before I realised I had lost a shoe in the mêlée! Now this was a real blow, what with the rainwater splashing around everywhere. I concentrated on the game but at half-time my thoughts started to turn again to the embarrassing journey home with one shoe in the pouring rain which awaited me. I then heard a shout above the general buzz of the half-time crowd. A hand was waved in the air, a considerable distance from where I was. What was that in the hand? Yes! It was my missing Adidas Samba (all the rage for teenagers at the time). I shouted, "Up here, that's mine!" Others around me all shouted as well and slowly but surely the feared lost training shoe was passed from hand to hand above the crowd all the way back to me.

'Other memories include the special display by Kevin Keegan in Alex MacDonald's testimonial against Rangers. Oh yes, and I was locked out of the Under-16 World Cup semi-final with Portugal with up to 5,000 others.'

Barry Didcock (Corstorphine, Edinburgh)

'John Colquhoun in full flight, taking on defenders at Tynecastle, was a joy to behold. Colquhoun had a nobility about him that is rare among footballers.

'At the other end of the scale was José Quitongo. What can you say about José? I thought he was mainly rubbish when he played for us but he had great dreadlocks. In saying that, he scored with a toe-poke to beat Celtic, something Hearts supporters will always be grateful to him for doing.'

Robbie Dinwoodie (Blackhall, Edinburgh)

'As a member of the "nae luck" club born just too late to have witnessed the Hearts glory days of the 1950s and early 1960s, I began going to Tynecastle, aged nine or ten, just as it careered over the precipice. I never clapped eyes on Conn, Bauld or Wardhaugh but I did see the likes of Johnny Hamilton, Davie Holt and Donald Ford.

'Over the years, I have watched games from all four sides of Tynecastle as the stadium changed out of all recognition. To be able to see the game as a wee boy I would get there early with pals and claim a space at the barrier above one of the big exit tunnels at the Gorgie Road end, which meant I was guaranteed a great view. Soon, though, that urge to be in with the bears on the covered terracings took precedence over actually being able to see much on the pitch.

'By season 1967–68, we had the great cup run and I was at all of the ties, including the remarkable 6–5 game at Tannadice, where the lead changed hands six times and Rene Moller scored twice. When it came to the quarter-final against Rangers at Tynecastle, my mate Dave Parnham and I got tickets for the stand. Just as well. I was 13 and hardly a giant. The ground was so packed that it was dangerous, so they allowed fans to sit on the track to get out of the crush. When Donald Ford scored late on to put Rangers out, the entire place went bananas. Of course, we then limped through against the might of Greenock Morton after a replay before the horror of losing to Dunfermline.

'A couple of years later, Ford scored eight goals in eight matches in the Texaco Cup. We were leaving the Ford era and entering the Ernie Winchester era. The Dark Ages.

'By the late 1970s, I was really only going to the games for the laughs. We had a pitch just inside the start of the cover at the McLeod Street End and, no matter how low things were getting, some of "Raymond's Rabble" would be there.

'One of the pals, Kenny Neal, was a primary teacher who could affect a booming, posh voice. That was the start of what might be called the Walter Kidd era and a favourite ploy of Kenny was to wait for a lull in the crowd noise and a piece of near competence from Kidd as the signal to yell, "That's it, Walter. You silence the boo boys!" and other bon mots adapted from *Roy of the Rovers* or *Gorgeous Gus*.

'I missed the famous Lokomotiv Leipzig tie at Tynecastle on 28 September 1976 as I was on a back-shift that night and couldn't get a swap. But I was there, in that very corner of the ground, for the great performance against Bayern Munich when Iain Ferguson drilled in the only goal from a free-kick. I couldn't afford to go to the return leg but it was the early days of satellite television and the Marina Hotel in Inverleith was promising to tune in to German TV to screen the game. The place was heaving as kick-off time approached and when they readjusted the satellite dish on the roof they finally managed to get a German channel.

'It was showing the American soap opera *Dynasty* dubbed into German. Christ, there was nearly a riot but they managed to get a feed off a live Radio Forth commentary, which calmed things down.

'I then began taking my kids to the games, so I was on the move again round different parts of the stadium. I think I had all three with me on the day of a memorable game against Dundee United. My mate Dave had his two sons with him, too, and we were treated to a memorable duel between Graeme Hogg and Mixu Paatalainen. At one point, Hogg put in a sliding tackle right in front of the family section, the old enclosure towards the McLeod Street End. He hit Paatalainen and the pair of them skited across the track and clattered into the hoarding in front of us. Both got up, dusted themselves down and got on with the game without a word. They're probably still picking bits of red grit out of their bums to this day.'

Bryan Dow

'I remember going with my dad, James, to Tynecastle when I was four, and when Hearts scored, the Main Stand started to shake. I also remember when we played Partick Thistle and Dave McParland scored for them straight from a corner.

'I became more and more involved in the club through the years and was on the testimonial committees for both Henry Smith and Neil Berry. I remember we wore hideous strips in both games. For Henry's match, we turned out against Everton in Inter Milan-type strips, which were dreadful. Justin Fashanu made his debut for us in that game and I remember Howard Kendall was impressed with Tynecastle.

'We played Neil's testimonial against Lyon and we tried to get Eric Cantona for the match, as he was godfather to one of Gilles Rousset's children. Unfortunately, he didn't play but it was still a good night. Once again, the strips were a hoot. I remember going down to Bradford to pick them up from the supplier and they were a hideous tartan colour. When I brought them back, Dave McPherson took one look at them and thought I was having a laugh.

'He was right. It looked like a white tablecloth had been covered in beetroot. We had 100 of them and we managed to convince the Hearts shops to buy them. I think they sold four.'

Alistair Duff (Edinburgh)

'I remember my favourite goal at Tynecastle vividly. It was my most memorable goal scored by Hearts, anytime, anywhere. I thought I had died when the ball went into the net. It was the quarter-final of the Coca-Cola Cup against Celtic back in September 1996. We had played Rangers the weekend before the match and had four players sent off. Things were so bad we had to introduce a teenage Gary Naysmith and Andy Thorn was brought in from Wimbledon and played for the first time that night.

'At the end of 90 minutes, it was 0–0 and each team had had a player sent off. We went into extra time and then moved into the second period with Hearts shooting towards the School End. There was an attack up the Hearts left wing and Neil McCann cut inside and passed it to John Robertson. Robbo let the ball roll across him without touching it just outside the box.

'I was right behind the Celtic goal. I will never forget the moment as Robbo opened his body up and let the ball roll across him to take a right-foot shot. At that precise moment, it was as if the entire crowd realised this was the opportunity we were looking for. There was a communal intake of breath and a second of what seemed to be utter silence. Robbo fired the ball and as soon as it left his foot we all knew it was going in. I could not even roar with excitement. My heart felt like it was going to explode in my chest. My mate Peter Winning, a smoker, had a cigarette in his mouth and when he made a sharp intake of breath, he almost swallowed it.'

Bill Duff (Washington, USA)

'I'm now based in Washington but watch Hearts' progress from afar. One of the funniest stories that I was told by my dad, who was the goalkeeper in the Scottish League Cup-winning side of 1954–55 and Scottish Cup-winning side of 1955–56, was about an event on the bus to an away cup game. Tommy Walker had banned the players from playing cards to pass the time, so they started playing 'I Spy'. It was Johnny Hamilton's turn and he said, "I spy with my little eye, something beginning with L L." Several minutes went by and no one came up with the answer, so they gave in. "Well, what is it, Hammy?" Back came the reply, "Lectric Lights."

Brian Fallon (Edinburgh)

'My Edinburgh Council ward of Murrayburn is in the heart of Jambo country and takes in Sighthill, Wester Hailes and Baberton Mains. I was one of the politicians involved in improving safety at sports grounds in the wake of the Taylor Report. I have known Tynecastle since supporters used to walk from one end to the other up to today when the stands surround the pitch. It is probably one of the few stadia which has retained its unique atmosphere, regardless of the changes that have been made to the ground.

'I have always had a season ticket in the Main Stand beside my friends Eric Milligan and Eric Gibson. We sat in the same seats for years until we lost them when the Main Stand was refurbished. I remember in the old days, there was a passageway behind the old School Road End and thousands of fans used to file through it. How there wasn't an accident back then I shudder to think.

'The two Erics and myself have had a ritual every time we go to Tynecastle. We meet at the Athletic Arms pub, which is known as The Diggers, at 2 p.m. every match day. We have a couple of pints of McEwan's 80 and head to the game. In fact, we were all in there when we drew 4–4 with Hibs on 2 January 2003. We left, like many others, when it was 4–2. We were walking out of the ground when it was 4–3 then heard a roar when we walked into Diggers to be told it was 4–4. Amazing.

'We go back to Diggers after every game and have another couple of pints and a pie and then head our separate ways.

'Hearts for me is Scotland's third biggest club. Hibs have a great tradition but Hearts for me is Scotland's main east-coast club. Supporters come from all over and once you've been to Tynecastle, you never forget it.'

Alan Faulds (Edinburgh)

'The funniest moment for me at Tynecastle was when Stefano Salvatori's family (mother, father, brother and two kids) came over from Milan to watch the cup final in 1998. I had to look after them as Stefano was away with the team in the Midlands. They did not speak a word of English and I did not speak a word of Italian (at that point). I had them for three days – it was like a lifetime and quite stressful! There was also the occasion after the 1996 cup final when Pasquale Bruno had just a little bit too much to drink – something he apparently wasn't used to doing – and paid the penalty.'

Hugh Ferguson (Edinburgh)

'Back in the early 1950s, I was one of the founder members of Merchiston Hearts Supporters' Club and was the beer and bus convener. A group of around 20 of us used to help the Tynecastle groundsman Matthie Chalmers after matches on a Saturday by helping to replace any divots that had been made during the game that day.'

Richard Fletcher (Trinity, Edinburgh)

'I remember reading a match-day programme at Tynecastle in February 1986 and noticed that Henry Smith's birthday was on 10 March 1956 – a day after mine. As any Hearts fan will tell you, 1986 was the year we kept winning game after game up until the last match of the season against Dundee – but the less said about that one the better!

'I was having a big party for my 30th birthday that year and I thought, "Why don't I invite Henry Smith?" Now, I'd never met Henry before but I wrote a letter to him care of Heart of Midlothian, Tynecastle Park, inviting him to my party. To my amazement, he phoned me up to tell me he would be delighted to come to my party and when he strolled in he was wearing a silver suit and carrying a bottle of champagne.

'Because I was certain we were going to win the league or the Scottish Cup that year, I decided not to open Henry's champagne and keep it for a celebration at the end of the season. Yes, I was that confident we were going to win something but I wasn't alone in thinking that.

'Sadly, everybody knows we didn't quite manage to lift a trophy that year but I decided to keep the champagne until we did. I put it away in the cupboard and the years passed. We won nothing, so I thought I should put it to good use. In 1994, I got down on one knee in the kitchen of my flat and proposed to my lovely wife Margaret. When she said yes, I pulled the champagne out of the cupboard, popped the cork . . .and it was flat as a pancake. I had kept Henry's champagne too long and it had lost its fizz!'

George Foulkes
(Hearts chairman, 2004–present day)

'Tynecastle has an atmosphere all of its own. Wherever you go in the world, you will struggle to find a more intimate place to go and watch a football match. Walking down Dalry Road onto Gorgie Road and heading towards the stadium on match day is a great experience and you can sense the anticipation as you get closer to the ground.

'Once you get inside, the crowd are right on top of the players and the noise at Tynecastle when the supporters get going is deafening. I love going to matches and my favourite period for attending was when John Colquhoun and John Robertson were in the same team along with the likes of Craig Levein and Gary Mackay. That was in the early 1990s and they were a great side. A picture of that team has pride of place in my house in France.

'My favourite game at Tynecastle was on 28 February 1989 when we beat Bayern Munich 1–0 in the UEFA Cup quarter-final first-leg tie. The atmosphere was electric that night and it was a thrilling win for us.'

Harvey Frew (Edinburgh)

'Many older supporters will recall when the season opened with the Scottish League Cup being played in sections of four teams, the winners proceeding to the quarter-final stage. At the start of the season 1961–62, Hearts were drawn in a section along with St Mirren, Kilmarnock and Raith Rovers. In addition, the opening league game of the season was played in the midweek following the first three League Cup ties. Hearts found themselves up against St Mirren three times within a fortnight, home and away in the League Cup and at home in the league.

'A bit of needle had developed between the two teams mainly due to the provocative antics of the then St Mirren and former Hearts goalkeeper, Jimmy Brown. It all started when Hearts were awarded a penalty in their first meeting at Love Street. Johnny Hamilton placed the ball on the spot about to take the penalty when Brown started removing blades of grass from the goalmouth that he had suddenly decided were distracting him.

'When the agitated wee Hammy eventually took the penalty, the ball ended up somewhere near the top of the terracings. St Mirren won the opening encounter 1–0 and Brown's antics continued in the opening league game at Tynecastle, with gestures to the Hearts fans.

'Results would have it that, when the final League Cup section game took place at Tynecastle, the winning team would progress to the quarter-final stage. On a warm late summer afternoon, Hearts ran out winners, Johnny Hamilton getting revenge on the provocative Jimmy Brown by scoring in a 3–1 victory.

'As my friends and I were leaving by the Wheatfield Street exit in celebratory mood, a big boy from Paisley, probably being all of 15 years old and there being no crowd segregation in these days, stole my maroon tammy off my head. My mum had spent much of the close season knitting the hat, as there was no such thing as a Tynecastle superstore back in those days. The St Mirren supporter was last seen running up Wheatfield Street with my tammy pulled down over his ears! That guy and Jimmy Brown have much to do with my lifelong dislike of St Mirren.'

Charles Girdler

'I'm probably one of the few people who can say they saw Barney Battles play. The record books show he scored 218 times in 200 first-team appearances. That is amazing. Also, people forget his first team was Boston AL in America and that he played for the USA at national level before coming to Hearts and getting a £20 signing-on fee and £9 a week. I think about 18,000 people turned up to watch his first match at Tynecastle and that was only a trial among Hearts players.

'Alex Munro was always my favourite player, although through the years I enjoyed watching Andy Black, Tommy Walker, Tom McKenzie and Bobby Flavell. I watched Hearts standing in the freezing cold in the old cowshed until I moved to the Main Stand with my season ticket in 1955. It's much warmer.'

Brian Gorman (Edinburgh)

'I can recall going with my dad to stand in the North Enclosure to watch the likes of John Cumming, Johnny Hamilton and Willie Bauld, who was one of my heroes. I used to go early to try to catch the players going in, so that I could get their autographs and I was standing with Dad one day when Bauld came past. I asked him for his autograph but he said he had to go inside but that he would come back out in about ten minutes. Needless to say I was really disappointed and thought my chance had gone. Imagine my delight then when he suddenly appeared, walked straight over to me and signed my book. What a man!

'Another recollection of the old Tynecastle is attending a Hearts v. Rangers cup replay in 1968. We were in a big crowd of well over 30,000 when there was no segregation, surrounded by Rangers supporters. They were crowing about how they had never been beaten in a cup replay. When Donald Ford rounded their full back and smashed a shot past Erik Sorensen, Tynie went ballistic. What a night!

'During the so-called see-saw years, when Hearts spent the time between the Premier and First divisions, I was a season-ticket holder in the North Stand during a period when there was very little to get excited about. Things were so bad that me and my mate would bring a flask of tea and have a picnic at half-time to cheer ourselves up.'

David Hadden

'I used to live in Danderhall and me and my friend would walk to Ferniehill to catch the No. 33 bus to Gorgie. Every second Saturday for home games, we would catch the same bus, and every Saturday, Drew Busby would be waiting to get on at the same bus stop. We never spoke to him; we just sat on the bus looking at him. When the bus got to Gorgie, we would get off, run ahead of him and wait outside the players' entrance to have our programme signed. This went on for nearly three months and not once did we speak to him at the bus stop. After all, we were just ten years old and he was our hero. All he ever did was give us a knowing grin and happily sign our programmes.'

HEARTS

Alan Hardie (Acomb, York)

'I was selling programmes for Jim Jefferies' first match as "home manager" at Tynecastle. It was not for the friendly against Newcastle in August 1995 when he took over at Hearts but against Kilmarnock in November 1989 when he was manager at Berwick Rangers. At the time, Northumbria County Council had declared the roof of the Main Stand at Shielfield Park unsafe so Berwick switched the match to Tynecastle.

'Berwick were owned by George Deans, the local butcher in the village of Lauder. Berwick's commercial manager was Rory Macleod, who also came from Lauder. The Berwick programme sellers wouldn't travel to Edinburgh, so Rory asked a couple of my friends, Sam and Ally Clark (Clyde fans), if they'd fancy selling programmes outside Tynecastle. The lads in turn asked if Ross Gilder and I would like to join them, as we were Jambos. So the four of us sold programmes with "Welcome to Historic Berwick-upon-Tweed" on them at 50p each to Berwick and Killie fans. The Berwick match was at 1 p.m. as Hearts reserves were due to play at 3 p.m. Hearts were playing Dundee United at Tannadice and we managed to flog a couple of programmes to unsuspecting Jambos going for buses, thinking it was the *No Idle Talk* or *Jam Piece* fanzine.

'As it was a 1 p.m. kick-off, only two Hearts ball boys had turned up, so we were asked if we wanted to do it. I jumped at the chance to grace the hallowed turf – well, the muddy trackside. I patrolled the Wheatfield Street touchline, just below the TV gantry and pie shop. I had to retrieve the ball from underneath benches and once from the Gorgie Road terracings. It took me about five minutes to clamber back through the gate onto the trackside. There were no fans to chuck the ball back, as the crowd was only 789. There were 200-odd Berwick fans in the Panini family enclosure as it was called back then and 500 Killie fans in the South Enclosure. Berwick, second bottom of the league, beat the mighty Killie 3–2. I didn't think I was watching a future Hearts manager at the time.'

Stephen Hendry (world snooker champion)

'I was brought up in Gorgie and first taken to Tynecastle by my dad, Gordon, who still goes along to watch them. I was five at the time and all I remember, to be honest, was the massive noise from the crowd and the very special arena they were playing football in.

'I used to go regularly with my dad up until I was around ten years old and I always enjoyed it and thought Tynecastle was a very special ground. Snooker started to take over. Then I started travelling a lot and I didn't have any real chance to get back to games. I always look for the Hearts results though and my dad still keeps me up to date with how they are doing.

'For me, Bobby Prentice was the best player I ever saw at Tynecastle. We used to always go to the Main Stand and it was great to see him run up the wing just in front of us. What a player and what a stadium.'

George Hutchison

'In 1958, the Scottish national team played two trial matches before choosing the squad to go to Sweden for the World Cup later that year. The first game was against Rangers at Ibrox and ended in a draw. The second game was against Hearts at Tynecastle. In a great match, "wee" Johnny Hamilton ran the Scottish team ragged and scored a screamer from 35 yards. Hearts won 3–2, with Dave Mackay scoring the winner in the last minute. That was the game that will always stand out in my memory.

'I was fortunate to meet Johnny before a league game against Kilmarnock in February 2005 and I reminded him of that great game. I said to the wee man that if the side had been chosen on displays that evening, he would have been the first name on the list. Dave Mackay and Jimmy Murray were the players from Hearts chosen to represent Scotland but Hamilton should have been with them.'

Hazel Irvine (Edinburgh)

'I remember my first game as a ball girl in a reserve match and what an embarrassment it was. I went to get the ball and

165

unfortunately tripped over a billboard at the School End and heard the roars of laughter coming from the old stand. Players on the park were laughing at me also, as did all my friends who were ball boys.

'Undaunted, I went to every other reserve game as ball girl and most first-team and reserve training sessions. I even went out on the players' annual Christmas fancy-dress day out. It was unforgettable. They had me dressed for the part as a schoolboy-come-Hearts fan. Brian Whittaker gave me a run up to my house in his car to borrow another school blazer. My dad thought I was having him on when I burst in saying, "Roger's in the car looking for a school blazer."

'The highlight for me came when Pilmar Smith helped to get my work permit which allowed me to become a ball girl at first-team matches in season 1989–90. John Frame said it was uncalled for, no girls – only boys.

'My most embarrassing moment came during the 1990 New Year's Day derby. After being up all night, I went to the game as ball girl and fell asleep leaning against the fence in front of the singing corner. Next minute, I heard someone shouting, "Move yourself, Hazel, hurry up!" Or words to that effect. Gary Mackay was standing in front of me shouting and the ball was at my feet. Those were the days.

'On another amusing note, I read an article in the fanzine *Always the Bridesmaid* which said: "Whatever happened to the obese ball girl who couldn't catch the ball at Tynecastle?" Amusing stuff!

'I had my wedding reception at Tynecastle and even my son David's christening was at Tynie, so the ground definitely holds a special place in my heart.'

Frank Johnston (Selkirk)

'I started going to watch Hearts in the late 1940s and saw great players like Willie Bauld, Dave Mackay and Alex Young at Tynecastle. I used to have to get the bus from Selkirk to Galashiels, get the train to Edinburgh then walk to the ground, so it took a wee while to get to matches. One of my most vivid memories is actually from the more modern times when John Robertson scored the winner against Celtic in a cup tie in the early 1990s.

'The best side I have seen at Tynecastle would have to be the Dundee team which won the league with Alan Gilzean in it.'

Alex Jones (Edinburgh)

'One game I recall fondly is Hearts v. Celtic on 29 January 1966. Willie Wallace was one of my favourites and he was to play a big role in our 3–2 victory.

'Hearts had returned from Zaragoza with a heroic 2–2 draw after extra time and playing with ten men for seventy-five minutes (due to Danny Ferguson's injury) while Celtic, on the other hand, had been to Tblisi and drawn 1–1 with Dynamo Kiev. Jock Stein's Celtic were well beaten by a Hearts side again reduced to ten men by an early injury to George Miller. Wallace grabbed a double, Don Kerrigan netting the other. Another hero of the day was veteran John Cumming (then aged 36).

'Sadly, the memorable triumph had dark undertones as Stein saw that Willie Wallace was the final piece in his jigsaw that was to win him European Cup glory some 16 months later. Celtic stole Wallace for the miserly sum of £29,000 shortly after the triumph at Tynecastle.

'Two derbies also spring to mind. The first was on 8 September 1973. New Year's Day of 1973 is best forgotten but revenge was sweet in the first home league match of the 1973–74 season. Hearts ended a five-year, ten-game league and cup jinx with a fine 4–1 victory over their rivals. The stars that day for the men in maroon were midfielder John Stevenson and Kenny Aird, a diminutive red-haired winger.

'The other Hibs game was on 3 September 1983, after Hearts had returned to the Premier League bolstered by old heads Donald Park and Jimmy Bone as well as ex-West Ham youngster George Cowie. John Robertson was the young gun the veteran Bone was to look after in this testing season, and to them fell the glory of defeating the wee team. Robbo twice equalised. The first was a thumping left-foot shot into Alan Rough's net, the second a toe poke after Ally Brazil had been short with his back pass. But it was the veteran Bone who became a Gorgie legend, heading the winner past the despairing Alan Rough. Victory was ours after five long years.'

Gordon Josey (New York, USA)

'It's mid-September 2004, I'm the last one left inside Tynecastle on a cold Wednesday evening, and I'm feeling distraught. The security men are ushering me out but I can't leave.

'I had returned to Scotland from my home in America to witness what I had thought would be my last game at Tynecastle. For everyone else in the crowd, that evening's rather dull 0–0 draw against Rangers would mean little.

'For me, it was my last trip home before Tynecastle was bulldozed, or so I thought. All the newspapers at the time were saying it was a sure thing that Hearts would be leaving Tynecastle and the 2004–05 season would be our last there. I wanted to make sure I visited the great stadium one last time and the midweek game against Rangers was my chance. I had made a special trip to the game to say goodbye to Tynecastle, the place which had given me so many great memories.

'Little did I know when I left Gorgie that night that the campaign to keep Hearts at Tynecastle would be successful. The ground was saved, thanks to the efforts of the Hearts supporters and Mr Romanov. It means I can have many more trips to Tynecastle from my home in the USA and the sadness I felt that September evening won't have to be repeated.

'It had been a long road travelled for me as a Hearts supporter. I was brought up in Alness in the Highlands and followed them from up there. Most people at my school were Aberdeen, Celtic or Rangers fans. They couldn't quite fathom why I supported Hearts.

'The answer was simple. My dad, Fred, was a loyal supporter. He had been born in Lewis and moved to Glasgow to work in the shipyards. He didn't want to support either of the Old Firm teams, so followed Hearts instead.

'I remember my dad, myself and our local Free Church minister, who was also a big Hearts supporter, making the long drives to and from games every other Saturday. I also remember the minister writing his sermons in the back of the car as we travelled back from Edinburgh on a Saturday evening after the game.

'When I was back in Scotland last September, I took my dad and my close friend Lawrence Randak to watch Hearts at Motherwell. The rain was pouring down but the supporters were there in their thousands, just as I remember it from the days when I used to go regularly.

'I moved to New York in 1994 and keep up to date with the team thanks to the Hearts website. Although I am far away, I still look out for their results. I'm delighted next time I come back to Scotland on holiday I can still go to Tynecastle to pay my respects to such a great ground that holds so many good memories for me.'

Grace Knight (Edinburgh)

'Davie Laing was the man I used to idolise. What a player. I was heartbroken when he left us for Clyde. I have had a season ticket since 1964 and miss being able to stand on the terraces with the opposition fans. We had lots of fun with them and the most fun was with the Celtic and Rangers fans with their Glasgow humour.

'My husband Alex and I have been at a lot of great nights at Tynecastle but the best for me was when we beat Lokomotiv Leipzig 5–1. We followed them all over Europe as well. Bologna, Prague, Madrid, Vienna, Braga, Rotterdam, Basle. We've been to them all but, wherever you go, the atmosphere at Tynecastle is second to none.'

Norman Lees (Edinburgh)

'I was so desperate to see Hearts play Celtic in a Scottish Cup tie in the early 1950s that I skipped the start of school one day to queue for tickets. I was about 15 years old and attending Tynecastle School, so decided to wait from around 6 a.m. on the morning the tickets went on sale at the ground. Back in those days the demand was huge and fans used to queue along Russell Road and into Roseburn.

'I got my tickets but when I went in late for my English class, the teacher, Hector McKenzie, asked me where I had been. Once I explained, he gave me six of the best! It was worth the pain to follow Hearts, though. The next time I came back into the classroom, someone who thought I had been hard done by had written a notice saying, "Justice For Norrie!"

'The thing about supporting Hearts was that you were always full of hope and one day that hope would come to fruition, as it did in 1956 when we won the cup. I went along to the North British Hotel in Princes Street to join in the celebrations, which was a great occasion. I had been at the match at Hampden when there was a crowd of something like 132,000.

'Other memories include seeing the birth of the Terrible Trio when they played for the first time together against East Fife. That was a momentous occasion and the start of an era. They were just young lads who had come into the team and I had no idea of the significance of seeing them together for the first time. I also saw the great Gordon Smith turn out for the first time for Hearts in a reserve match against Dundee in 1959 – there was an incredible crowd of 12,000 there for that game.'

Marilyn Leishman (Edinburgh)

'In the 1970s, I remember going to a game with my husband – I can't remember the opposition or even the score but Tynie was packed to the gunnels! The game started and so did this guy behind me. For the next 90 minutes, all he shouted was, "Cruikie, Yer Majic!" Not another word passed his lips and because it was packed we couldn't move anywhere else. By the time the final whistle went, I could have taken one of Jim Cruickshank's gloves and rammed it down this guy's throat.

'Another memory is from 20 June 1989, when Tynecastle played host to the FIFA Under-16 Scotland v. Portugal game. It was a lovely sunny evening and the kick-off had to be postponed because of the huge crowd waiting to get in. The day, though, was one of shock for me. I was the mum of two boys aged 10 and 12, who were both with me at the game. Earlier that day I had been to Simpson's only to be told I was expecting twins! I had phoned my friend earlier in the day to let her know and unknown to me she had phoned her sister, who just happened to be about five rows in front of me in the then family section in the Gorgie Road stand. When Ann saw me, she shouted up, "I hear it's twins – congratulations!" I promptly burst into tears and sobbed all the way through the game, much to the consternation of those all around me – especially my boys.'

Mark Lennie

'New Year derby matches long before segregation was introduced were great events, when young Hearts and Hibs fans with their dads would stand shoulder to shoulder. I have good memories of the rival banter as my dad would have a swig from a half bottle before passing it around a few of the dads next to him.

'One of the dads ran a sweep and for 20p a pick you put your hand in a hastily made bag, pulled out a piece of folded paper and whatever name was on it, whether it was a Jambo or a Hibby, that was your pick for first goalscorer of the game. Being a Jambo, I always hoped I that I would pick a Hearts player and it was a bonus if it was Drew Busby or Donald Ford.

'Tynecastle on the day after we won the Scottish Cup in 1998 was also special. I thought I would never see a Hearts trophy-winning team (unless you count the Tennents Sixes). I remember the glorious sunshine, the fact that the newspapers had Hearts on all the front pages and the roar when the players and management came out.'

Jurek Leon (Perth, Australia)

'I went to live in Perth in Western Australia in September 1974 and left with great memories of my top player Donald Ford. It wasn't too difficult to get Hearts results, as the Australian newspapers always had a Scottish round-up on a Monday morning, although they used to concentrate on Celtic and Rangers. As years went on, and with the birth of the Internet, I registered with the Hearts website and managed to get all the up-to-date news from there.

'From 1974 up until January 2005, I didn't see a Hearts match, as whenever I came back to Scotland, it was during the close season. I went to the 1–0 win over Aberdeen on 29 January 2005 and that was my first game in 30 years. It was a great experience. The three new stands have made a big difference and I think there is maybe a better atmosphere now than there was when I left in 1974.

'I heard all about the attempts to save Tynecastle and I can see why everybody was up in arms about the possible sale. Take it from me, a Hearts fan who hadn't seen a game there for 30 years, it is worth saving. Going there fresh after such a long time was fantastic. It is one of the best stadia in the world to watch football at and people shouldn't forget that.'

Craig Lumsdaine (Edinburgh)

'I used to play for Berwick Rangers and I was part of their reserve team which played Hearts in a second XI League Cup tie. We were always going to be struggling but things got worse when we realised that Peter Marinello, who they had signed the day before, was going to play to get some match practice. This was October 1981 and we got stuffed 4–1.

'Although I was a midfielder, I was pushed back into defence to try to keep the score respectable. Marinello was brilliant but Hearts also had Gary Mackay and Dave Bowman – it was the era when Hearts had a lot of good young players.

'I actually played at Tynecastle in a cup-winning side when I played for Civil Service Strollers, who beat Gala in the King's Amateur Cup. I had a trial for Hearts but they never signed me. It was disappointing, as I loved the club, but it never put me off watching them play. The night they took on Bayern Munich in the UEFA Cup and won 1–0, I couldn't get a ticket. That didn't put me off and a group of us descended on a mate's flat which overlooked Tynecastle to hang out of the window and watch the game. To see the crowd and hear the roars from way up high was an amazing experience.'

Lord Macaulay of Bragar (Edinburgh)

'I actually started supporting Hearts in the west of Scotland. Willie Bauld was my man of that time and I don't think I've ever seen a better header of a football. I was captivated by the team and they were a side which you wanted to get out of your house to go and see.

'I remember being at Glasgow University on a night out with some fellow Hearts supporters and our girlfriends at the students' bar. A couple of us stood up, raised our glasses and said, "To the King of Hearts!" I think the girls, who didn't know us too well at that stage, thought we were a couple of head cases!

'I can also remember some comical songs the supporters used to sing. One was about crowning Willie Bauld the King of Scotland and Alfie Conn the Prince of Wales, the other went along the lines of: "I'll raise my hat to Willie Bauld, although my heid may feel the cold!"

'He was an outstanding talent but it shouldn't be forgotten that the likes of Tom McKenzie, Bobby Parker, who didn't do wingers any favours, and Freddie Glidden added grit to proceedings.'

Grant McDonald (Edinburgh)

'I remember a game against Clydebank back on 26 April 1986 when we were going for the championship. We were playing superbly at the time and for the first time that I could remember they opened the away end and filled it with Hearts fans, as it was vital we got all three points. I remember Gary Mackay scored in front of 20,000 people. The atmosphere was incredible.

'The match against Hibs we won in the New Year of that season is one I remember as clear as day. Ian Jardine, John Robertson and Sandy Clark all scored. We had a special song we sang about the game for a few years afterwards.'

Ian MacDonald (Elie, Fife)

'Watching the football results in a crowd gathered round Radio Rentals in Gorgie Road will always live with me. We used to pour out of the stadium and head towards the television rental shop to watch the rest of the football results through the shop window. People would jeer if a team that was close to Hearts in the league had won and cheer if they had been beaten. They were great times.

173

'As a boy, I was desperate to go to Tynecastle on my own and my folks granted my wish when Willie Bauld had his testimonial match. Davie Holt was my all-time favourite player but Bauld was also a hero. His testimonial was on a Wednesday night and I was incredibly excited. I think about 15,000 folk were there and we played Sheffield United and drew 2–2. I remember the papers at the time said he got about £2,800 from the night but the board took £1,000 off that in match expenses. No wonder he never returned to Tynecastle for years.'

Peter McGrail (Edinburgh)

'I always remember Willie Jamieson scoring a blinder in the last minute against Celtic at Tynecastle when Tommy Burns was their manager in the mid-1990s. Hearts were losing 1–0 when the ball dropped to him about 30 yards from goal. It was one of the early magic moments for my son Michael, as we were right down at ground level in front of Jamieson when he struck this wonderful shot straight into the back of the net.'

Graeme McIver

'Hearts v. Morton on Saturday, 20 September 1980 was my first proper Hearts match. Segregation meant that Hearts fans now no longer occupied vantage points on the famous Gorgie Road terracings and with drink banned from inside stadiums for the first time, a handful of Morton fans stood emptying beer cans and bottles into the bins at the turnstiles.

'As I watched the small group drain the last drops of beer before entering, I was held spellbound by the sign above their head. Since that day, I have seen some of the world's most famous football stadiums – I have stood on the pitch at Old Trafford, walked up Wembley Way, watched the finishing touches being put to the Stade de France – but nothing has come close to impressing me as much as the giant painted board that Hearts had erected over the turnstiles in the Gorgie Road: "Heart of Midlothian Football Club Ltd. Tynecastle Park".

'I cannot remember too much about the actual game itself other than Morton's winning goal. My overriding memory is the swearing and general lambasting of the Hearts players by the old men surrounding us. As we travelled back to the Borders, I re-read the programme. According to manager Bobby Moncur, that very week Hearts had signed a promising young talent by the name of John Robertson. "I wonder if he'll be any good?" I thought to myself.'

George McKechnie (Wales)

'Following Hearts, I've had to get used to disappointments. I remember being in Kenya back in 1986 when we were going for the league and I had no way of finding out how they were doing. I knew they were playing Clydebank at Tynecastle then Dundee away in the final game of the season. I got on a plane from Nairobi to Amsterdam and saw some Kenyan government officials with a newspaper. I looked over their shoulder and saw Dundee 2, Hearts 0. I was devastated. I remember repeating to my wife, "I think Hearts have lost the league; I think Hearts have lost the league." I can still remember running through Schipol Airport looking for another newspaper, hoping the one I had seen was wrong. Sadly, it wasn't.'

Calum MacKenzie

'On match days, I am with the bike section of Lothian and Borders police at Tynecastle. It is a real labour of love for me. I first went to Tynecastle when I was 14 with my schoolmates Dougie Ross and Richard Bell. We used to get into the ground dead early and stand next to the Hearts punks in the Shed before games. I've always had a season ticket but when I joined the police, with the shifts, I couldn't go to all the games. However, when I joined the bike section, I volunteered to cover matches on Saturdays. I'm paired with my mate, Bob "Sparky" Martin, who is a big Hibs fan. The banter between us is great and whenever I go to Tynecastle I wind him up and whenever we go to Easter Road I get it in the neck. My favourite player? It has to be John Robertson. I've met him through work and had a cuppa with him at the training academy at Riccarton when he was manager. A great guy and a great player.'

Nicholas McLaren (Glasgow)

'My dad first took me to a match at Tynecastle in 1967. After trying a few spots, we settled on a position at the Gorgie Road End. We would arrive by 2.15 p.m., park in Wheatfield Place, and be amongst the first in the ground to get our place. At the end of the game, we would make a dash for the car and be home in Corstorphine by 5 p.m. for the results on TV. Our car didn't have a radio.

'As I grew older, we would join the exodus changing ends to stand behind the goals we were attacking. However, that all came to an end after the Hibs riot in 1978. We turned up for the next match against Morton to find the Gorgie Road End closed off and allocated to visiting fans.

'One of the funniest matches I remember was on the last day of the season in 1977. We had been relegated for the first time and thought the world was coming to an end. Surely the powers that be wouldn't let it happen! It was a lovely sunny day and we beat Motherwell 3–2. Malcolm Robertson scored a sensational own goal, hammering it past Brian Wilson from about 25 yards.

'Stan the Fossil Man was a colourful character in those days. He had entered the ground with a placard on a pole protesting against the board and shortly after the start the police had had enough. They marched him around the track and out of the ground to warm applause as he tilted his hat to the crowd. I also remember Ally Hunter, the Motherwell keeper, being injured. He lay in his six-yard box trying to attract the referee's attention by waving. The crowd waved back shouting, "Coo – eee!" as play raged on at the other end.'

David McLetchie (leader of the Scottish Conservatives)

'It was on 8 April 1961 that I first set foot in Tynecastle. It was for a game against Third Lanark and Hearts won 1–0, with John Cumming, one of my favourite players of all time, getting the goal.

'Willie Gibson, Bobby Prentice, Jim Cruickshank and, of course, Robbo are some of the players I have marvelled at through the years. Politics takes up a lot of my time but I still go as much as I can. For me, the intimacy of Tynecastle sets it apart. When I was going there as a boy, it was the smell of the hops from the brewery that I remember and the roar of the crowd. As far as I am concerned it is the best place in Scotland to watch a football match.'

Mindaugas Majauskas (Vilnius, Lithuania)

'I watched Liverpool play Kaunas in a Champions League qualifying match at Anfield in August 2005 and before I went, people told me that the atmosphere at Anfield could not be beaten. I went to Tynecastle a few days later to watch Hearts play Hibs and the atmosphere was the best I had ever experienced. Much better than Anfield. The Hearts fans were incredible. I had never heard so much noise. I was in the directors' box and everybody was shouting the name of Vladimir Romanov before the match. It was easily the best football match I have ever attended. I had my Hearts scarf on and we won 4–0. To make things even better, my countryman Saulius Mikoliunas got the final goal. It was a game I will never forget.'

George Meikle

'I was nine when I went to my first game with my dad in 1948 and have been hooked on Hearts every since. My first match was a match on 26 February 1949 against Falkirk and we won 3–1. Charlie Cox scored the first goal and Davie Laing, who was one of my heroes, got the other two.

'Up until 1969, I used to get the train up from Gala to all the matches. For evening games, I used to get the train just after 6 p.m,, which used to get me into Edinburgh at around 7.10 p.m. I used to run down to Tynecastle and never missed the kick-off. Afterwards, I dashed back to the station to get the 9.55 p.m. train back to Gala.

'For me, the greatest ever Hearts player has to be Willie Bauld. He was magnificent. I used to have a Hearts strip with No. 9 chalked on the back. This was long before you could get names and numbers printed on shirts but it was a way for me to salute one of the best players Scotland has ever seen.'

John Miller

'I was first taken to Tynecastle when I was seven years old but didn't start going regularly until I was in my thirties. That was because music became my big love and I was in a band called Fags and Matches, who were introduced on *Opportunity Knocks* by the former Hearts player George Donaldson. George was my brother-in-law and after he signed from Rangers all my family used to go along to watch him at Tynecastle. The band also had close links with the club and we played at their centenary concert in the Usher Hall. I also remember George and Jim Jefferies rushing from Tynecastle and getting changed in the car as they wanted to see Paul McCartney and Wings play the Usher Hall. My favourite player was always Eamonn Bannon, although I also liked Dave McPherson and Walter Kidd.

'I always go to the John Robertson Suite on match days as the banter in there is brilliant. I may have been a late starter when it came to watching Hearts on a regular basis, but I love it.'

Eric Milligan
(former Lord Provost of Edinburgh)

'There are those who become Hearts supporters. There are others who are born into the faith. I was lucky enough to be one of the latter. My mum and dad, Duncan and Amelia, were fanatical supporters of the club and my dad used to say it was great that I came into this world at 2.30 p.m. on a Saturday, as it still allowed him time to get to the match.

'I was brought up in Robertson Avenue and my granny lived in Gorgie Road. I went to Tynecastle Secondary School with Willie Bauld's son and still love the history and romance of the club. Just think about it. How long does it take to come up with the name Aberdeen Football Club or Glasgow Rangers or Glasgow Celtic? Compare that to Heart of Midlothian. It is a poetic name and the name of Sir Walter Scott's best novel.

'There is something of Edinburgh about Heart of Midlothian and after 13 years as Lord Provost, the longest serving civic leader ever in the city, I feel I know what makes the capital tick. There is a bit of pretentiousness about the name Heart of Midlothian, a bit like Edinburgh people themselves, as we always think we are a bit better than we really are. We aspire to be more than we can be and love the faded glory of the football team.

'Even our colour, maroon, is magnificent. It is a traditional colour, a royal colour, and a colour which is always linked with Heart of Midlothian. I don't even like it when they change the colour of my season-ticket book from maroon.

'One of the best games I remember was a pre-season friendly back in the early 1960s against Torpedo Moscow. Here was this great team from Russia and we beat them 6–0. I remember Willie Hamilton tore them apart. He was a wizard on the ball.

'It goes without saying that John Robertson was great for Hearts but for me Dave Mackay was king. He was my greatest football hero and I am honoured that I now regard him as a friend. Willie Bauld was another master and I remember the excitement I felt just watching him walk across the Gorgie Road.

'Family ties to a football club last for ever. The ties that bind me to Hearts were there from the start and they remain strong.'

Kevin Moffat

'Standing shivering on the terraces as a boy watching Norwegian Raold Jensen terrorise defences was a good way to start a lifetime of watching Hearts. He was a great player and it was a tragedy when he died of a heart attack at just 44.

'I used to love going to the old enclosure with my cousin Robert Finnie and now my own sons are Hearts fans as well. Like many youngsters who were taken to Hearts games by their relatives, my other abiding memory is standing outside the Murrayfield Bar with a bag of crisps and a bottle of juice waiting for the men to come out to go to the game.

'The match which sums up Tynecastle for me was a 2–2 draw against Rangers in the league back in 1984. We were losing 2–0 with a few minutes to go before Derek O'Connor scored, then Robbo popped up with the equaliser. The place went mad.'

Stewart Morrison

'Wednesday, 30 September 1992. Slavia Prague were the visitors in this first-round, second-leg match. We won 4–2 to just beat them on aggregate. That was one of the best games I have ever witnessed at Tynecastle. From the highs to the lows, high again to low again, then ecstasy. It summed up Tynecastle for me.'

James Mullins (Edinburgh)

'My first memory of Tynecastle is from a Hearts match in 1980 against Dunfermline. I was three years old and my brother took me. The game ended 3–3 but all I remember is crying throughout the match due to the volume of noise, which I had never experienced before. I have since seen many brilliant matches and European nights in particular hold a special place with me. Velez Mostar and Stuttgart were two of my favourites in terms of atmosphere and drama and I still can't believe Gordan Petric missed that chance right at the death against Stuttgart.

'Hibs games are always great, too. John Robertson's goal in the first game against them since returning from Newcastle was priceless – and I'll never forget him running to the corner of the Shed to celebrate. Graham Weir's two in the last minute on 2 January 2003 had the ground rocking.

'We have all seen some smashing goals at Tynie, too. A Gary Naysmith 25-yarder against Aberdeen stands out for me but Iain Ferguson's wonder strike against Bayern Munich wins hands down in my book. The best player ever to be seen at Tynecastle – who else but wee Robbo – say no more.'

Dougie Napier (Edinburgh)

'I remember going through to the UEFA Cup tie against NK Zeljeznicar at Tynecastle just when all the talk was going on about how we would have to play our European games at Murrayfield. I was in the School End when one of their players came across to take a corner. The Hearts fans gave him pelters and that moment showed just what a great atmosphere Tynecastle can generate. The Zeljeznicar player could only take one step back to take the corner.

If he stepped back any further, he would have been in the crowd. Tynecastle is a real bear pit, a great place for football. I thought playing our European ties at Murrayfield was disastrous.

'For me, the greatest ever player has to be Donald Ford. The only thing I didn't like about him was his haircut. He looked like he should have been a dentist rather than a footballer. He was the antithesis of all the trendy footballers at the time. What a player, though.'

Andres Padilla
(foreign visitor to Tynecastle from Colombia)

'I remember being on holiday in Edinburgh in 2003 visiting relatives and I had the chance to go to Tynecastle to watch a game. Being from South America, I'm a big football fan and wanted to see the stadium. I would have liked to be there with a capacity crowd but this was a reserve match with Hibs, so there weren't many people inside the ground. I could still sense it is the kind of stadium which would have a great atmosphere when full, though. I also spoke Spanish to another fan who was there, so the evening had a real international feel for me, which was great.'

Gordon Paterson (aka Hearty Harry, the Hearts mascot)

'I made my debut against Partick Thistle at Tynecastle on Boxing Day 1994. I thought I would be there for just a couple of games but eight years later I had made 182 appearances! In the winter it was fine but I was so hot during warm days in the summer that sweat would run into my eyes and I couldn't do anything about it. The only occasion I didn't appear during that spell was when Ally McCoist took my place!

'I'll never forget the open-top bus ride after the Scottish Cup win in 1998. I was standing there head and shoulders above everyone on the top deck and had to hang on to Stefano Salvatori to keep my balance. All good things come to an end, though, and I decided enough was enough in 2002.'

John Proudfoot

'Playing at Tynecastle was always a dream for me and I've now done it twice. The first occasion was a charity match arranged by Football Aid, and Dave McPherson and Jimmy Sandison played. Things got even better in December 2004. We all paid a minimum of £150 to take part in the match, with all the proceeds going to the Hearts Youth Development Fund, so it was money well spent all round. We won 7–3 and I got a couple of goals. I was in a team which beat a side containing John Robertson at Tynecastle. Now not many people can say that.'

Rod Ramsay (Glasgow)

'Willie Bauld is a player who was the real "King of Hearts" for me. I remember a great day back in September 1958 when he scored five goals against Third Lanark and we won 8–3. I also remember meeting Davie Holt, who was another of my favourite players from the early 1960s, years later and playing golf with him. He was a real gentleman and a fantastic player. I used to love watching him and Alex Young, who had more skill than most. Years later, I took my son Alan down to the ground on a non-match day and we were allowed out on the pitch. He was three and watching my son toddling about a deserted Tynecastle was a great feeling.'

Graeme Renwick (Edinburgh)

'The day we won the cup in 1998 was pretty special, given the fact that I'd a broken leg at the time. Thanks to his SFA connections, my dad had got me a seat behind the dugouts, unfortunately right in among all the Rangers fans. When the final whistle went, I couldn't contain myself and ended up getting a police escort out of the section as I was getting a bit carried away.'

Ian Richardson (Bearsden, Glasgow)

'The date was 29 January 1949. I was nine years old at the time and lived in Glasgow. On a visit to my grandfather in Edinburgh, my father had promised to take me to see Hearts at Tynecastle.

'The stadium had no floodlights, so the match started earlier than the now customary 3 p.m. kick-off. We made our way to the terracings opposite the Main Stand and headed for the corner flag. My heart leapt when the Jambos ran out on to the field. My hero at that time was Willie Bauld and I was thrilled to see him give his all for Hearts. Hearts led 2–1 at half-time. Bauld scored during the second half and was denied a second when he was brought down in the penalty area by the Motherwell goalkeeper as he was about to put the ball in the net. We scored from the penalty and Hearts went on to win 5–1 to make a very memorable afternoon – and a wee boy very happy.'

Kevin Riddell (Edinburgh)

'I always go back to the night we beat Bayern Munich in 1989 and I don't think anything will ever surpass that occasion. There was just such a buzz about the whole occasion and the ground was bouncing as we'd given ourselves a real chance of going through.

'Winning the Scottish Cup was obviously another unforgettable experience and it was great just to be part of the celebrations the following day in the centre of Edinburgh. I was in Princes Street and along Gorgie Road but couldn't get into Tynecastle on the Sunday as it was jammed out. I actually don't think I got back home until the Monday afternoon but it was worth the sore head I had for the next couple of days.'

Alex Salmond (leader of the Scottish National Party)

'Watching Willie Wallace play at Tynecastle was a joy. He glided past opponents and oozed class. Jim Townsend and Jim Cruickshank were also great favourites of mine.

'The best debut I ever saw was Tommy Murray, who scored two goals against Dunfermline on 11 September 1971, when we won 4–1. I thought we had signed the new George Best, as Tommy was so good that day.

'My political commitments mean I don't get along to Tynecastle as often as I would like nowadays but between 1966 and 1974 I followed them home and away and went to every reserve game. In fact, the best goal I ever saw scored at Tynecastle was in a reserve match and was scored by Donald Ford, who hit one in from 35 yards.

'It was my dad, Robert, who took me to my first game at Tynecastle when Hearts beat Airdrie 3–1 on 14 January 1961, and Willie Bauld was among the scorers. I remember my dad saying that Willie Bauld was such a good player he could score with a header from the halfway line. I believed him and was disappointed that he didn't that day.'

John Sanderson

'I was at a scout camp at Colinton on the outskirts of Edinburgh as an 11 year old when I went to my first game. The scout leader took a whole group of us to an evening game between the Hearts first team and reserves. It was in 1939, just before the outbreak of war, and it was the first time I got the chance to see the great Tommy Walker play. He was magnificent. I also remember on the way back watching the searchlight operators practising by spotting our own planes in the sky in preparation for the war. Tommy Walker was a genius and as for Conn, Bauld and Wardhaugh, what can you say? Top class.'

Stuart Sherry

'My grandfather died in 1995, having suffered from Alzheimer's disease for several years. I wanted to raise a bit of money for the Alzheimer's charity by doing something a bit different, so I decided to ask Chris Robinson, the then chairman of Hearts, if he would allow me access to the stadium one Sunday so that I could sit in all the seats in what was the then relatively new Wheatfield Stand. He permitted me to do my sponsored sit, so I turned up with my wife Alexandra in tow, ready for my challenge. It was more of a challenge than I had expected but I sat in all the seats in both the Wheatfield and School End stands and raised, if I remember correctly, about £400. It was more of an ordeal for my wife, who spent about five hours bored by my recollections of more than 20 years of games I'd seen at Tynecastle.

'A further memory of the day was that Alan Rae, the club physio, was doing some work on the pitch with Jeremy Goss, who was injured at the time. Having asked them if I could use the gents under the Main Stand, I was able to come back out into the arena down the tunnel for the one and only time in my life. Like many Jambos and, indeed, football supporters, I'm just a wee boy at heart and it was a real thrill to come out of the same tunnel as Robbo, Rab Prentice, Jim Cruickshank, Kenny Aird, Derek O'Connor and the rest of my heroes from down the years. From Hearts' point of view they got about 10,000 seats buffed by my bum free of charge and the jogging bottoms I wore never saw another day.'

Bill Smith
(club historian, Bonnyrigg, Midlothian)

'Having been a Tynecastle regular since 1957, my memories of the ground are plentiful. Unfortunately, they are not all pleasant and the first one was a defeat against Rangers. My one regret is that I rarely saw the Terrible Trio play together at their peak, as the 1956 cup-winning side was breaking up.

'The 1962–63 season saw me introduced to the finest player I have witnessed in a Hearts jersey, Willie Hamilton. He was signed from Middlesbrough for £3,000 and his skill with a ball was unbelievable. Unfortunately, however, Willie reportedly liked wine, women and song, and that affected his fitness.

'In the mid-1960s I was a member of the Danderhall Hearts Supporters' Club and a regular under the famous Shed. The entertainment was poor, though, despite the likes of Cruickshank, Shevlane, Holt, Anderson, Cumming and Wallace, to name but a few, being regulars in the side. The football was so poor that the fans used to vent their feelings on the police:

> Who's the – with the helmet on, Dixon, Dixon,
> Who's the – with the helmet on, Dixon of Dock Green,
> On the beat all day, On the – all night
> Who's the – with the helmet on, it's Dixon of Dock Green

'The men in blue would take it for so long, then would move in for a couple of victims. I never found out if they were charged, however, or just ejected from the ground.

'In the 1970s, I purchased a season ticket for the Main Stand and my seat was next to Hearts legend Barney Battles, who I became very friendly with until he sadly passed away. What the great man must have thought about the entertainment on the park I don't know, as he never said a bad word against any individual.'

Mike Smith (author and Hearts enthusiast)

'When Wallace Mercer took over in 1981, the heavy clouds of depression which had settled over Tynecastle began to lift as a new era was welcomed in at Gorgie. Alex MacDonald was appointed manager a year later and the likes of Sandy Jardine, Jimmy Bone and Willie Johnston, former internationalists in the twilight of their careers, were recruited to help stop the rot of the yo-yo syndrome which had seen Hearts flit between the Premier and First divisions.

'While the elder statesmen were seen as a short-term fix, it was in the youth policy, however, that Hearts saw the long-term future of a club that had faced oblivion at the beginning of the 1980s. Gary Mackay, David Bowman and John Robertson were regulars in the side that gained promotion to the Premier Division in 1983 and there was hope that, at last, Hearts had a team good enough to compete in the top division.

'The acid test came in September 1983, when Hearts faced Hibernian at Tynecastle in the first Edinburgh derby for four long years. It would prove to be a game that spawned a legend. Hearts' biggest attendance for nearly seven years – almost 20,000 – swarmed to Tynecastle in eager anticipation and, for once, they weren't to be disappointed.

'Hearts began in positive fashion with youngsters Robertson and Bowman both forcing Hibs and Scotland keeper Alan Rough into action. But it was Hibs who drew first blood. After 11 minutes, a Gary Murray shot cannoned off Hearts keeper Henry Smith only for former Gorgie favourite Ralph Callachan to lash home the rebound. Hearts boss Alex MacDonald brought himself on to replace Mackay and the transformation was immediate. Within two minutes, Hearts had levelled the score with one of the best goals ever scored in an Edinburgh derby – and it proved to be the first of a derby record for Robertson.

'Henry Smith launched a long ball forward and with wind assistance it landed at the feet of 18-year-old Robertson. With a breathtaking piece of skill rarely seen by Hearts fans since the golden age of the 1950s, Robbo, with his back to goal, controlled the ball with his right foot. With deftness of touch, the wee man turned Hibs veteran Arthur Duncan, spotted Rough off his line and curled a magnificent left-foot shot past the startled keeper and into the net to make it 1–1. It was one of those goals that remain etched on the memory and those Hearts supporters who witnessed it still talk about it to this day.

'Willie Irvine scored to make it 2–1 for Hibs and as they tried to hold on for two points, Ally Brazil was short with a pass back to Rough. Robertson raced to get to the ball first and poked it past an aghast keeper to level the score at 2–2.

'Tynecastle was now in a frenzy as the huge Hearts support acclaimed the birth of a star who had been banging in goals in the First Division the season before but who was now proving himself in the top league.

'Robertson sprayed a 25-yard cross-field pass which landed at the feet of Donald Park. He gave it to Jimmy Bone, who made it 3–2. It was Hearts' first victory over Hibs in almost six years, their first derby win at Tynecastle in almost a decade and, remarkably, only their third league win over Hibs in Gorgie in two decades.

'The terracings rocked and the jubilant Hearts fans in the old stand rose as one to applaud their team and one player in particular. John Robertson would go on to become "the Hammer of Hibs" over the next 15 years. Many Hearts fans are still proud to say they were there when a legend was born.'

Ian Somerville (Edinburgh)

'Willie Johnston was a player I loved to watch. The pitch was so close to the crowd at Tynecastle you felt you could reach out and touch him. My favourite Johnston moment was when he was giving a poor full-back a real torrid time. He was getting past him time and time again. The man was pulling his shirt to the extent that the referee had to keep stopping the game. It got so bad that one time Willie got past the player and was fouled yet again, he got up, took his top off and presented it to the full-back. You just never knew what would happen with him. He was great in a Hearts jersey. And the one thing that shocked me? Seeing Henry Smith's perm for the first time.'

John Somerville (Edinburgh)

'Back in 1946 I remember getting lifted over the turnstiles by my dad Walter for my first game against Third Lanark. I remember it well. We won 4–1 on 17 August and there were more than 24,000 people there.

'Going to a Hearts game was a real event for everybody. We used to get the No. 8 bus from Juniper Green to Shandon and walked down to the ground from there. We used to be in there by 1 p.m. We were OK if Hearts were shooting towards the Gorgie End, as that was the end we would be behind. In the second half, we simply walked round behind the opposition goal. There was no segregation and we just walked from one end to the other.

'Out of all the games at Tynecastle the match against Rangers in a Scottish Cup quarter-final replay in March 1968 will always be the best match for me in terms of atmosphere. The first game at Ibrox on the Saturday had been a 1–1 draw and Jim Irvine scored for us.

'More than 44,000 folk were at the replay and it poured down. The crowd were in great voice and Donald Ford netted the winner in the last minute. Magic.'

David Speed (Murrayfield, Edinburgh)

'My earliest memory of Tynecastle was not actually of watching the games but of playing football with a paper cup that had Willie Bauld's face on it. We used to be able to wander freely around the terracings back then and it was a tremendous time. When there was a big crowd, I used to go to the back of the terracing under the Shed and hang on to the metal bars of the distillery windows. I could then see above the fans to watch. Alternatively, we used to climb up the floodlight pylons.

'My earliest recollection of a game was seeing Willie Hamilton score a fantastic goal for Hearts against Dundee in a League Cup tie in 1962. He had joined us from Middlesbrough for £3,000 and I had never seen anybody like him before. He must have beaten five men in a great run from the halfway line before scoring a stunning goal which brought the crowd to its feet. I remember asking my dad if they all played like that in England! A remarkable player who could dribble with the ball and take on opponents, he became something of a hero who unfortunately let his career go to waste. He made a huge impression in two seasons at Hearts before joining Hibs and I know many fans regard him as the best player they have ever seen at Tynecastle.'

Craig Stewart

'Hearts played Falkirk on the last game of the season 1991–92 and had to win to qualify for Europe. Celtic played Hibs at Parkhead and Celtic just had to win or draw for their place in Europe. It was right in the middle of "crisis" seasons for Celtic, when they won nothing.

'The chances, however, of Hearts qualifying were slim in the view of the fans that day and hardly any turned up to watch the game. Midway through the second half, Hibs somehow had a two-goal lead at Parkhead and Hearts predictably were 2–0 up against Falkirk. Well, when the news came through to the fans at Tynie the place just erupted. You had plenty space to jump about and me and my mates just went mental. We couldn't believe it.

'At the end of the game, it was announced that we were definitely in Europe and the place was in raptures. The irony, of course, was that it was Hibs who put us there. Classic!'

Ken Stott (actor, London)

'My dad David was a mad keen Hearts supporter and took me to my first game when I was six years old. For a young boy, it was an amazing experience that I still remember with affection. There I was, perched on my dad's shoulders at an Edinburgh derby, looking down from on high on thousands of men crushed in beside each other. They were all handing round caps of whisky and roaring on their team. At the end, I remember looking down and below me was a sea of empty brightly coloured McEwan's Export and Pale Ale cans. I also remember I couldn't quite grasp the concept of Tynecastle. I was disappointed there was no castle at Tynecastle.

'I have great memories of watching Heart of Midlothian through the years and being brought up in Newington I used to make the pilgrimage as often as I could. One of my earliest memories was sitting in the stand with my dad on the day Hearts lost the league to Kilmarnock on the last day of the season back in 1965. When the final whistle went, my dad turned to me and said, "That's it. Hearts will never win the league." I was so certain that they would and shouted back at him, "Yes they will, Dad, yes they will!"

'My favourite player was Arthur Mann, who was a very skilful and poised full-back. Also, Willie Wallace was a real favourite. He moved from Heart of Midlothian to Celtic! As a kid I couldn't understand why he would want to do anything like that. I couldn't believe it when he left.

'In the 1970s, I didn't see much of Hearts as I was a penniless actor living in London. Money was so tight there was no chance of me getting back to Scotland much to see them play. As anybody who has lived south of the border will realise, trying to get details of Scottish football down there is near to impossible. I tried my best, though. As things improved for me professionally I started to come up more and I still have two season tickets for me and my son. I only get up four or five times a year due to work commitments but I would never give them up. Also, don't ever call my team Hearts. They are Heart of Midlothian. When I mention their name to people in the acting profession from home and abroad many of them claim not to have heard of my team. When they say that, I accuse them of ignorance. After all, Heart of Midlothian isn't just a football club; it's also the name of Walter Scott's greatest novel. They should know that.

'I'm excited about the new era at Hearts. I think Rangers and Celtic should be worried. The "axis of evil" can be broken.'

Kingsley Thomas (Edinburgh)

'Tynecastle is a vital part of Gorgie and a vital part of Edinburgh, and as the local councillor I know what Hearts means to people. Many people forget that the future of the ground has been in the balance on a number of occasions in the past and as local councillor for the area I remember them well and the furore moving away would have caused. There was a plan by Wallace Mercer to move the club to Millerhill and another time there was talk of going to Ingliston. The planning department also heard proposals that if Hearts moved from Tynecastle there would be a Gorgie relief road going straight through the stadium site, which would have been terrible.

'I go with my son Andrew to games now and tell him what a great player Drew Busby was and what a great night it was when we beat Lokomotiv Leipzig.'

Len Todd (Lauder)

'Coming from Lauder, I live in Jim Jefferies' country and one incident I recall spoke volumes about the man. My next-door neighbour in Oxton was Willie Nisbet, who was terminally ill in 1998. Jim surprised him one day by bringing the Scottish Cup to his house. Jim had known he was very ill and decided to try to give him a wee lift. It certainly boosted Willie for a wee while but unfortunately he died not long after he got his hands on the cup. Another occasion saw Jim bring a handful of first-team stars all the way to Lauderdale for a supporters' club player of the year function. Despite the travelling involved, Gary Locke, Thomas Flogel and Paul Ritchie were among those who turned up, which was greatly appreciated.

'Best goal ever seen at Tynecastle has to be Iain Ferguson's wonderful effort against Bayern Munich. I've been going to Tynecastle for years and while the redeveloped ground is much better for the fans, I did like it when we used to be able to change ends at half-time by just walking round. You wouldn't dream of doing that now. The old stadium was a bit primitive in some respects, though. I remember standing on the old terracings and having to be careful I didn't get someone peeing down the back of my leg.'

Elaine Turner (Edinburgh)

'I got hooked on Hearts after we lost a Scottish Cup semi-final against St Mirren at Hampden in the 1986–87 season. I was a teenager sitting my exams and my dad asked me along to give me a break from studying. We played them off the park and still lost 2–1. The injustice got to me and I've been following them ever since. I have a season ticket and have followed them all around Europe. My only regret is that the day after Hearts won the Scottish Cup I forgot to take my season ticket down to Tynecastle and they wouldn't let me in to see the trophy being paraded round the ground. Still, I was there on the day when we won the cup and that was extra special.'

Tommy Walker (Edinburgh)

'Being the son of a famous Hearts manager was often quite hellish. While I was very proud of my father, at the same time it caused a lot of hassle. By hassle I mean people would always phone me up looking for tickets. They just seemed to think I would be able to get them from nowhere and didn't realise that a manager only had his own allocation, like everyone else at the club. I was the easy option, or so people thought. They soon found out differently.

'We had all gone to London in 1945 just after the end of the war when my father signed for Chelsea for a record fee. He came back to Hearts as assistant manager to Dave McLean in 1949 when I was 11 years old.

'I used to go along to Tynecastle every week with my father and had a permanent seat in the stand. I would be in the boardroom after matches and would stay for a while before going to meet friends in the evening. I also travelled away with the team as well and I don't think I missed a game between the ages of 11 and 17. That was when I went to the army. After I came out I played a bit myself and then had family to think about so didn't really go back that much.

'I have so many good memories of that era but I suppose the best one has to be the 1956 Scottish Cup win. I was 18 years old and it was a fantastic day. The bus came back to the Maybury and then there was an open-top bus parade through Gorgie, which ended up

The Scottish National War Memorial match between Hearts and Celtic at
Tynecastle on 22 May 1920. (Photo courtesy of John Kerr)

Alex Young jumps to it
during training at Tynecastle.

Snow puts paid to a Hearts v. Kilmarnock game
at Tynecastle in February 1960. Referee Tom
'Tiny' Wharton carries out the pitch inspection
watched by manager Tommy Walker (right) and
groundsman Matthie Chalmers.

Hearts stars John Cumming (back row, fifth from left) and Alex Young (front, second from left) pictured at Scotland training at Somerset Park, Ayr, before the Home International against England in 1960. (Photograph © Tom Purdie)

Dave Mackay meets up with John Harvey again at Wembley in 1963. (Photograph © Tom Purdie)

Tynecastle favourites John Cumming (left) and Billy Higgins (back) get in a spot of putting while at Turnberry Hotel with the Scotland squad. (Photograph © Tom Purdie)

Hundreds of supporters queue to get into Tynecastle 25 minutes after the start of the Scottish Cup quarter-final replay against Rangers on 13 March 1968.

Tynecastle legend Tommy Walker wasn't a man to sport headgear that often but here's a rare sight of him wearing a Scotland tammy with wife Jean on the way to Wembley Stadium in 1979. (Photograph © The Walker Family)

Jim Jefferies and Cammy Fraser celebrate together with the First Division championship trophy, won in the 1979–80 season.

An aerial view of Tynecastle before any of the new stands went up.

Work begins on the Wheatfield Stand.

The imposing Gorgie Road Stand nears completion.

The modern-day Tynecastle has been described as
a tremendous arena for a football match.

Tottenham Hotspur's
Paul Gascoigne shoots
for goal in a friendly
at Tynecastle.

The foreign legion: French striker
Stephane Adam (left) and
Austrian midfielder Thomas
Flogel, both vital parts of the
Hearts team which won the
1998 Scottish Cup.

It's party time at Tynecastle the day after the Jambos'
famous Scottish Cup win over Rangers in 1998.

Steven Pressley celebrates scoring Hearts' first goal in the pulsating
UEFA Cup first-round second-leg clash against Stuttgart in
September 2000. The Jambos won 3–2 on the night
(aggregate 3–3) but went out on the away goals rule.

Craig Levein shares a joke with Finnish goalkeeping star Antti Niemi.

It's a derby dream for Mark de Vries after he nets his fourth goal in the 5–1 victory over Hibs at Tynecastle in August 2002.

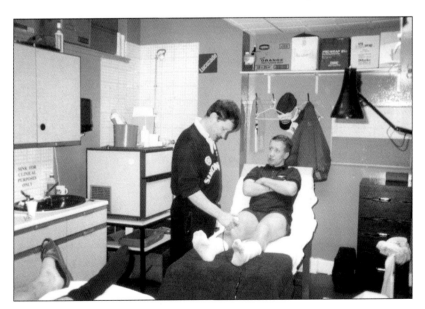

John Robertson undergoes treatment from physio Alan Rae.
(Photo courtesy of Alan Rae)

George Foulkes, the Hearts chairman, and then chief executive Chris Robinson make their way to the Gorgie Suite as the future of the ground is put under the spotlight by angry shareholders.

Thousands of fans protest against the controversial proposal to move to Murrayfield by marching along Gorgie Road in March 2004.

in a function suite in South Charlotte Street across from the Roxburghe Hotel in the West End. I was downstairs with Mum and a few others and that whole occasion stands out for me, as that was the start of some real success for Hearts – some special years for the club.'

Craig Watson (Glasgow)

'It wasn't so much the goal as the celebration that I remember more than any other. The occasion was the UEFA Cup quarter-final against the mighty Bayern Munich in 1989. Hearts had gone on a fantastic run in Europe but the game against Bayern was the big one, bigger than any other that had been played at Tynecastle. When Iain Ferguson let rip with a 25-yard drive which flew into the net, the whole ground seemed to erupt in surprise as much as joy. The corner of the old Shed, where I was standing, was simply bedlam and somehow I ended up at the bottom of the terracings near the perimeter fence after originally standing near the top, such was the uncontrollable sway of thousands of bodies. Thankfully, I had the presence of mind to video the game and therefore could watch the goal again and again. And there, in the scenes that followed the goal, I could clearly make out an over-excited Jambo hurling his distinct cream-coloured jacket from the top of the corner to the bottom.'

Karen Weir (Edinburgh)

'I started going to see Hearts in 1996 and used to sit quite close to the front of the stand from where I could actually hear what the players were shouting to each other, which was quite amusing. It's a great stadium to watch a game of football as it's just the right size and spectators do get a feeling of being right in amongst it, as they are so close to the action.'

Chris Whitehead (Edinburgh)

'The best memory I have is when we got to the quarter-finals of the UEFA Cup and faced Bayern Munich at Tynecastle. I was still at school at the time and did well to persuade my parents to allow me to go to the game with my mates. The ticket cost £10 a head, which was a lot of money back then, and I don't recall there being any child concessions. What the club did, though, was give you a voucher for each of the three games leading up to the European match. I managed to get my ticket for £7 – imagine trying to get £7 out of your mum and dad when you're only getting £2-a-week pocket money. It was well worth it, though.

'It was obviously the old Tynecastle and everyone wanted to go into the Shed back then. I can't honestly remember much about the game but I do clearly remember Iain Ferguson's goal. I couldn't have been more than five feet tall at the time so it was a case of seeing glimpses of the action.

'When his shot went in, the whole place went berserk and someone bigger than me caught me in the face with their elbow and bloodied my nose. I had a brand-new cream jumper on that night which I had just been given for my 15th birthday and it was ruined by all the blood – I had some explaining to do when I got home as my parents thought I'd been involved in a fight! I lost all my friends in the celebrations and didn't see them until after the game. I have kept a video of the game and still have the ticket stub and programme – the works.

'For a team like Hearts to get to the quarter-finals of a European competition was fantastic. And who knows, if we hadn't had to play our home UEFA Cup games at Murrayfield in 2004–05 and Craig Levein hadn't walked out on us before it all really kicked off, we might have made it into the last 32.'

Scott Wilson

'As well as being a Radio Forth presenter, I also work as the stadium announcer at Tynecastle. What makes Tynecastle special for me? The smell of the brewery, the roar of the crowd, the closeness of the pitch. The place can't be beaten.

'I started to go to Tynecastle with my brother Tom and my best mate from school, John Davidson. We used to jump into his white van at Burdiehouse about 2.45 p.m. and somehow managed to make kick-off more often than not. I'm still not sure how we did it! Everybody loved John Robertson but my other favourite player was Jim Cruickshank. What a goalkeeper he was. He made me want to be a goalkeeper and I had a trial for Dundee United but they released me because they thought I was too small at 5 ft 10 in. – the same size as Andy Goram.'

Alex B. Young

'I have been a supporter for over 50 years. I still have two friends who are season-ticket holders and we have attended nearly all our home games together during these years.

'Now our families and their friends come with us and have to put up with all the old guys' tales of the "good old days". We have seen some fantastic games at Tynie during these times. The 1956 Scottish Cup game against Rangers when we won 4–0 is still my favourite; Willie Bauld was absolutely brilliant and had big George Young tearing his hair out. I can even recall that we used to get a bit fed up with having to go to Hampden for another League Cup final.

'My own claim to fame actually happened at Easter Road in October 1959. We were playing against Cowdenbeath in the League Cup semi-final and, as usual, a crowd of us went to the match and held a correct score sweep, no bookie odds on results in these days. I won the cash of about £1.50 with the correct score of 9–3 to Hearts. I can't really recall much about the match except that Ian Crawford scored four goals and, as usual, we ended up at Hampden.'

Ray Young

'I swear to this day that I saw Jim Townsend burst the net with a shot at Tynecastle. The game was a friendly between us and the Dallas Tornadoes; Jim hit a great shot and there was a hole in the net. It was at the Gorgie Road End and the ball went straight through it. We all just looked on and realised we were there when a footballer burst the net with a shot.

'I was born and brought up in Leith but moved to Wheatfield Place in Gorgie when I was two years old. It was a lucky escape. Like all Hearts fans of my generation, I marvelled at how good a player Donald Ford was and loved the European nights against teams like Lokomotiv Leipzig and Bayern Munich.

'Also, does any other Hearts fan out there remember the horse that used to be kept in stables at the Gorgie Road End? As far as I remember it was kept there to pull the rollers to flatten the pitch. Changed days indeed.'

CHAPTER TEN

THE PRESS BOX

Mike Aitken
(one of Scotland's most respected sports journalists with over 30 years' experience of covering football and golf for the *Scotsman* newspaper)

'Out of all the games at Tynecastle, three really stand out. The first was against Bayern Munich on 28 February 1989, when Iain Ferguson scored the winner. It was significant in that Hearts had beaten one of the major forces in European football. What is forgotten, though, is that Munich won 2–0 at home in the return and Hearts went out, so in that context it comes in as my third favourite game involving Hearts.

'My second was when John Robertson laid down a marker to Scottish football. The date was 3 September 1983 and it was the first Edinburgh derby since Hearts had been promoted. Jimmy Bone scored that day but Robbo was truly magnificent and got the other two. People may not have noticed him the year before when he was scoring goals in the old First Division. When he got back into the Premier Division, they couldn't fail to see how good he was. For me, that game brought to everyone's attention the talent of John Robertson.

'My greatest match involving Hearts was the win over

Lokomotiv Leipzig in the UEFA Cup back in 1976, which they won 5–1. It was a reasonable Hearts team, nothing more than that, although they did have some good players like Drew Busby and Bobby Prentice. There is nothing better in football than a night when a home team in a great, atmospheric stadium is going all out for victory. That's what happened that evening and Hearts beat the German side with a performance full of style and flair. It was the best match at Tynecastle I have ever witnessed.'

Jim Black
(former football writer with *The Sun* and president of the Scottish Football Writers' Association)

'Gordon Smith was a Tynecastle great I remember. He went on to play for Dundee, which was my club, and he was magnificent. He had great pace, could shoot and had all the attributes that a top player needed.

'During more than 30 years in journalism, mostly with *The Sun*, I saw my fair share of great matches at Tynecastle. I am currently president of the Scottish Football Writers' Association and Hearts, especially during Wallace Mercer's days, looked after us well. He brought panache to the club, which they deserved.'

Martin Dempster
(former Hearts reporter and ex-sports editor of the *Edinburgh Evening News*)

'As the Hearts reporter for the *Edinburgh Evening News*, I spent a fair bit of time at Tynecastle – both inside and outside. Waiting patiently for a player to emerge after training or a match for an interview was an accepted part of the working week. There was many a time, too, when I'd find myself standing at the entrance as Jim Jefferies crossed the Ts and dotted the Is on a new signing inside.

'On one such occasion, I arrived to be told that the player in question would get the whole of Scottish football talking. Jim had already brought Gilles Rousset to the club and the Frenchman, of course, was to prove a superb signing for the club. "This one will give you even more to write about," smiled Jim before disappearing into the ground to finalise the deal before unveiling the player to the press. Pasquale Bruno did, indeed, give us plenty to write about, the one-time hardman of Italian football proving hugely popular with the Tynecastle faithful.

'Fittingly, it was on the Gorgie ground where Bruno gave one of his best performances for the club. It came in the second leg of a European Cup-Winners' Cup tie with Red Star Belgrade, whose tricky right-winger had proved a real thorn in Hearts' side in the first leg.

'The day before the return tie, Jefferies took Bruno aside and told him he had a special job for him in the match. "I know," replied the Italian in a flash. "You want your best player to mark their best player!" Yes, Bruno was given that marking job and he performed it brilliantly, the Red Star danger-man being subbed in the second half after his threat had been snuffed out.

'When Bruno himself was withdrawn shortly afterwards, he went over to the Red Star winger and shook his hand – one of my many great memories of Tynecastle.'

Mark Donaldson
(Radio Forth sports editor)

'When the authors of this book asked me to provide them with my favourite memories of Tynecastle, my initial thought was how on earth was I meant to abbreviate them into just one or two from over four hundred matches I must have attended in Gorgie? I am sure this dilemma rang true with every contributor to this book!

'My first ten years following Hearts at Tynecastle (1985–95) were spent in the old Family Enclosure (where they gave away free Panini stickers!) before "graduating" to the Shed, where fellow supporters became close bosom buddies at the onset of inclement weather!

'Since then, the press box has been my permanent abode on match days. First, it was the dilapidated wooden hut at the back of the Main Stand; presently, the refurbished old executive seating area just in front of the directors' box, just along from my old seat in the Family Enclosure.

'I want to pick one memorable match from the "scarf around my neck" days, and one from the "trying to stay neutral in the press box but finding it hard" days.

'You always remember your first game – I was taken along to Tynecastle by my father on 19 October 1985 and witnessed a 3–0 victory over St Mirren with two goals from John Robertson and one from Gary Mackay. There are obvious matches at Tynecastle that are recounted elsewhere in this publication – Bayern Munich and others – but I want to single out another UEFA Cup tie with special memories. Following a 1–0 defeat in Czechoslovakia, Hearts entered the second leg of their first-round match with Slavia Prague in September 1992 as underdogs. I arrived at Tynecastle slightly later than usual, about 15 minutes before kick-off, and decided to stand in the away end on Gorgie Road due to the length of the queues around the ground.

'The hardy bunch of around 30 visiting fans were housed in the Main Stand that night and I recall them being annoying as hell with constant chants of "Slavia", but they were still singing as the game approached its conclusion. Hearts were leading 3–2 but Prague were through to round two on away goals. However, Glynn Snodin – the most unlikely goal hero – struck a free-kick from way out to both silence the Slavia supporters and send the home fans into raptures, including us in the away end at the other end of the park.

'It was one of those moments where we could not really see what was happening. We watched as Snodin let fly but had to rely on the rest of the crowd's reaction to tell us that, indeed, the ball had ended up in the back of the net and we were through to face the Belgian side Standard Liège.

'My favourite memory as a commentator? Not too difficult a decision!

'Hearts, having just conceded a goal to trail Hibs 4–2 in stoppage time on 2 January 2003, pulled one back through substitute Graham Weir. Jambos heading to the exits in the Wheatfield and Gorgie stands stopped in their tracks. I screamed, "Wait a minute, there's a minute left" in the final part of my commentary on Radio Forth. I could mention it was said more in hope than expectation but surely neither I nor anyone else at Tynecastle that January afternoon thought anything could still be salvaged from that match.

'Looking back, it seems apt that I ended my commentary that day with these words, "Can you script it? No, you can't." Kind of sums up being a Hearts supporter, don't you think?'

Roddy Forsyth
(Radio Five Live commentator and analyst and *Daily Telegraph* sportswriter)

'Tynecastle is easily my favourite ground in Scotland. I like the idea that the stadium is part of the local community and you make your way there through narrow streets past people's houses. It is a true neighbourhood stadium.

'Once inside, it is a maroon fortress where I have seen some great games. I was brought up in Maryhill and used to go to Firhill a lot, and, for me, Tynecastle has a similar feel.

'As a commentator it is a great place to broadcast as you are right on top of the action, although there is a big pillar which does obstruct your view. I used to commentate a lot with John Greig when I worked with BBC Scotland and as a boyhood Hearts fan he used to sing the club song before kick-off. I must admit the Hearts song is by far the best in Scottish football.

'The most significant game for me was when Hearts played Celtic on 14 December 1985, the year they lost the league to Celtic on the last day of the season. Hearts were ahead through John Robertson and then Paul McStay equalised with 14 seconds left. If Hearts had held out for those last 14 seconds things could have been so much different.'

Martin Geissler (ITN's Scotland correspondent)

'Hearts against Queen's Park on a cold March day in 1982 isn't the sort of match that you would think would be a favourite Tynecastle memory. For me, though, it was a magical day. It was the day I finally got the chance to be the Hearts mascot.

'I was supposed to be mascot at the same game way before Christmas. I was really excited the night before and got all my stuff ready and headed down to Tynecastle. I always remember the programme sellers were out in force but when I turned up at the door I was told the game was off. I was crushed. I had been looking forward to it so much. The rearranged fixture couldn't come quickly enough for me on 20 March 1982 in front of only 3,777 people. We won when Pat Byrne scored and I was the mascot. A great occasion.

'I got my first season ticket when I was nine and have followed them ever since, although as an ITN correspondent I am all over the place and have missed some games I would love to have been at. Everybody remembers the game against Bayern Munich but for me it was extra special as it fell on my 18th birthday. I remember having a few drinks legally in my local before the game and the look of shock on the barmaid's face when I told her I was celebrating my 18th birthday, as she had been serving me for at least two years!'

Richard Gordon (BBC *Sports Sound* presenter)

'My first memory of Tynecastle was as a teenage Aberdeen fan. It was the time when Jim Leighton was making his breakthrough into the first team and I used to go to watch them as much as I could.

'On this particular day, it was chucking it down. Tynecastle was an intimidating place to go as an away supporter at the best of times and in this game, which we won, we were behind the goals near the Hearts fans.

'As it became clear Aberdeen were playing the better football, the Hearts fans started to taunt us and ended up chasing us from the ground at half-time. We sought sanctuary back on our supporters' bus and listened to the second half of the game on the radio with the Hearts supporters outside baying for blood.

'Working at Tynecastle has always been enjoyable. I was there when they returned with the Scottish Cup in 1998 and was part of the media company commissioned to make a video of the victory. That meant I was lucky enough to be on the open-top bus that took the players through Gorgie to Tynecastle the day after the game. It must have been the slowest bus journey I have been on in my life because of the massive crowds which lined the route.

'Commentating at Tynecastle is an experience in that you feel part of the action. Our position is right above the dugouts and because of that you can feel the intensity of the game. Granted you struggle to see two corner flags but it's a small price to pay.

'I can't think of a ground I have been to in Europe that creates such a great atmosphere. There are three identikit stands at Tynecastle which many other grounds have but the steepness and the closeness of them to the pitch makes Tynecastle a very special place to watch football.'

Iain King (chief football writer with *The Sun*)

'Back in 1989, I was covering a game between Partick Thistle and Morton, and playing for Thistle that day was Billy Dodds. Billy was on loan from Chelsea and his time at Firhill came when Ken Bates, the Chelsea chairman, was considering buying the club. Billy, by his own admission, had a nightmare game that day. He just couldn't score. To make matters worse, the crowd were on his back as they saw him as Bates' boy. He just couldn't win.

'Afterwards, we had a chat and he said he was hoping my match report wasn't going to be too hard on him. He must have liked it because we struck up an immediate friendship. He told me that as a thank-you for my match report that day and for not giving him too hard a time he would give me his Scotland international jersey when he scored his first goal for his country.

'Now the years went on and Billy and I remained good friends. He started to gain international caps and I moved up in the world of journalism to become chief football writer with *The Sun*.

'When Scotland was playing Estonia at Tynecastle in 1998, we were praying for anybody to score for us, as we were 2–1 down. Then Billy popped up and scored two goals, and Scotland won 3–2. I was delighted for him. When I met him on the Monday after the game he handed over to me his yellow Scotland shirt with the number 17 on the back that he had worn against Estonia. After all these years, he was true to his word and I have it framed and in my office at home.

'The 4–4 derby on 2 January 2003 was another game which I remember well. It came against a background of Bobby Williamson having a rotten record against Craig Levein. I remember Bobby was wearing a green suit that day and was getting dog's abuse from the Hearts fans behind his dugout. He must have thought he was going to get his first win against Hearts but then Graham Weir popped up with two late goals. The place went mad and you saw then the great atmosphere Tynecastle generates.'

David McCarthy
(sportswriter with the *Daily Record* and former Hearts reporter with the *Edinburgh Evening News*)

'I took over covering the Hearts beat for the *Edinburgh Evening News* around 1991, just after Wallace Mercer tried to buy Hibs. I fought like cat and dog with Wallace at times but really he was a newspaperman's dream. If I was struggling for a back-page lead, I would just phone him up and I always knew he would say something quotable.

'I saw some great matches at Tynecastle but the one that sticks out for me was the game against Slavia Prague in the UEFA Cup first round back in the 1992–93 season. Hearts had gone to Prague and had been beaten 1–0 when their Russian midfielder Tatarchuk scored direct from a free-kick.

'The return at Tynecastle was just one of these really special nights. I remember Gary Mackay scored first but they equalised through Silhavy before Ian Baird scored after a great one–two with John Robertson. Craig Levein made it 3–1 just before half-time and everybody thought that was it, especially after one of their players called Penicka got sent off. However, Kuka scored for them before Glynn Snodin cracked home a magnificent free-kick to make it 4–2 on the night and take Hearts through 4–3 on aggregate. It was a classic and one I remember well.

'I still enjoy going back to Tynecastle as a sportswriter with the *Daily Record* and the atmosphere created remains superb.'

Kenny MacDonald
(chief football writer with the *News of the World*)

'I first went to Tynecastle as a cub reporter with Doug Baillie, the former Rangers player turned journalist, to do evening newspaper reports for the *Sporting Post* in Dundee. We used to be stuck in a glass hut at the back of the Main Stand but it got so busy that you were forever rubbing the windows to see out as they always got steamed up.

'An ever-present back then was John Fairgrieve, the legendary journalist and huge Hearts fan. He used to sit there usually moaning about how the present Hearts players weren't good enough to lace the boots of people like Conn, Bauld and Wardhaugh, who he used to watch as a kid. In saying that, the minute the referee gave a bad decision against his team he was spouting conspiracy theories against Hearts.

'I moved on to become chief football writer with the *News of The World* and for me the game between Scotland and Estonia showed just how great an atmosphere Tynecastle can create. The score was 2–1 for Estonia and then Billy Dodds scored. The crowd really got going after that and urged the team on to their 3– 2 win. It was a great atmosphere.'

Jim McLean
(chief football writer for more than 30 years with the *Daily Express*)

'In 30 years of working for the Scottish *Daily Express* I've seen my share of great Tynecastle matches. Also, I can lay claim to bringing John Robertson to Tynecastle for the first time. His brother Chris was with the club and I picked John up from school to get a picture of the two of them together at Tynecastle. It goes without saying there have been plenty pictures of John Robertson at Tynecastle since then.'

Archie Macpherson
(doyen of football commentators in Scotland)

'Hearts supporters may not like to be reminded about this particular match but the first game I covered at Tynecastle in my early years as a commentator with the BBC was the day they lost the league to Kilmarnock. It was 24 April 1965, Hearts were beaten 2–0 and Killie won the title on goal average.

'I've always enjoyed covering matches there despite the problems with the famous Tynecastle pillars. The cameras were on top of the covered enclosure opposite the Main Stand. In the early days of broadcasting the cameras would swing from side to side as we covered the action. However, at Tynecastle you had these big pillars holding up the stand in the way.

'Every time the camera followed the ball, the picture would be interrupted with a view of a big pillar. They became such a problem that Alistair Milne, who was head of BBC Scotland at the time and went on to become the controller of the BBC throughout the UK, was asked to try and find a solution.

'Despite that difficulty, since the early days I've always found Tynecastle a great place to cover matches as having the crowd so close creates a great atmosphere.'

Arthur Montford
(legendary Scottish Television commentator)

'Going to Tynecastle was always a pleasure for me. In the early days, the media used to go in the same gate as the fans and I always made a point of getting there early to talk to some of the regular supporters.

'One of the biggest games we covered was when Kilmarnock pipped Hearts to the title on the final day of the 1964–65 season. Archie Aikman did the commentary that day, I did the stories surrounding the game and we had cameras in both Edinburgh and Kilmarnock to get reaction.

'Tynecastle was not the easiest of places to cover games as there were big pillars in front of the brewery wall which obstructed our view. As far as atmosphere, though, it was second to none and I always enjoyed covering games there.

'Throughout all my years in football Tommy Walker was one of the greatest men I ever met. He had the chance of becoming a minister but became a football manager instead. He never swore, was always polite and a great man. I remember doing an in-depth piece with him and the final line was Tommy saying to camera, "Heart of Midlothian is my life." Three days later he was sacked!

'He was a great man and I never felt he got the credit he deserved. Even when he died, the obituaries in his honour were scandalously short. He deserved better.'

Derek Rae
(former BBC Scotland commentator and now with ESPN, USA)

'We broadcasters are a pernickety lot. The atmosphere at a game has to be just right and frequently much hinges on the peculiarities of stadium design. I think I can speak for everyone in the Scottish electronic media when I say Tynecastle ranks as one of the best-loved venues as far as we commentators are concerned. A true football atmosphere can practically be guaranteed.

'When covering games in Gorgie, I would normally take the train to Haymarket, so as to enjoy the brisk walk up Dalry Road. Maroon scarves would become more prevalent after the right turn on to Gorgie Road and you knew you were in honest football territory.

'Tynecastle has always given me the feeling of being the beating heart (if you'll excuse the rotten pun) of Gorgie as a whole: an antidote to the modern trend of soulless suburban stadia.

'I was fortunate to commentate on Hearts' matches during invigorating times. There were many memorable games but one stands out above all the others. That was the UEFA Cup quarter-final first leg against Bayern Munich in 1989. What made me especially proud that night was that our commentary was going out all over the UK.

'Under such circumstances, it's always nice to be the bearer of good news. Hearts were truly magnificent and the Tynecastle crowd got behind them like never before. The noise was deafening and could probably be heard as far away as Tranent! Even the likes of Bayern Munich's Klaus Augenthaler and Stefan Reuter looked as though they would rather be somewhere else.

'After the match, I compared notes with Gerd Rubenbauer, who was commentating for Bavarian Radio. He told me he wished he could cover games from Tynecastle more often, so passionate and noisy were the fans.

'Tynecastle deserves its special place in the Scottish football history books. Working with ESPN in the States, I'm often asked by football fans planning to visit Scotland, which grounds they should make a point of travelling to. You'll have deduced by now that Tynecastle is always high on that list. Besides, it's also the home of the catchiest football song ever written.'

Brian Scott
(former chief football writer for more than 30 years with the *Daily Mail*)

'I always remember my great sporting summer of 1953 when my grandfather took me to watch Scotland take on Australia at cricket at Raeburn Place, then to Easter Road to watch Hibs take on Third Lanark and then to watch Hearts play Hamilton Accies in the League Cup on 8 August, which Hearts won 5–0. I got my first taste of football at Easter Road but I was hooked on Hearts. There was something magical about the colours and of course the players. Who could forget Willie Bauld, who was one of my heroes?

'The game I remember most from these early years was when Hearts beat Rangers 4–0 in the Scottish Cup quarter-final on 3 March 1956. Ian Crawford scored twice and Willie Bauld and Alfie Conn got the others. I was jammed behind the goals and couldn't see much. What I do remember is that Rangers had a star-studded side but Hearts played them off the park. They had a big South African in their team called Don Kitchenbrand, who stomped about like a rhino. He was a hard player and I remember him chasing the ball to the touchline but he couldn't put the brakes on and landed in the enclosure in front of the Main Stand.

'Over more than 30 years as chief football writer with the *Daily Mail* in Scotland I have travelled the world to cover matches and I think Tynecastle has amongst the best atmosphere of any of them. Valencia's ground has a similar feel and Borussia Dortmund's creates a good atmosphere but Tynecastle remains special. I also remember doing a newspaper feature on the flat-owners whose homes overlooked Tynecastle and who used to let people in to watch the matches from their front room. They had their very own executive boxes before they were invented. When the new stands went up, that put a stop to it but it was fun for them while it lasted.'

Graham Spiers
(award-winning chief sportswriter with *The Herald*)

'I have good, albeit random memories of Tynecastle. As a boy, my first memory, and Hearts fans may not enjoy being reminded of this, was the 7–0 defeat to Hibs. I watched the game on my granny's television in Hawick and I remember I thought Tynecastle looked a gloomy sort of place.

'I was a great reader of newspapers in my youth and used to go out and get four or five a day and read all the football match reports. I remember reading about one row at the time when an opposition team complained about a "blazing" floodlight at Tynecastle which was too bright and had put them off. I remember thinking at the time they probably needed incredibly strong floodlights so the players could see through the Gorgie gloom.

'My formative years were spent watching games from Tynecastle on television with Archie Macpherson or Arthur Montford commentating. The one player who stood out during those television days was Rab Prentice. He came comet-like onto the scene but quickly petered out. I remember one game he played against Celtic when he ran amok and it made great television.

'It wasn't until I was 25 that I started to go to Tynecastle as a journalist on a regular basis and have always enjoyed the atmosphere generated there. Perhaps one of my favourite occasions was the Under-16 World Cup semi-final when Scotland played Portugal at Tynecastle and won 1–0 in June 1989. The place was packed and they managed to get 29,000 people into the ground. There was a 45-minute delay in the kick-off time to allow the crowds to get in.

'Kevin Bain was the Scotland captain and was plying his trade with Brechin City by the mid-1990s. Like him, the rest of the

Scotland team which started that game never really made a big breakthrough at professional level. Compare that to the Portugal side and the way the career of Figo and the rest of their squad, which also included Rui Costa, really took off.'

Gordon Waddell
(chief features writer of the *Sunday Mail*)

'Hearts ruined my dad Ken's wedding day. He got married on 30 November 1957 and was a mad keen Falkirk fan. His best man told him that Falkirk had been beaten at Tynecastle that day 9–1 and that didn't help his mood. For me as a Falkirk fan and as chief features writer with the *Sunday Mail*, it is always a pleasure to go to Tynecastle. It is one of the last examples of what a real football stadium should look like. Other clubs have built new stands at their grounds and lost the atmosphere but somehow Hearts managed to retain it and also the integrity of the ground. I remember going with my dad a few years ago and although we were on the top tier of the away stand at the School End, we still had a great view and felt part of the game.

'As a journalist, I remember having a run-in with Joe Jordan when he was manager, as I had not asked his permission to interview Alan McLaren. Joe took me outside and we had a face-to-face row. Although I held my own, I did think to myself I was arguing with one of Scotland's toughest ever centre-forwards!'

Chick Young
(BBC Scotland football correspondent and
newspaper columnist)

'As a boy, I had a bit of a soft spot for Hearts. When you are younger, you are always influenced by the teams that are doing well. This was back in the 1950s and Hearts had Conn, Bauld and Wardhaugh, so they were the team to watch. Also, I really felt sorry for them when Kilmarnock beat them to the league flag on the last day of the 1964–65 season.

'As a youngster going to Tynecastle, I always saw the stadium in black and white. For me, it epitomised Auld Reekie and the old image of Edinburgh. I believe that the introduction of the new stands in the early 1990s really improved the atmosphere at Tynecastle and brought the place alive.

'As BBC football correspondent, there is no hiding place for me at Tynecastle. I am so close to the dugouts on either side when I work there as a touchline reporter.

'In all my years covering football there, the small laundry room just before the tunnel is a place I have passed with interest. For years it was the place where players used to go for a fly cigarette before kick-off. That happened a lot in the past and in recent years Claudio Caniggia, when he was at Rangers and Dundee, used to nip in there for a quick puff of his fag before kick-off.'

CHAPTER ELEVEN

THE ODD COUPLE: DEANS AND ROBINSON

Chris Robinson and Leslie Deans were the Edinburgh version of *The Odd Couple*. The quietly spoken, rather dour catering boss and the small, charismatic lawyer combined forces to usher in one of the most turbulent periods in the history of Hearts. When they were thrown together, they were mutual acquaintances rather than close friends. That was just as well, as they ended up bitter enemies.

It was Robinson alone who made the first approaches to buy Hearts. The then owner Wallace Mercer remembers his move came during a pre-season tour to Germany: 'He told me he was interested in buying Hearts but I told him his offer wasn't good enough to meet my valuation of the club. I told him to go away and come back again with a bigger bid, and find some big players from the business world to support him. That was when he got involved with Leslie and got back to me.'

When the chance to invest in Hearts arose after Robinson approached him, Deans had to think long and hard. Although he was a dyed-in-the-wool Jambo, he had no real ambition to get involved in football. He had a busy lawyer's property business to run, which was going from strength to strength. Robinson also had a successful business career. He had founded Wheatsheaf Catering and his involvement in the trade earned him the nickname 'the Pieman'.

In the early days, they formed a grudging respect for one another, but the only thing they really had in common was a love of Hearts. Eventually, even that failed to keep them together.

The joint plan to buy out Mercer was hatched when Deans and Robinson met in the office of Edinburgh lawyer Fraser Jackson on a Tuesday evening in early October 1993. Jackson was a senior partner at the respected Edinburgh law firm Henderson, Boyd, Jackson and was Robinson's lawyer.

Despite willingness between Mercer and Robinson and Deans to do a deal, things dragged along at a snail's pace. Many times in those early days, Deans came close to throwing in the towel, frustrated by the amount of time it was taking, time he could be spending on his law firm. Even now, as he looks back, he describes the amount of time it took to conclude the take over as 'torturous'.

Finally, however, in July 1994, a deal was concluded with Mercer. Mercer had spent 13 years at the helm and, by his own admission, was suffering from burnout. Trying to run the Tynecastle club plus his property business was getting on top of him. 'They offered me around £2 million for my controlling interest and I decided to take their money and take a break from football,' remembers Mercer. 'I had had a great time but it was time for me to move on. I was tired both physically and mentally.'

Deans and Robinson, who had been thrown together by accident more than design, finally saw their hope of buying the club they loved turn into reality and to begin with everything ran smoothly. They even agreed to take turns at being chairman, with each spending two years in the role so they could both experience the excitement of being in the hot seat. So far, so good, and for the first five years in charge they got along. They even had plans to increase the capacity of Tynecastle to 25,000 and create a mini-village-style development with hotel and associated leisure facilities but these never came to fruition.

The breakdown in their relationship started during what should have been the most exciting period in the recent history of Hearts and it resulted from a lack of trust on both sides.

For a few years, things ticked along, but in 1997 their decision to float Hearts as a company on the stock market didn't look too clever when the shares, which started out at 140p, soon ran into selling pressure and fell to 98.5p. The first half-term results Hearts produced as a quoted company showed a loss of £1.3 million but came against the background of the opening of the Hearts superstore at the stadium, as well as the installation of a new playing surface.

While all that was going on at the club, Robinson was carving himself a niche at the SFA. He was also becoming one of the leading lights in the plans to set up a Scottish Premier League of elite clubs, which came to fruition on 6 May 1998. With Hearts in the Scottish Cup final of that year, his star was very much on the rise.

A few weeks later, he and Deans shared their finest moment. The sleeping giant that was Heart of Midlothian Football Club came alive after the Scottish Cup win over Rangers. More than 200,000 people took part in a massive Edinburgh street party and over 15,000 of them crammed into Tynecastle to watch the team parade the trophy around the ground. Lord Provost Eric Milligan hosted an informal reception for the team at the City Chambers, where Hearts manager Jim Jefferies turned up with the cup in a 1952 maroon two-litre Bristol sports car driven by Robinson. The players followed in a flotilla of taxis and John Robertson had to hitch a lift in a police car to get him through the crowd.

As Robinson and Deans joined with Milligan in the City Chambers to sing songs and drink champagne, they thought the club would go onto the next level and challenge Celtic and Rangers. If you had told them back then that Deans would resign as chairman of the club he loved, that Hearts would run up debts of £19.6 million and that a Lithuanian millionaire banker who did his national service on a Russian nuclear submarine would take over the club, they would have thought their drinks had been spiked.

THE ODD COUPLE: DEANS AND ROBINSON

The first official signs of supporters' anger at Robinson, who appeared to take most of the flak over the way the club was being run, emerged in November 1998 when he started being booed at games. A section of them were unhappy at the lack of progress since their Scottish Cup win, which was made worse by the loss of players like David Weir and Neil McCann. Officials of the Hearts Supporters' Association, which represented 2,500 fans, expressed their displeasure at their own internal meetings over what they perceived as Robinson's high-handed attitude and he was criticised for not handing Jim Jefferies more funds to strengthen a squad depleted at the time by injury.

Robinson put the problem down to a 'relationship difficulty' between himself and the supporters' group but it soon became apparent that Jefferies, who was being linked with a possible move to Aberdeen to replace Alex Miller, also had a problem with a lack of money for new players.

Just before Christmas 1998, only seven months after he had coached Hearts to their Scottish Cup win, Jefferies insisted on a special board meeting to work out how much cash he could expect for new players. He didn't get answers that would inspire confidence. Robinson told him that the club didn't have the money to 'go to the next level' and it was clear that Jefferies felt let down.

The euphoria over the Scottish Cup win had passed and it became clear to Jefferies that the sleeping giant that was Heart of Midlothian Football Club looked likely to return to its slumber unless more money was put in to strengthen the squad.

That meeting was a key one for Hearts and the manager who had brought the Scottish Cup to Tynecastle for the first time in 42 years. From then on, things would never be the same and it was after that meeting that the relationship between Deans and Robinson fell apart for good.

Both men had been unhappy at the other's role at Hearts. It was a simple breakdown in communications between the pair, with Deans unhappy at the direction in which the club was going in terms of its rising debt.

On Christmas Eve 1998, Robinson announced that he would be

the club's only official spokesman and journalists were not to contact Deans, who, up until that point, had taken calls on Hearts matters both in and out of working hours.

As a result of Robinson's announcement, the Federation of Hearts Supporters' Clubs added their voice to the clamour for change, calling on the board to 'get their act together' in a statement made after one of their many meetings.

Throughout his time as chief executive, Robinson had a sign up in his office that stated, 'I have a responsible position around here. When anything goes wrong, I'm responsible.' With debts of £5 million, partly as a result of increased spending on players' wages, many supporters felt it was time for him to act on that statement.

Despite the off-the-field problems, Robinson was awarded a new one-year contract by the Hearts board in March 1999. They put faith in him to pull the club back from the brink. At the same time, he said that in future he might take 'a less active role' in the running of the club but that proved not to be the case.

On Tuesday, 15 June 1999, Deans resigned as chairman after the working relationship between the two men collapsed completely. He also had major concerns about the growing debt at Tynecastle.

His resignation was no surprise and despite attempts to suggest that there wasn't a problem between them, nobody was fooled. Deans continued as a member of the Hearts board and remained part of New Hearts Limited, the company set up by himself and Robinson, which had shares in the club. Businessman Doug Smith took over from Deans as chairman but Hearts had lost a man who cared passionately about the Tynecastle club.

To try and make Deans' resignation a less bitter pill to swallow, Robinson came up with an ambitious five-year plan costing £15 million that included rebuilding the Main Stand and setting up a state-of-the-art training complex. Although Hearts don't own the training centre at Heriot-Watt University, at least that proposal happened. The Main Stand at Tynecastle was not replaced under Robinson's reign.

It was around this time that Robert McGrail, a well-known Hearts supporter, started making his voice heard. The Edinburgh businessman was concerned about the finances of the club and wanted Robinson out. He started his attempt to oust him on 7 July 1999 and only let up when Robinson's shares were bought over by Vladimir Romanov in February 2005.

'I have always maintained that I would step aside and sell my shares if someone would come in who would provide major investment for Hearts,' said Robinson when McGrail made his interest known. 'I decided that McGrail was not that man. I did not have the impression that he would be ready to make major investment in the club, nor does he want to pay the market price for the shares which would give him a controlling interest. He is trying to buy into Hearts on the cheap.'

It was a mantra that Robinson would repeat time and time again as the dogged McGrail did his best to try and buy his way into Hearts so he could take the club in a new direction. He even paid out £250,000 to boost his holding to 4.3 per cent in July 1999, which made him the third-largest shareholder and he continued to invest more, but this still left him trailing behind Robinson and Deans, who held just over 45 per cent between them.

He had an ally in Deans, with whom he had done business in the past, and saw him as a potential partner in any efforts to get rid of Robinson. Both men worked closely together on attempts to buy control of the Tynecastle club.

It was against this background that Robinson was trying anything he could think of to increase the revenue stream at Tynecastle. He had experimented by bringing rugby league to the ground, when London Broncos beat Bradford Bulls in front of 7,000 spectators back in 1998. A year later, Wigan Warriors played Gateshead Thunder with a view to a rugby league franchise coming to Tynecastle but only 5,000 people turned up. The franchise never materialised and the experiment was deemed a failure.

Much more interesting was a story broken in the Scottish edition of the *News of the World* in August 1999. 'Souness set to launch takeover at Hearts', proclaimed the headline.

Graeme Souness confirmed that a group with significant

financial resources had contacted him when he was still employed as manager of Benfica and asked if he would be interested in going to Hearts as technical director. A document commissioned from property consultants Knight Frank, which also found its way into the newspapers, suggested that Hearts would consider moving to Murrayfield, the home of Scottish rugby, to clear their debt and that several unnamed Edinburgh businessmen had been asked to put in up to £1 million to help the club financially and bring Souness back to Scotland. That was the first time the spectre of Hearts moving to the national rugby stadium raised its head.

It was a topsy-turvy time for Hearts, with the next major shock a pleasant one, or so everybody but Deans thought at the time. On 5 September 1999, broadcasting company Scottish Media Group (SMG), at the time also publishers of the *Herald*, *Sunday Herald* and *Evening Times* newspapers, invested £3.5 million in the club and gave them a £4.5 million loan. The deal was that SMG could convert the loan into shares in the club if the share price rose high enough to allow them to make a profit on their investment. This bought SMG a 19.9 per cent stake in the club with an option to increase to 37 per cent over five years.

Their investment came against a background of anticipated growth in television revenue, as Sky were still making positive noises about the future of Scottish football. SMG's £8 million bought them a seat at the table on the football financial gravy train, or so they thought. At the time, the company must have believed that football clubs would soon be in a position to negotiate their own television deals. They never took up the option to increase their shareholding and their investment risk was not a success for the club or the company.

Supporters believed, rightly or wrongly, that SMG had invested £8 million in the club and that this money would bring the good times back to Tynecastle. Hearts immediately said they would use the new cash to 'improve on-field performance and help create a youth academy'.

Amid all the euphoria, Deans further distanced himself from the club, resigning from the board to 'relax and enjoy his football', although he did maintain his shareholding. He left the stage with the minimum of fuss and only now has he broken his silence on the reasons for his decision in an interview with the authors.

'It was a popular misconception that SMG had invested £8 million in Hearts,' remembers Deans. 'They never invested £8 million. They invested £3.5 million and loaned Hearts £4.5 million. We were going to spend all the money but I asked the question at the time: what if SMG want their money back?

'I was told they would turn their £4.5 million loan into shares but at three board meetings in a row I kept asking what we would do if they didn't. How would we repay them the money if we had already spent it? It was a crazy decision to take all their money and spend it, assuming, quite wrongly as it turned out, that they would not want their loan back. SMG had an option to convert their loan but history shows that they never did. I told them time and time again to be wary. That is why I walked away. I was deeply concerned that the SMG money would put the club further into debt. Time has proved me right, as the interest on the £4.5 million kept going up and up and SMG did ask for their money back. It was a situation which could have been avoided.'

Trying to keep a lid on the row between Deans and Robinson was now proving difficult. Once the restraints of being a board member had been removed, Deans revealed that Robinson had attempted to get rid of Jefferies as manager in March 1999 when the club was faring badly but had failed to gain enough support. Jefferies now had proof to back up what he had thought all along which was that, despite bringing the Scottish Cup to Tynecastle, he did not have the full backing of his board.

Robinson claimed, with support from board chairman Doug Smith, that their priority with the SMG money was to release funds to buy new players. There were even rumours that Jefferies was going to be handed £4 million but, as with most of the stories flying around Tynecastle at this time, it proved to be false.

In total, around £1.2 million was given to Jefferies for new players and more was spent securing existing players on long-term contracts. Cash was also set aside for the soccer academy and the redevelopment of the Main Stand.

As far as many supporters were concerned, the only real attempt to secure a player of note for big money came when they tried to sign Motherwell's Lee McCulloch. Jefferies had hoped a bid of around £850,000 would take him to Tynecastle but back in the strange days of an over-inflated transfer market the Fir Park club said no. It proved to be one of the last tastes of real, big money to buy in new signings that Jefferies got.

In saying that, Antti Niemi was bought from Rangers for £400,000, Gordan Petric from AEK Athens cost £500,000 and Robert Tomaschek came from Slovan Bratislava for £300,000. Robinson said that £1.2 million had been spent on transfers, £1 million on signing-on fees, £300,000 in agents' commissions and the balance on funding wages.

The whole sorry mess was getting worse, with the Federation of Hearts Supporters' Clubs, made up of 49 different groups, passing a vote of no confidence in Robinson at one of their meetings on 10 November 1999. It was the first of many attempts made by supporters' groups to oust him as chief executive.

One major misjudgement at boardroom level came when the club refused a £850,000 bid from Rangers for defender Paul Ritchie in the summer of 1999. At the end of his contract, a year later in 2000, the man who had been part of the Scottish Cup-winning team walked away for nothing. It was a miscalculation that was lampooned by the *Daily Record*, who printed a picture of Robinson with big ears and a donkey nose.

The mistake took the spotlight off the fact that, in February 2000, Hearts announced they had found a site for their long-awaited youth academy and would invest £3.5 million into building it at Heriot-Watt University's campus at Riccarton on the west side of Edinburgh.

Only eight months after the investment by SMG, Robinson was warning Jefferies that he would have to sell before he could buy because the wage bill, running at around £5 million a year, was not sustainable. Colin Cameron, the club captain at the time and a Scotland internationalist, was so frustrated that he spoke out about the difficulties in trying to build a side when cuts were being made in the playing budget.

Plans were put in place to cut the first-team squad from 28 to 21 to save money and overall things were going from bad to worse. Jefferies conceded he would listen to offers for all his first-team players, as the Tynecastle club were losing in the region of £250,000 per month, even though they had secured the SMG money.

Deans tried to find a way back into the club and fronted a consortium willing to invest money. Even now, estimations of the sum which they were going to invest vary, with Robinson claiming it was £2.5 million while those close to the consortium claim it was nearer £4.5 million.

Their interest provoked an angry response from Robinson, regardless of the real financial value of their bid. In what was the most open interview with the chief executive during that period, he spoke of his concerns to Alan Campbell of the *Sunday Herald* in an article published on 30 July 2000.

'Leslie Deans' ego is severely bruised and he and his partners are trying to harness supporters and their contacts in the media to make life uncomfortable for me because of the last few years,' Robinson told Campbell. 'It's time for people to know what's really been going on. Everyone should see them for what they are. A frustrated group who bought equity last summer and were trumped by the SMG deal.'

Campbell prised every last detail out of Robinson during the interview, which tore asunder any pretence that there was anything other than bad blood between himself and Deans.

With slur and accusation flying between the two men, the fans were getting angry. 'What's more important, the egos of Deans and Robinson or Hearts football club?' wrote a Mr Rick Quinn of Edinburgh to *The Scotsman.* 'The fans want some peace so that we can start really challenging for trophies again. Instead, we're getting a ridiculous public wrangle which no doubt will drag on and on.'

It was a prophecy that proved correct, with no let-up between the pair. When Gary Naysmith left for Everton in October 2000 for £1.75 million, Hearts fans saw another one of their heroes depart from Tynecastle. After Neil McCann, David Weir and Paul Ritchie, it was becoming a regular occurrence and no real surprise. But with losses running at £3.7 million and a 6–2 defeat by Hibs on 22 October 2000 to cope with, the Hearts supporters were galvanised into action.

At a match against St Johnstone on 28 October, around 5,000 of them flashed red cards at Robinson in protest at the way he was running the club. At the end, around 1,000 people noisily demonstrated outside the ground against him. It was the first of many similar protests that were to follow.

At this stage, the row between Deans and Robinson started to get really petty. After a 5–2 midweek defeat against Celtic on 1 November 2000, Deans tried to talk to Jefferies in his office at Tynecastle but was ordered by a senior official to leave. Club sources at the time claimed that as Deans was no longer a board member he had to be treated like any member of the public and that was why he was asked to leave. Robinson refused to comment on the matter but clearly such a decision to ask Deans to leave would have had to be cleared at boardroom level.

It was all becoming too much for Jefferies, who had had a 28-year association with the club. On 8 November 2000, sick of the in-fighting at the club and not having as much money to spend as he would like, the man who had been a player and manager at Hearts left 'by mutual consent'. His loyal assistant Billy Brown left, too. It was a sad day for the man who brought the Scottish Cup to Tynecastle. He left the club twenty games into the season, nine of which they had won, seven of which they had lost and four of which they drew.

With Jefferies gone and about to take over at Bradford City, that left the way clear for former Hearts player Craig Levein, manager at Cowdenbeath at the time, to come in. Regardless of what people will tell you now, there was more than a bit of trepidation about his appointment felt among Hearts supporters. Many felt they were trying to appoint a manager on the cheap and, despite his strong Hearts links, his lack of top-level management skills was a concern.

Looking back, it is clear all these fears were unfounded, as he ushered in a successful period on the pitch. Hearts may not have won a trophy before Levein left for Leicester City in November 2004 but their forays into Europe, as a result of finishing third in the SPL two years on the trot, brought excitement to Tynecastle. Indeed, the success of the Levein years took the heat off Robinson for long periods as the fans were mollified by good results. That was lucky, as just before Levein was appointed, Hearts reported a £3.7 million loss to the Stock Exchange and their shares slipped to a new low at the time of 77p. They also revealed that further cuts in playing staff and the wage bill were necessary to ensure the club's financial future.

The Levein era began on Friday, 1 December 2000, and his starting salary was only a fraction of the £140,000 a year Jefferies had earned. The figure of £45,000 was bandied about but, whatever the sum, the man who had spent 14 years at Tynecastle as a player turned into a bargain managerial buy. Indeed, his appointment, it could be argued, was the best piece of business Robinson did when he was in charge.

Robinson had not given up his grand plans for the club and just before Christmas 2000 revealed outline plans for a multimillion-pound 30,000 all-seater stadium in the west of Edinburgh to replace Tynecastle. He hinted that the new state-of-the-art complex, built in conjunction with a leisure development company, could include a roof over the structure and be built at Braehead Quarry. He called it his 'Towards 2005 Initiative'. It came to nothing.

Robin Beith, vice-president of the Federation of Hearts Supporters' Clubs, always felt that would be the case and made it clear at several meetings and in the press that most fans were strongly opposed to a move away from Tynecastle. Later events would prove that he was spot on in predicting the way the majority of fans would react to the thought of leaving their spiritual home.

Deans was still working away behind the scenes at the time to try and oust Robinson from the club. He called for a meeting between himself, his fellow investor Robert McGrail and the club to discuss putting new money into Hearts but his call fell on deaf ears. He wouldn't go away, though. In August 2001, he went public over his role as head of a consortium whose £8 million takeover bid for the club had been rejected two months previously. His group insisted it wasn't a takeover bid per se and the money was more of a cash injection. The consortium had planned to put in £4 million in the first year, £3 million the second and £1 million in the final year. They also wanted to create a new swathe of shares, at 75p each, which, under their plans, would give them around 40 per cent of the shares at the end of the first year. That would give the group more than 55 per cent and a controlling interest. There was also a clause calling for Chris Robinson to be removed as chief executive to allow the investment to happen.

Robinson's attempt to resurrect his plan for a new £22 million stadium at Braehead Quarry and get the SFA to pay for part of it didn't get off the drawing board. On the one hand, Robinson was talking up plans for the new stadium at Braehead Quarry, while on the other the club was losing lots of money. For many, the sums just didn't add up.

The rank-and-file Hearts supporters were losing patience with the board, as they had no idea what the future held for their club. On the evening of 25 September 2001, before the CIS Cup defeat at Ross County, a supporter yelled obscenities and attempted to throw a chair at Robinson as he ate with club officials in a local hotel. The chair missed him and Hearts security chief, Tom Purdie, managed to defuse the situation.

The AGM of 2002 stuck to the now-familiar formula of Robinson having a go at Deans from the platform and the lawyer having a go right back from the body of the floor. Even Wallace Mercer turned on the club's board at the AGM, accusing them of mismanagement.

Despite having a chair thrown at him, death threats, attacks on his home, being whisked out of Tynecastle in the back of a police van for his own protection and having fans shouting at him every other Saturday, Robinson simply wouldn't leave the club. The pressure on him increased when Deans claimed that he had tried to bankroll a deal to keep Ricardo Fuller at Tynecastle. The striker, who had been on loan from the Caribbean side Tivoli Gardens, had been a great success but although Deans claimed he had been willing to put up £1 million to keep him at the club, no deal could be reached and the man who had been banging in the goals headed towards the exit door. The only silver lining was the fact that the Hearts £6 million youth academy at the Heriot-Watt University campus was granted planning permission early in 2002.

While all this was going on, Robinson refused to be drawn on reports that he was involved in talks to sell his shareholding in the club to an English-based consortium.

Despite the financial mess Hearts found themselves in, it was clear that the club was a brand name in which sponsors wanted to invest. Leading UK sports retailer all:sports and manufacturer Reebok agreed a joint three-year sponsorship agreement worth £1 million in February 2002, a link-up that marked Reebok's first venture into Scottish football, although they already manufactured strips for Liverpool and Bolton in the English Premiership.

Hearts may have had their own financial problems but Robinson was fighting battles within the SPL as well and became spokesman for the ten SPL clubs who took on the Old Firm in a row over television money and threatened a breakaway league. Despite all the posturing from both sides, a compromise was always going to be reached and the breakaway league failed to materialise. In the end, the SPL agreed a two-year deal worth £16 million with the BBC to broadcast matches, and the ten clubs made their peace with the Old Firm.

Back at Tynecastle and just before the club's AGM in 2003, there was talk of yet another 'mystery' consortium about to bid for the club. Once again, it came to nothing. The financial figures Robinson reported at the AGM hardly inspired confidence but the loyal shareholders who filled the Gorgie Suite at Tynecastle were well used to bad tidings.

This was a time when the typical accompaniment to an annual general meeting at Hearts was a call for Robinson to resign but he survived time and time again. The club may have reported annual losses of £2.7 million on a turnover of £6.1 million but bad financial news was becoming the norm. Around the time of the 2003 AGM, Hearts shares closed at 37.5p. Five years before, when the club floated on the Alternative Investment Market, they stood at 140p.

With money tight and the debt at Hearts growing, Robinson made a decision which further alienated him from the supporters. While denying a ground-share plan with Hibs was on the cards, he claimed it would be a 'sensible proposition'. His comments came after the Tynecastle club pulled out of plans to build a 30,000 all-seater stadium near Turnhouse Golf Club, close to Edinburgh Airport, the latest in a long line of false starts about finding a new ground.

Robinson said he was now looking at two new sites, also on the west side of Edinburgh, and Hearts would still be moving out of Tynecastle come what may. He cited UEFA regulations concerning pitch size due to come into force in 2010, which Tynecastle didn't meet, as one of the reasons for moving, although a special working group set up by Hearts made it clear that problem was not insurmountable. Robinson was clearly flying a kite back in March 2003 to see what sort of reaction he would get from Hearts supporters and the Easter Road club and their fans to the possibility of them sharing a stadium.

Despite all the negativity surrounding Hearts, Robinson remained bullish about the future of the club, claiming they should be trading profitably by 2005 without having to rely on player sales to shore up the bottom line. It was a prediction that failed to come true.

His pledge came as interim figures showed that he had chopped nearly 20 per cent from the club's salary bill. Excluding player trading, turnover fell 12 per cent to £3.42 million in the six months to 31 January 2003, partly reflecting lower season-ticket sales. However, the critical wages-to-turnover ratio dipped to 72 per cent, down from 78 per cent in the same period in 2001–02.

The consensus among analysts is that football clubs should

spend no more than 60 per cent of their income on pay. John Moore, a football analyst at Edinburgh stockbroker Bell Lawrie White, said Hearts had to find a way to attract more spectators to balance the books, as they had taken wage costs probably as low as they could go.

It could be argued that sharing a stadium with Hibs wasn't the best way of attracting new fans but in the summer of 2003, a few months after he had raised the proposal, Robinson admitted the clubs had opened talks on sharing a new ground. Not surprisingly, opposition was swift and venomous from both sides of the city. The thought of more than a century of tradition being swept away when Tynecastle was sold off for housing development trampled on the football memories of tens of thousands of Hearts supporters and they responded angrily.

For all their emphatic denials that groundsharing could lead to a possible merger, the fact that both clubs had sizeable debts showed that such a future scenario could not be dismissed out of hand. Debt figures of almost £15 million for Hearts at the time and marginally less for Hibs had been mentioned, and a move to a new 20,000-seater stadium, which was to be built at a cost of £15 million at Straiton, near the Ikea superstore on the outskirts of Edinburgh, would significantly reduce their financial problems. The site earmarked for the shared stadium was owned by Straiton Park Ltd, a company in which Sir Tom Farmer, the Hibs owner, had an interest, a fact which didn't help sell the plan to Hearts supporters.

Robinson denied that his desperate attempts to take the club away from Tynecastle were connected with the rise in debt, although the vast majority of Hearts supporters thought otherwise. 'The possible move to Straiton is the result of a straightforward assessment of where Hearts are going,' said Robinson. 'I don't think it's relevant to tie these two issues together.'

Robin Beith, the vice-president of the Federation of Hearts Supporters' Clubs, thought otherwise and did not subscribe to the claim that the proposed move was driven by a change in UEFA guidelines which would render Tynecastle unfit to host European football.

After weeks of failed public relations offensives to try and convince their supporters, both Hearts and Hibs threw in the towel regarding a shared-stadium plan. Robinson may have lost that battle but he was still convinced that in order to cut debt, Hearts had to move away from Gorgie.

In September 2003, he broke cover to suggest that Hearts could move to Murrayfield and be tenants of the Scottish Rugby Union. All hell broke loose when he let that particular cat out of the bag. It was bad enough to suggest that Hearts share with Hibs but at least with that option they had a stake in any new ground. Moving to Murrayfield would see them being tenants and just renting their ground rather than owning it.

Throughout his time in charge of Hearts, one of Robinson's favourite expressions was 'sweating the asset', a term which in a football sense refers to a club making money out of its stadium seven days a week, instead of once a fortnight on a Saturday. He always claimed there was little scope for that at a cramped Tynecastle, whereas at Straiton, for example, the planned development would have included leisure and restaurant facilities that, theoretically at least, could have brought in much-needed revenue for Hearts and Hibs.

If any move to Murrayfield were to work, Robinson suggested it would mean the SRU having to lease the football club some of their extensive conference and banqueting facilities on match days to allow them to offer corporate hospitality packages. He claimed Hearts could also generate considerable extra revenue on match days through car parking charges and, more contentiously, beer tents on the Murrayfield training pitches.

With the SRU having debts of £9 million at that time, a shared stadium made obvious financial sense to both parties but, quite rightly, the Hearts supporters saw it as a ridiculous idea, akin to selling their birthright. That didn't stop Robinson and the Hearts board pushing ahead with their plans to play UEFA Cup football at Murrayfield.

On 10 October 2003, Hearts made history when they played a behind-closed-doors bounce game against Dundee at the home of

228

Scottish rugby. In part, it was to help both teams prepare for their UEFA Cup ties later that week; however, it was also about road-testing Murrayfield for SPL football. Craig Levein tried to put a brave face on things but joked he would like to win the lottery and spend some of the money to keep Hearts at Tynecastle rather than see the club move to Murrayfield.

The Hearts Supporters' Trust told Robinson it would oppose leaving Tynecastle unless flitting could be demonstrated as the only genuine option. Despite that, Robinson kept delivering the Thatcherite message 'There is no alternative' as he pressed the case for a move to Murrayfield.

The Hearts board chose to launch a pre-emptive strike, issuing a document, entitled 'Tynecastle Stadium: Not Fit for Purpose' on their official website on 18 December 2003 as the prelude to outlining their claim that their pitch in Gorgie no longer complied with European regulations and that rebuilding the ground would cost an estimated £36 million. It was ironic that respected stadium architect Jim Clydesdale, who helped design the new stands at Tynecastle, felt it would cost just £100,000 in improvements to the Main Stand to keep the club at Tynecastle for another five years so they could have time to work out their long-term proposals.

Nobody had the faintest idea what Hearts, a team with an average support of 12,000, would gain, beyond short-term fiscal relief, from playing around 20 matches a season at a rugby ground with a capacity of 67,500. Deans, who had adopted the tactic of allowing Robinson to stew in his own juice, felt his old business colleague had once again made the wrong decision. Pushed on the possibility of Craig Levein's side playing league matches at a near-deserted Murrayfield, Robinson said, 'We would look at ways of masking or blanking out the top tiers, so that the impression of the stadium is much smaller and more compact than during Six Nations rugby fixtures.'

One man who wasn't impressed was Robert McGrail, who was steadily building up his shareholding in Hearts. He felt renting Murrayfield would kill the club. 'I believe,' he said, 'the current board will be the end of Hearts and the undertakers will be in

229

within a few months of a forced move to Murrayfield, and up until then the club will be playing in a mausoleum. Season ticket sales will fall, as the move is not based on optimism or ambition but necessity. I'm no David Murray by any means, and I don't want to be portrayed as a white knight or saint, but I'm fortunate enough to have had a certain level of success which allows me to do something about this situation.'

He wanted to buy the ground, build a new Main Stand, put in better corporate facilities and then lease it back to the club, giving Hearts a buy-back option at a later date. That way the club could stay at its historic home while addressing the massive debt burden that had put them under so much pressure.

'To stay at Tynecastle is to die,' said Robinson, while claiming the club would be choked at a stadium which 'gives this football club no room to breathe'. 'Tynecastle can be made to pay,' was McGrail's response. 'We have a ground with a capacity of over 17,000 and we get average crowds of around 12,000. Clever marketing needs to be done to galvanise fans to come back to Tynecastle.'

Derek Watson, the secretary of the Hearts Supporters' Trust, said at the time Robert McGrail's plan to buy the ground and lease it back to the club should have been listened to but it was never considered seriously by the board.

Bizarrely, McGrail's plan came up against opposition from his own brother, Peter. Peter McGrail was not a major shareholder or investor and didn't have the financial muscle to make his plan happen but he had spent a lot of time and effort on doing his homework on a masterplan to keep Hearts at Tynecastle. He had spoken to stadium designers and Edinburgh City Council, and felt there were good grounds for simply keeping the club in a regenerated Gorgie with a new stadium being built 200 yards from the existing one. His brother Robert simply wanted to keep the ground where it was and upgrade it. Having two brothers with conflicting plans did confuse some supporters.

The club's AGM in January 2004 was the usual stormy affair, with shareholders venting their fury, but there was no movement in the board's position: they were adamant that a move away from Tynecastle was vital.

Robinson was shouted down on a number of occasions and called 'a Muppet' and 'a clown' by certain shareholders, but he later tried to put his own public relations campaign to rectify his image into full swing. He talked of the positives of the youth academy in various Sunday newspapers but that came against the background of the fact that Levein had had to cut £3 million from his player budget over three years, a fact that was revealed around the same time.

The youth academy with its six outdoor pitches, one of them artificial and floodlit, a mile-and-a-half jogging track around the site, ten changing-rooms up on the first floor to house the club's five squads of youth players, up to 200 kids in all, was a big positive for Robinson, who was delighted when it was opened. Even now, it is hard not to be impressed by what the academy has on offer but it was a risk and, with debts of £17.6 million at the time and continued cuts in the playing budgets, many supporters felt the stadium issue should have been addressed first.

'Ten years ago, when I first came to Hearts, we had no facilities,' Robinson said in his defence. 'The coaching staff would spend half an hour every morning phoning around schools and local authorities trying to find a pitch we could train on. In the spring of 2004, that officially came to an end.'

All the talk of the benefits of the youth academy clearly gave Robinson confidence and he pressed ahead with his plan for moving away from Tynecastle. However, there were still many false dawns to come. There were suggestions that Hearts could move to a 20,000-seater stadium to the west of Edinburgh and share it with Edinburgh Rugby, the professional district team. Nothing happened. Again.

Through it all, Deans was working away quietly in the background and on 14 January 2004, Robinson and Deans shared a platform together for the first time at a meeting organised by Hearts supporters to allow both men to put their points of view across. It was standing room only when the public meeting took place and it didn't disappoint.

Insults flew and the meeting at the Orwell Lodge Hotel in Edinburgh dragged on. Deans was looked on as the all-conquering hero, as was Robert McGrail, who had come up with the buy-and-lease-back scheme for Tynecastle. But the evening was most notable for the fact it was the first time Robinson admitted that the club was on the brink of administration.

The comments sent chills down the spines of the Hearts supporters in the audience. Deans made an impassioned speech, claiming a move to Murrayfield would be the death knell of the club. Deans said, 'The board has no sustainable business plan and Chris Robinson is just picking figures from the air. If the big earners have to go if we stay at Tynecastle, it would be unpalatable but the reality is that this is the position we are in.

'If we have to go down a peg or two to come back up, then so be it. Motherwell and Dundee have done that, and Motherwell sold James McFadden and Stephen Pearson for substantial sums of money because they invested in youth.'

It was like old times as the pair of them verbally slugged it out, with Deans the crowd favourite against Robinson the hate-figure but ultimately the one with the power at that time. A few days later, he showed that power when he secured an agreement in principle with the SRU for the club to play at Murrayfield beginning in season 2004–05 and revealed Tynecastle was going to be put on the market. For many Hearts supporters, this was the low point. All their protests appeared to have been for nothing. It was the news they had been dreading.

'I honestly feel that if we move, it will be the death knell of the club and lead to our extinction. Just watch how many fans refuse to buy season tickets if he remains at the helm,' said John Borthwick, secretary of the Federation of Hearts Supporters' Clubs.

His comments summed up the views of the majority of Hearts supporters. Fans' groups called for a 15-minute 'withdrawal of attendance' at the start of the home match against Dundee United on 21 February 2004, while thousands of extra 'Robinson Must Go' posters were printed and handed out to supporters.

In one last attempt to try to stop the move, Save Our Hearts –

which had been set up by the Federation and the Trust – signified its intention to buy up Scottish Media Group's 19.9 per cent shareholding in the Edinburgh club. There was even talk of a mystery consortium but like so many plans of that era it came to nothing.

The venom towards Robinson continued and the Hearts team bus was attacked by their own fans on 15 February 2004 after an Edinburgh derby in which they drew 1–1 at Easter Road. The supporters were trying to get to their under-fire chief executive, who wasn't actually on board.

Regardless of any plans for a new stadium, the move to Murrayfield looked inevitable. A survey carried out by Save Our Hearts revealed that 65 per cent of fans polled wouldn't renew their season tickets at the home of Scottish rugby. A ballot was taken of 3,774 fans, with 2,172 not in favour of renewing. This was in direct contrast to Robinson's hopes that all 12,000 season-ticket holders would remain loyal and give them a £75,000 profit by moving to Murrayfield.

As one sage pointed out, what was the point of having a season ticket for a stadium which held 67,500 people for matches involving a club which only had an average attendance of 12,000? It was never going to be the case that you needed a season ticket to ensure a good seat.

Robinson may have been on the ropes but he found an ally in businessman Calum Lancastle, who acquired 250,000 ordinary shares, representing 1.9 per cent of the issued share capital in February 2004. It took Lancastle's shares up to 452,629 and his total share holding to 3.6 per cent. Crucially, Lancastle supported the move to Murrayfield and this diluted the chances of having the decision to move reversed. It was a huge boost for Robinson, who had been trying to garner support for the move despite overwhelming opposition from the home fans.

Lancastle's involvement was a massive blow to Robert McGrail and Deans, as it meant they would have to find even more money to get rid of Robinson. In frustration, Peter McGrail, Robert's brother, wrote to Hearts directors, including Robinson, asking them to give personal assurances that the club's financial forecasts were accurate or face the prospect of legal action. His scepticism over Hearts' income forecasts if they moved to Murrayfield prompted his actions.

While all this was going on, Robinson was backing more and more extravagant, some may say desperate, money-making schemes. In early March 2004, a plan was hatched for Hearts to play Celtic in an SPL match in Melbourne, Australia, in either August or, if that wasn't suitable, the following January. Although some sportswriters and television commentators quite fancied a trip to Australia, the idea was rejected out of hand by Martin O'Neill, the Celtic coach, and fans of both clubs.

Permission for Hearts to play football at Murrayfield in the 2004–05 season was given by the board of the Scottish Premier League on 30 March 2004. On returning from that SPL meeting at Hampden, Robinson was assaulted by a supporter outside Tynecastle. More than 50 Hearts supporters had protested outside Hampden before the SPL board meeting, which ratified the controversial proposal, and after the meeting Robinson left the national stadium by a side door before being driven away. When he returned to Edinburgh, he was surrounded by a number of supporters and backed into a doorway outside Tynecastle. One of them hit him several times in the head, face and body, but no charges were brought.

Although representatives of the SPL clubs had rubber-stamped the move to Murrayfield, a legally binding agreement between Hearts and the Scottish Rugby Union had still to be lodged with the SPL and a deadline of 30 May 2004 had been set for that to happen.

The proposed go-ahead for the Murrayfield move was the issue that proved too much for Hearts chairman Doug Smith. The plan had never sat well with him, although he remained loyal to Robinson for a long time before his patience snapped. He became more and more distant from Robinson and on 5 April 2004 made clear his intentions of resigning. He told a Hearts board meeting that evening of his plans. His resignation was a huge embarrassment and left the Hearts chief executive even more isolated. Smith issued a short statement which said: 'The success of the move [to Murrayfield] will ultimately hinge upon the board's ability to build broad support among Hearts fans and I am disappointed that we have not yet been able to achieve this.'

The morning after his resignation, with Hearts protest groups camped outside the ground, George Foulkes was brought in as chairman. Foulkes was no stranger to Tynecastle. He was a regular in Gorgie despite the fact he represented an Ayrshire constituency as an MP. He travelled miles following his beloved Jambos, both home and abroad, so, at last, Hearts had one of their own as chairman.

He had been approached to take the job by Brian Duffin, who was a Hearts director at the time, and recommended for the post by Jim Gilchrist, a Tory councillor whom he had known since the early 1970s. The fact that thousands had seen Foulkes at matches meant it proved to be a popular appointment with the fans.

At his first press conference, it was easy to see the pride on Foulkes' face. At the age of 62, the long-time Hearts fan and season-ticket holder had the job any self-respecting Jambo would love. The MP, who had announced his decision to retire from Westminster at the general election of 2005, having entered Parliament in 1979, said he would explore the possibility that the club could postpone any move to Murrayfield for at least a year. He was true to his word.

Foulkes resembled a UN peace ambassador as he said he would speak to anybody about the future of Hearts, and that included Deans, a man who was *persona non grata* with Robinson. The MP made it clear that he would be his own man on the Hearts board and denied he would be a mouthpiece for Robinson. It was another promise which he would keep.

Gary Mackay, the Hearts midfielder and leading light in the Save Our Hearts campaign, had a private meeting with Foulkes and felt he was a man who could be trusted. Foulkes also met other supporters' organisations and from that moment on he was looked on as a clean pair of hands and a man without a preconceived agenda. He certainly managed to sway the Hearts board. Within a few weeks of Foulkes becoming chairman, Robinson said it was 'looking increasingly likely' that the club would stay at Tynecastle for at least one more season and at the same time the board would be setting up a working party to try and find a new ground for Hearts.

There was clearly a softening of attitudes after Foulkes was appointed club chairman in place of Smith. However, it may have just been that the board realised that their lack of plans for a new stadium was causing concern amongst supporters and that a new site had to be found sooner rather than later before a temporary move to Murrayfield could be forced through. Protests against the move were becoming more and more high profile. More than 11,000 fans held a well-organised placard protest during a game against Celtic on 25 April 2004, which was broadcast live on television.

The SRU seemed to accept that Hearts wouldn't be playing at Murrayfield during the 2004–05 season. David Mackay, the SRU chairman, warned that Hearts would have to renegotiate any agreement to use Murrayfield in the season after that.

All the Hearts fans wanted to know was where their beloved club would be playing football. The majority just wanted a sense of belonging, preferably at Tynecastle but if that was not possible then at a new stadium. Moving temporarily to Murrayfield with no other plans in place wasn't the answer. Foulkes was astute enough to realise that.

He met businessman Peter McGrail to discuss his vision of a new stadium being built on the Edinburgh City Council's roads depot, 100 yards from the current ground, in a regeneration of the area. Another option he pursued was to try and find Hearts a home in a municipal stadium in the Sighthill area of the capital, jointly financed with the local council.

On the pitch, Hearts were in the process of securing third place in the league for the second time in a row. The spectre of European football being played at Murrayfield moved a step closer.

In the summer of 2004, Hearts officially set up an independent working party to try to find a permanent home for the club, with Lord Macaulay of Bragar, a Hearts season-ticket holder, brought in to chair the group.

'I want to stress that there is no option which is off limits for the group in looking for the best options for Hearts,' said Foulkes. 'Every potential solution, including staying at Tynecastle, has to be examined. Many proposed solutions and potential sites were looked at in exhaustive detail before but I thought it was prudent to give this working party absolutely free rein in considering this crucial issue.'

It was also around the same time that clashes between Robinson and Foulkes became more prevalent. Foulkes was very much his own man and stood up to Robinson over many issues, including a possible move away from Tynecastle.

Foulkes claimed there was a problem with Robinson remaining as chief executive of Hearts while he was also a major shareholder in the Tynecastle club. 'It is normal practice for major shareholders to be involved in running the business,' was Robinson's reply. 'For instance, Bill Gates is a shareholder in Microsoft. Why should football be any different? There is no logic in suggesting it should be.' With that, Robinson flew off to Vancouver with Craig Levein and the first-team squad for the start of their 2004–05 pre-season tour to Canada.

When Robinson was away, Foulkes used his business and political contacts to try to open up new avenues for Hearts. Two Thai politicians visited Edinburgh and expressed an interest in trying to facilitate a deal which would see young Thai players arrive at Hearts' training academy. Similarly, Foulkes hoped to engineer another deal with a contact in Ghana, although nothing came of either plan. He was putting in phone calls both home and abroad to try and find other new investors but he realised time was not on his side.

Just as the 2004–05 season kicked off, so did the row between Robinson and Foulkes over the proposed sale of Tynecastle, which was announced to the Stock Exchange without Foulkes' knowledge. Foulkes was angered that the announcement was made public on 4 August 2004 before he knew about it. The statement said that the ground would have to be sold by the end of August to keep the club's bankers on side. Robinson insisted that the statement was released as a matter of urgency and there had not been time to forewarn Foulkes, who was told 'within a few hours' of it going to the Stock Exchange. The announcement was like a red rag to a bull for Deans, who described himself as 'baffled' by the goings-on.

With the sale of Tynecastle imminent, the match-day protests were stepped up. When Hearts announced that their directors had recommended that Tynecastle, their home for more than 100 years, should be sold to Cala Management Limited, a housing developer, the temperature rose even further.

Foulkes insisted that any Tynecastle sale document should have a clause included that would allow the club to pull out if they came up with a plan to remain in Gorgie. He was once again true to his word. 'Whether Tynecastle is sold on, we will still have a clause in that contract to give us until 31 January 2005 to try and find a resolution to try and keep us at Gorgie,' said Foulkes. 'Lord Macaulay, who is a lifelong Hearts supporter, is chairing a working party at present and working to these ends. Maybe the club will find a foreign backer, as Chelsea did. Either way, regardless of whether we give the go-ahead for the sale of Tynecastle, we still have six months' grace to find a way to stay in Gorgie.'

His hint was the first time any indication had been given that a foreign businessman was considering investing in Hearts. Soon the name of Lithuanian Vladimir Romanov would be known to one and all.

Without knowing about Romanov's interest at the time, Gary Mackay and the Save Our Hearts Group pressed on to try and save enough money to buy out the Scottish Media Group's shareholding. The group raised around £650,000 in donations from more than 1,200 supporters but that was still a long way short of the £1.2 million needed to make SMG consider the offer.

On 18 August 2004, it looked like doomsday had arrived for Hearts and their supporters. It was the day that Hearts Football

Club, proud tenants of Tynecastle Park, announced they had reached a conditional deal to sell their spiritual home to Cala Management Limited for £22 million. The Hearts board released a statement to the Stock Exchange outlining the Edinburgh club's plans to start the procedure to sell the stadium to the developers. The sale had to be confirmed by a vote of shareholders on 13 September 2004 but Hearts at least had the right to withdraw from the agreement before 31 January 2005 if a preferred alternative was found. Although Foulkes warned fans not to expect a last-minute reprieve and that a move to Murrayfield looked likely, privately he was working hard to convince Vladimir Romanov to invest in Hearts and stop the sale.

Angry reaction from supporters was swift, with a group laying a wreath at the main door of Tynecastle when they heard the news of the proposed sale. It summed up the mood. Deans described the proposed sale as ' a sad day for Hearts' and called on supporters to rally to stop the plan. With borrowings standing at £13.72 million and around £5.4 million owed to investors Scottish Media Group, Foulkes admitted the club had been close to going into administration and the possible sale of Tynecastle had to be considered to keep Hearts alive.

Around 46.3 per cent of the club's issued shareholding backed the plan to sell the ground to Cala Management Limited, despite the fact that the vast majority of supporters and small shareholders were against the sale. Halifax/Bank of Scotland had a 5 per cent share in the club and did not vote against the plan, which meant those in favour of the sell-off had the majority.

The Hearts board remained in turmoil through it all. A document leaked to *The Herald* revealed that Robinson was firmly against a plan for the club to sell Tynecastle and lease it back – a proposal put forward by Deans and Robert McGrail. Gary Mackay described the leaked document as devastating and said it illustrated the Hearts board weren't even paying lip service to the views of the supporters.

Against a background of growing anger, Hearts pushed ahead with their plans to hold their first UEFA Cup match at Murrayfield against FC Braga on 16 September 2004 and agreed to pay the SRU £40,000 to play there plus £5,000 as a hospitality access fee and a levy of £5 per spectator over 18,000. More than 19,000 turned up for the match.

On 31 August 2004, Graham Bean, deputy sports editor of *The Scotsman*, broke the story that Romanov was interested in investing in Hearts. The back-page story was the first time his name had been officially linked with the club and the exclusive report caused great interest throughout Scottish football. Back then, nobody could have foreseen the impact Romanov was to have on the Tynecastle club and how he would save them from financial ruin.

His interest would bring an end to Chris Robinson's involvement in Hearts in the summer of 2005, a decision which was applauded by the majority of rank-and-file supporters, who blamed him for taking the club to the brink of administration and close to a move away from Tynecastle.

Deans welcomed Romanov with open arms and sold some of his shares to him to help pave the way for the Lithuanian to become the biggest single shareholder in the club. Romanov's involvement brought the curtain down on the reign of the Odd Couple and started a new era where the power base of Heart of Midlothian was now in Lithuania.

CHAPTER TWELVE

EASTERN PROMISE

Vladimir Romanov didn't look at the popular, groundbreaking music of the early 1960s by artists such as Elvis Presley, The Beatles and The Rolling Stones simply as a form of entertainment. For the 15 year old who had to leave school early following the tragic death of his father, it was a way of making money. Lots of it.

Romanov, by his own admission, was not a big music lover but made his first tentative steps into the business world through the pop charts of 1964. It was a brave thing for a teenager in old-style Russia to do. Particularly for one whose father Nikolai had been a war hero and whose mother Zinaida had been a loyal factory worker, both of them dedicating themselves to the Communist way of life.

Vladimir, their only son, was very different. He had the ambition and guts to challenge the state system of his homeland. His endeavours would eventually make him a multimillionaire, enabling him to plough some of his fortune into Hearts.

When he started out selling his records, many older Russians of the time bought into the propaganda that America was the evil empire and musicians like Presley were a symbol of Western decadence to be avoided at all costs. However, for the kids behind the Iron Curtain, music became a way to rebel, and the more authorities did to outlaw Western pop music the more they wanted to hear it.

Romanov spotted the opportunity and when he started to buy and sell records, the roubles came flooding in. 'My very first venture in the business world was when I was 15 and I bought records wholesale, like ones by Elvis Presley,' he remembers. 'Back then, the records were not available in shops but they were brought into the country by collectors and I bought from them.

'There was a real demand for Western music and I knew that. If I bought one record for 5 roubles from a collector, I could sell it on for 25 roubles. That was the start of my business career.'

A constant in his business life has been his willingness to take risks and investing in Hearts, a Scottish football team with debts which peaked at £19.6 million, could be looked on as the ultimate gamble. But it was as a teenager that his willingness to speculate to accumulate first began to surface. After amassing a considerable amount of money from selling records, he didn't rest on his laurels. 'I took the first lot of money I got and invested it in finger-puppets,' said Romanov. 'I used them to put on puppet shows for children. They were very successful and made even more money.'

A record-selling, puppet-theatre-creating businessman who then made his fortune in the textile industry after a spell on a Russian nuclear submarine off the coast of Britain and who was chased out of Russia by the authorities for being too rich is the man who bought his way into Hearts. A more colourful character with an equally interesting past would be hard to find.

Romanov entered Scottish football at a difficult time, as there was a general climate of suspicion about foreign investors when he started sniffing around Hearts. Giovanni di Stefano, the controversial Italian lawyer who was part of Saddam Hussein's defence team and who was asked by the deposed Serbian leader Slobodan Milosevic for legal advice, had expressed interest in investing heavily in Dundee but the money didn't materialise and soon afterwards the club went into administration. Raith Rovers had been left in turmoil after the departure of Frenchman Claude Anelka, who had invested £300,000 and appointed himself manager in March 2004, but left only five months later. To top it all, former German internationalist Berti Vogts had had a disastrous time as Scotland manager and there was a huge sense of relief when he was replaced by Walter Smith. Due to this failure of foreigners to deliver in Scottish football around that time, matched with Romanov's lack of English, there were many who wondered how successful he would be.

In an astute move, Romanov appointed Weber Shandwick, the respected worldwide public relations agency, to represent him. They assigned one of their most experienced executives, Charlie Mann, who also worked part time as a football broadcaster with BBC Scotland, to help him become known to the Scottish public and get his story across.

Mann had his work cut out but slowly the feeling of distrust disappeared, partly because of Mann's efforts to get Romanov's plans out into the public domain. However, such is the fragile state of football, someone who is one day the saviour of a football club can become the villain the next.

Only now, due to a series of exclusive interviews with Romanov by the authors and trips by them to his home city of Kaunas in Lithuania, as well as extensive independent research, can his story now be told in full.

Many will believe that Vladimir Romanov is the first Russian-born millionaire to control Hearts. Bizarrely, however, that isn't the case, as back at the turn of the twentieth century, Elias Furst took over the Tynecastle club when they were on the verge of financial collapse in 1904 and restored them to rude health.

The current Russian-born head of Hearts is notoriously publicity shy, similar to his countryman Roman Abramovich, the owner of Chelsea. Up until his interest in Hearts became public there were only a few pictures of him in circulation and no personal details were known.

Romanov was born in 1947 in Russia's Tver Province to parents who helped forge his personality and encouraged him to walk his own path in life. His mother, Zinaida, was a strong woman who didn't suffer fools gladly while his father, Nikolai, had been a commander in the Russian army frontline forces which helped take Berlin in 1945. His mother's parents came from St Petersburg while his father's came from Tula in the Russian Provinces. They had a daughter, Olga, Vladimir's sister, who he is still close to and who works with her brother at the family business base back in Kaunas.

His mother in particular had a very difficult and traumatic time during the war years. She lived through the Leningrad blockade when the German army pummelled the city in an attempt to grind its people into submission. Towards the end of the siege, she was sneaked out in the dead of night and sent to work in a munitions factory near Lake Ladoga in north-west Russia. While she survived, many of her fellow citizens and family members left behind in Leningrad died.

While his mother was escaping to the north-west of Russia, his father was fighting with the Soviet army as they advanced towards Berlin. Nikolai had studied at the military institute at Tula, a city famed for making Russian tanks, and was hailed as a war hero.

'I was extremely proud of my father and what he did. I can't remember any situation where officers in the Russian military would compromise their position. There was great respect for the uniform and great respect for the period. He was a role model for me,' recalls Romanov.

'I remember him telling me stories from the war: how he was in the Soviet army commanded by General Zhukov and was part of the capture of Berlin. It was a very difficult operation, as the city was so heavily fortified. Some people thought it was impossible but the Russians divided Berlin up into small segments. Each unit had the task of taking a certain part of the city.

'My father's unit had to take an area that included a museum and they were given a few days to carry out their task. The problem was getting past the German defences that guarded the building but my father's unit did their work well and kept battling through the night. It took them 24 hours to capture their segment of Berlin rather than the few days that was expected.'

Both his parents survived the war and moved back to the Tver Province, where their son was born. 'My childhood was a happy time,' he remembers. 'I was born while we were staying with relatives in the Tver region. Later, my father served for some time in East Germany and I went to school in Wittenburg, not far from Berlin. When I was nine, my father received a commission in Kaunas, which was still part of the USSR back then, and we stayed on there after he left the army.

'People in the West thought that the Russian people did not enjoy life and had no money or food. That was all just propaganda. I had a happy time and there were no shortages. It was a wonderful childhood and I have only seen such a great childhood depicted in the movies.

'Sometimes I look at Scotland, and the weather, and ask who had the worst of things? I spent my childhood running barefoot in shorts held up with just a piece of string. It was a carefree existence and the only worry my parents had was whether we would drown or not, as there was a lot of water around in the area where I grew up.'

Romanov was streetwise at a very early age, mainly because his parents worked very hard and their double shifts meant that they weren't around much.

'They were at work all the time and I grew up in the street. My mum worked double shifts and remained with the same factory unit making radio equipment until she retired. My dad died of a heart attack just before my 16th birthday and because of that I was given permission to start work and joined my mother in the factory. Usually in Russia you have to wait until you are 18 to start work. But I went to evening classes at the same time from the age of 16, so I didn't miss out on schooling.'

Romanov always had the urge to travel and when he was called up for military service he chose the navy, where he stayed for three years. He remembers being based in Murmansk and it was there he met his future wife Svetlana. The couple have one child, Roman, who has done well academically. He received a Bachelor's degree from Marietta College in the USA and also finished a Masters degree at the Moscow State Institute of Industrial Relations before going on to study at Pace University in New York. He became a

Hearts director when his father became the club's single biggest shareholder.

When Vladimir finished his time in the navy, he had been given a good grounding in electro-mechanics but his love for the sea continued and he joined the merchant navy and travelled the world. He saw every continent, bringing back all sorts of consumer goods from countries like Australia, Africa and Canada to trade back in Russia. It was his trips abroad that showed him that the world was a small place and that merchandise could be bought in one country and exported to another to make a profit. It was an idea he found very easy to come to terms with, although in Russia at the time making money was frowned upon.

With his sharp entrepreneurial brain, he quickly built up a decent amount of cash by Russian standards. He made his base in Kaunas, which was still part of Russia but was later to become a major city in Lithuania when the Baltic republic was given independence in 1990. With Kaunas a major industrial centre, Romanov decided to invest in local industry. Working on the assumption that everyone needed clothes and once again realising that the American influence in Russia was growing, he decided to invest in a number of textile and clothing factories. Many of the clothes he produced had Western slogans on them.

'Under the law of the time, people were allowed to take out a patent on a specific form of business activity,' he remembers. 'The textile industry was huge in Kaunas and there were various opportunities there for me. I started up a production line with looms in a knitting factory producing clothes. I looked at the newspapers for inspiration and came up with clothing with various emblems on them. Some of the tops I produced had Marlboro on them after the American cigarette brand and Montana after the state.' Business went so well that he created the biggest knitting factory in the whole of Kaunas and at one point had 14 giant looms in operation in the one factory.

Such success didn't go down too well with the men in the Kremlin. Private enterprise was still frowned upon, as was anyone who made a profit without giving the state a major slice of the pie.

They could not understand how such a young man could be so successful.

'The Kremlin were interested and included me on a blacklist compiled by President Yuri Andropov but my neighbour, who was working as an auditor for the Soviet authorities, warned me I was in danger and that my businesses were under threat.'

Things got so bad that he had to leave Kaunas before the authorities closed in on him.

'I had to relocate to the Caucasus in Dumbai, which is an autonomous region near Chechnya. I took my son Roman with me and my wife, and we headed south to get there. With the Kremlin people crawling all over the business in Kaunas, I stayed away for a while and left local managers to get on with things. I was out of the way but did learn to ski, which was a useful skill and great fun.'

Without Mikhail Gorbachev, it is unlikely that Romanov would have succeeded in taking his business plans any further than the borders of Russia because of Soviet reluctance to embrace capitalism. Gorbachev changed that when he introduced a 'cooperative' law that broke down trade barriers.

'The law allowed me to expand my textile operation and acquire wool from Russian republics like Kazakhstan that produced it,' he says. 'It meant I could control every level of production and I had links with wool-producing companies all over the place. It meant I had a bigger say in all aspects of clothing production.'

Because of the change in the system and growing consumerism, inflation was spiralling out of control, which was good for Romanov. 'I would buy in a particular commodity, say wool, but it always took a while for it to arrive, so by the time I had received it the value had gone up ten or maybe 100 times compared to what I paid for it. Back then, they called what I did speculating, which was negatively perceived in the Soviet Union.'

Because businessmen could trade in different goods, Romanov, who had by now returned to Kaunas, started to take risks and invest in the metal industry, the oil trade and in other companies from which he felt he could make a profit. 'Speculate to accumulate' was his motto. The risks paid off.

There were moments, however, when vagaries of the Russian banking system nearly scuppered his plans. It was no surprise that later in his business career he decided to invest in a bank in Lithuania to make sure his money would always be safe. 'I remember one time I had tens of millions of roubles in an account but they went missing. I panicked and transferred large amounts of the money I had left to my friends, giving them 50,000 roubles each. Rather than risk losing the roubles, I thought they might as well have it. Around 5,000 roubles bought a car back then but I'm not sure how they spent the money. In fact, only one of them did anything with it business-wise and used it to build his own company. The others were young and spent it.'

Such largesse showed how Romanov's fortune was growing and how he could afford to write off vast amounts of money, confident that he could make even more.

As he invested further in the wool trade, the textile industry and in oil and metals, so the interest in his activities from the Russian authorities grew. 'My businesses kept growing and growing. If I had been buying wool and selling it on, it would be counted as speculation and I would be thought of as a criminal under Soviet law. I was buying it and producing thread and other things like clothes, so they could not take action against me.

'Despite that, I had big problems with the police. I remember one time they were ordered to check my operations. Remember, I was producing things on a large scale and my warehouse was full of wool in one place, metals in another. In one factory they searched, they did all sorts of checks but found in just one instance just a six-kilogram difference in the amount of wool I had compared to what I should have had according to their records.

'Driving them was this mentality of hatred towards me, as they thought, how could one man be making so much money? The directors of my warehouse where the audit was taking place with the police watching went grey as a result of all of the attention.'

Romanov's embrace of private enterprise was unpopular with the Russian authorities and even today he has a mild contempt for their activities and attempts to keep him down. 'Whenever the head of the inspection teams came to my factory, they made accusation after accusation. I used to say to them, "You are making these people who work here suffer," and ask them "What good is all this doing?" I never saw eye to eye with the Russian authorities. We were old enemies.'

Although Romanov looks a tough customer, talking to him it is clear these were difficult times when his will to keep going was severely tested. From 1986 to 1990, he was kept under surveillance by the authorities but they never ground him down completely.

'These were the toughest times psychologically for me. Everything was under scrutiny and people couldn't understand how I could have so much money. They would not leave me alone.'

Things changed on 11 March 1990. Events from that day on were to turn Romanov into one of the wealthiest men in the country. 'Lithuania was the first Soviet republic to become independent and allow the privatisation of enterprises. I used that process to provide raw materials like wool to outlets that needed the product all over the country.

'The next logical step was for me to acquire a production licence and I bought dozens of clothing production licences by way of auction, which meant I had factories all over the country. To make things even better, I owned the first company in Lithuania to receive an export licence, which allowed me to conduct foreign trade.'

With the shackles removed by the authorities, Romanov moved onwards and upwards. Around that time, he made his first investment in Lithuanian football. He had always been interested in sport, being a keen swimmer as a boy and skier in later years. However, he had always loved football and the glamour of European Champions League nights. For all his cash, it was a small team sponsored by one of his factories which first caught his interest.

'I never played football professionally but I've always been passionate about it, even as a boy. I still have very fond memories of the season that my favourite team of the time, Zalgiris, took third place in the Soviet championship and I'll never forget when they beat Spartak Moscow by five goals to two.

'I started getting involved in Lithuanian football in the early 1990s. There was a club called Banga attached to one of the state-run factories. After the collapse of the USSR, most enterprises became loss making and couldn't cope with the burden of having to support a football club, so I was asked to help finance it. At first I just supplied money but then I started wondering why a team that had twice the cash of all their opponents could only finish fifth. I became more involved and got hooked. Then, when FBK Kaunas, my local team, started to win the Lithuanian championship on a regular basis, I turned my attention and support to them.'

FBK Kaunas played both Rangers and Celtic in the UEFA Cup in different seasons and Romanov was there when Scotland played Lithuania in Vilnius. It was at that game he met Steve Cardownie, the deputy Lord Provost of Edinburgh, and it was he who talked up Scottish football to Romanov. The atmosphere and excitement he had experienced on all three occasions appealed to the man who had travelled the world in the merchant navy and he was impressed by the passion of Scottish football fans.

The football experiences with FBK Kaunas started him thinking about the chances of investing in a team abroad but he had to put that plan on the back burner for a while as he had enough on his plate. He was about to become the main stakeholder in Lithuania's fifth biggest bank, albeit in a roundabout way.

'I was buying up enterprises and companies and each of them had a shareholding in the bank. One firm might have had a 5 per cent stake, another a 10 per cent stake. I was interested in their business, not their balance sheets, and I didn't realise I was slowly acquiring a big holding in the bank. I had a large number of business interests at that time and I had to leave management teams in charge. Eventually, the representatives I had put in place to look after my banking interests came to me and asked me to get involved in the recovery process in the bank that was called Ukio Bankas.

'The most important thing in my business life has been putting the correct management teams in place. In the past, some have behaved dishonestly and that caused me problems. When that happened, I made a promise to myself to make sure it didn't happen again. I surround myself with the right people. I did that with the bank and have done it with Hearts.'

The Ukio Bankas, a privately run bank, is now a major player in Lithuania and its investment arm has made major acquisitions in Bosnia and Herzegovina as well as its own country. Its main branch in Kaunas is a magnificent building just off the city's main street. It has a beautiful oak entry door and a magnificent winding staircase takes you up to Romanov's office on the first floor, which has a simple plaque reading 'Room 202' on the door. He has a 20-seat boardroom table in the centre and works of art on the wall.

'By chance, the colour of the logo of Ukio Bankas is a shade of maroon, just like Hearts,' laughs Romanov. 'Maybe it was destiny that I was going to buy into them because of the team colours.'

Now with a successful bank, a textile mill, a clothing factory and interests in the metals industry, Romanov's wanderlust returned. He wanted to combine his interest in football with his interest in making money. He felt he had taken FBK Kaunas as far as he could. He had invested tens of thousands of pounds into the club but time and time again saw no return on his investment because players moved to the Russian leagues from Lithuania for nominal fees rather than to the more lucrative markets of the West like the English Premiership and La Liga in Spain. Romanov remembered how impressed he had been with Scottish football supporters and the passion they showed for their teams. He felt investing in a Scottish team was the way forward.

'It was clear to me that Hearts was the best team to invest in as they were in Scotland's capital city. Our bank had financial interests in Edinburgh and we thought it would be good to put money into the football team in the capital city. Ever since FBK Kaunas played Celtic and Rangers and Scotland played Lithuania I had been thinking about investing in Scottish football. FBK Kaunas had won the league title five years in a row and we had good players but there was a ceiling in terms of us progressing. Basketball is the main sport in Lithuania and always will be. Football wasn't well supported. It is very well supported in

Scotland and I realised that investing in a Scottish football club was an exciting prospect.'

His time at FBK Kaunas wasn't without its controversy, with a row erupting on the last day of the 2003–04 season. With only eight teams in the Lithuanian league and with Kaunas swallowing up the best players, they were usually well ahead of the rest, which bothered other clubs that couldn't compete with them. The other problem was that many key people in Lithuanian football also had key positions in Romanov's bank.

Kaunas went into the last game of the season level on points with FK Ekranas, which was surprising in itself as they usually had the league secured by then. On the eve of the game, however, the National Football Club Association (NFCA), whose acting president Gintaras Ubinfskis is deputy CEO of Ukio Bankas, intervened to award a 3–0 victory in favour of FBK Kaunas, amid unsubstantiated allegations that Ekranas officials had attempted to bribe unnamed Kaunas players. Then the Lithuanian Football Federation, whose president Liutauras Varanavicius is chairman of the supervisory council at Ukio Bankas, overruled that decision to insist that the match be played after all.

The match went ahead and FBK Kaunas secured the title and a Champions League qualifying place by virtue of a 2–0 win. At the end of the match, the referee and players had to escape a hail of bottles from disgruntled home fans.

Ritas Vaigimas, a businessman and politician who is also head of the regional Vilnius Football Federation, was furious both before the match and especially afterwards.

'You can do nothing new in Lithuanian football because it is all down to one man, Vladimir Romanov,' claimed Vaigimas at the time. 'The Ekranas and Kaunas scandal has brought big shame to Lithuanian football.' Romanov was insulated from the row due to his distance from the boardroom at Kaunas. He only supported the club, allowing other people to run it on his behalf. In the end, the title was settled on the park and the row died down.

So just who should be looked on as the man who introduced Romanov first to Scottish football and then to Tynecastle? Clearly

Steve Cardownie, whom Romanov met at the Scotland international match against Lithuania, had a major influence on him deciding to spread his wings and invest in Hearts. Also influential were Leslie Deans, George Foulkes, Chris Robinson and Jim Connor, the former Dundee director.

However, when asked directly who he believes made the first contact with him, Romanov replies with an old Lithuanian proverb. 'There is a saying that goes: "If you put seven blind men in front of an elephant and ask them what it is, they will all touch different parts and all identify it differently as something else but really all think they are correct."' In other words, he doesn't really care who takes the credit at all.

For Romanov, investing in Scottish football was yet another business challenge and the pace of his life means he has little time to relax. Such was his busy schedule that he gave up tennis in 2001, as he had no time to play it.

Wine is one of his great loves and he has a well-stocked cellar. A good white is his preferred tipple and he can get quite contemplative when he has time to relax with a glass of his favourite drink.

'My greatest satisfaction in life is seeing a project through to the end and realising one's personal potential. In 2001, I started writing poetry, as I don't enjoy being on the road or flying and it took my mind to different places. It was good to put down on paper what I was thinking. Poetry helps me to switch off and it is something completely different. I'm not interested in the beautiful words of poetry but the idea, the essence and philosophy in it. You can't write a poem unless you have an idea and find the truth, as the words won't come. That's the thing you have to overcome.

'I have often wondered how much of my success has been down to just hard work and what element luck and possibly higher spiritual forces had played. It's a subject I have thought about a lot. Thinking is what distinguishes us from animals and once you think about things you realise you have responsibility towards yourself.'

Anything can set him off writing poetry, a chance to see Mick Jagger and The Rolling Stones in London being one prime example. 'I went to see them and it was with a sense of regret I had not done that earlier, as when I was growing up, the Stones and The Beatles and Elvis Presley were the anthems being played. They were also the records I sold when I first started out in business. I don't listen to them much now but they were a constant presence in my childhood years. When I went to see the Stones in London a few years ago, they inspired nine of my poems.'

Hearts supporters have also been impressed by his poignant poems, which were read out at the war memorial at Contalmaison commemorating members of the Hearts first team who were killed during the First World War. No doubt because of his father's past, Romanov has strong feelings about those who fight for what they believe in.

'You can never create an empire out of evil. An empire can only be made out of people going forward to realise their ambitions. Whether it is Bosnia or Kazakhstan, I tell the people in my companies to go forward and show what they can do. If you try and build an empire out of evil, you will fail. Hitler tried it and failed, and it is important that the actions taken by men during the war to defeat such evil are remembered for ever.'

Romanov's appearance at the war memorial at Contalmaison created a favourable impression amongst many Hearts supporters, who began to feel that they could trust such a man. But it was a trust he had to work on, as, before they met him, many could not understand what he hoped to get out of his investment in Hearts. They also thought it strange that he had tried to invest in Dundee and Dundee United before turning his attention to Hearts.

His approach to Dundee and Dundee United came against the background of Lithuania becoming part of the European Union on 1 May 2004, which allowed freedom of movement for everyone within that country. Lithuanian players no longer needed work permits to play in Britain, which meant they could be imported with no red tape or problems. As the average wage of a Lithuanian player was £1,000 a month, it meant that a Scottish team could pay them just a little bit more, which wasn't terribly much for a professional footballer in Britain, and pick up the best of them on the cheap. Romanov, with his knowledge of football in Lithuania and the other Baltic states, knew he was in a prime position to bring the best players from these countries to Scotland.

John Yorkston, the Dunfermline chairman, was an early point of contact for Romanov. The pair had met after the East End Park side went looking for players in Lithuania.

'We had Andrius Skerla from Lithuania, who proved to be a good signing, and he told us there were many good young players from his country,' remembers Yorkston. 'I went across to Lithuania with Jim Leishman [who was then the Dunfermline general manager] and we had a good meeting with Liutauras Varanavicius, the president of the Lithuanian Football Federation, who in turn put me in touch with Mr Romanov and his people.'

'There is an untapped football market in Lithuania. Players are keen to get out because there is a poor standard of living outside of the main centres and if you think playing facilities are bad in Scotland, they are at least 30 or 40 years behind in Lithuania. We wanted to bring a few Lithuanian players back to Scotland but the Lithuanians wanted us to invest £500,000 in the Kaunas youth academy as part of the deal. We weren't on for that. At no time did we discuss the possibility with Mr Romanov about him investing in Dunfermline. What we thought we had agreed was to get their players for a nominal sum and split any subsequent transfer fees with the Lithuanians, but the goalposts changed. Things suddenly appeared that weren't in the original discussions, including us investing a substantial sum in youth development in Lithuania. We couldn't even afford that for our own club, so we weren't going to do it across there. In saying that, through all the discussions I found Mr Romanov charming.'

When the Dunfermline link fell through, Varanavicius was advised by his counterpart at the SFA, John McBeth, whom he knew through UEFA meetings, that a number of other Scottish clubs were in financial difficulties and might appreciate a link-up. Tom Burton of Ernst & Young, who was the administrator for cash-strapped Dundee, met Romanov and Varanavicius in London on the afternoon of 22 December 2003. At first it was assumed that the Lithuanians were merely interested in investing up to £2 million of working capital into the struggling Tayside club but then it became clear they wanted to take it over completely. Varanavicius said at the time they knew Dundee had debts of around £20 million and their main creditors were Halifax/Bank of Scotland (HBOS).

The quid pro quo for Romanov bailing out Dundee would be the placement of Lithuanian footballers at Dens Park, which he did at Hearts when he first took over. Those who were good enough would then be transferred on to England or one of the other major European football markets, with the new Lithuanian owners benefiting financially.

When the Dens Park club rejected that plan, Dundee United chairman Eddie Thompson arrived on the scene. He put forward the proposal to exchange players and coaching advice but no deal was reached, although the Tannadice outfit was the closest they got to investing before Hearts came along.

So what does Romanov remember of the period when he was searching for a Scottish club to put money into?

'In Dunfermline's case, there was never any issue of acquisition,' Romanov remembers. 'As for Dundee and Dundee United, in the end I decided that there were better opportunities in the capital city of Scotland.

'By way of comparison, imagine what it would do for the development of your business to be working in Moscow, compared with, say, Novosibirsk. Of course, in Scotland, the difference between the standard of living in the capital and the provinces is not so great as in Russia but my feeling was that Edinburgh still offered much more scope as a successful place to invest my energies than Dundee. What's more, Edinburgh has two clubs but I always thought Heart of Midlothian had much more potential and a bigger fan base than Hibs. Compare that with the situation in London, where there are several big clubs, or even Glasgow, where Celtic and Rangers have an equal fan base.

'Edinburgh is an ancient and beautiful city: the atmosphere is unique, the people are very special and, believe me, in terms of football the city deserves better.'

EASTERN PROMISE

On 1 May 2004, the European Union (EU) welcomed 10 new states into the fold, including Lithuania, swelling its 25 members and granting freedom of movement to millions under the Treaty of Rome. The only problem was that some of the existing member states were rather concerned about citizens of these new member states gaining unfettered access to all of their labour markets and chose to retain certain restrictions on selected industries like sport for a so-called 'transitional period'. The UK resisted this, withdrawing only the entitlement of incoming workers from eight of the accession countries to claim social security benefits but left Lithuanians alone, making it easier and more enticing for them to come to Britain.

Romanov was quick to realise that the British government's refusal to impose any 'transitional' restrictions on the football labour market for EU accession states opened up many opportunities to the enterprising entrepreneur with a bit of local knowledge. The flip side was the worry that cheap foreign players from countries like Lithuania would flood the Scottish game. The Scottish Professional Footballers Association's secretary, Fraser Wishart, had always been concerned at the influx of foreign players into the Scottish game and now alarm bells started ringing.

'I don't know that anything can be done with regard to players coming into Hearts or anywhere else but what we said to the EU and the British Government is that they should recognise the specific nature of sport,' said Wishart. 'With football being such a global game, and with the involvement of agents and national associations, there is obviously a concern this could be seen as an opportunity to bring guys in on lower wages. The problem is that we are now getting into an individual country's labour laws. Our own Scottish players would perhaps be at a disadvantage because of our weak national laws, where they would allow the influx of these players from these countries. It is a strange situation to be in, because you don't want to be seen as some sort of jingoistic maniac.

'Although these guys that come over are welcome, the system has to look after itself. They have to recognise the specific issues of sport for a country like Scotland that, even before the recent financial problems, was already overrun with guys from the EU, never mind elsewhere. I am talking in general terms here and not specifically just about Hearts, although clearly what happened with them was a good example.'

Romanov believed Hearts was the club for him and by the summer of 2004 he had set his sights on buying the 19.6 per cent shareholding owned by Chris Robinson. 'I had FBK Kaunas and also an interest in MTZ-Ripo Minsk in Belarus, and when you have three clubs, including Hearts, it is easier to manoeuvre the players, to gradually prepare them for the next move up the ladder and test them at different levels,' said Romanov. 'We saw investing in Hearts as a very good idea.'

The club was in huge debt and the supporters wanted Robinson removed. Romanov was further enticed towards the club through the sterling work done behind the scenes by George Foulkes, who worked tirelessly for the cause.

The Hearts chairman showed Romanov around the House of Commons and convinced him of the benefits of putting his money into the club. The two men had a number of follow-up meetings in London and the commitment was made. The main obstacles in his dealings with the other Scottish clubs in the past had been that Dundee was in administration and in a real mess, while Eddie Thompson did not want to relinquish total control at Dundee United.

At the time of the first sign of interest from Romanov, the campaign to keep Hearts at Tynecastle was gathering pace. Gary Mackay, the leading campaigner, remembers, 'We had suffered enough under Robinson and a new man at the helm was long overdue. We all welcomed Romanov with open arms. We knew there might be risks involved but what was the option? There was no way we could remain with Robinson in control, a man who had suggested that Tynecastle be sold and we play football at Murrayfield as a tenant of the Scottish Rugby Union. We could not let that happen.'

But despite such a positive reaction, the negotiations regarding

Romanov's investment in the club proceeded at a very slow pace and this led to frustration all round. Craig Levein, the Hearts coach, was clearly sick of the time it was taking to sort things out. 'For some reason we seem to be known for our off-field circus more than anything,' he told the club's official website, which gave an indication of growing concern within Tynecastle regarding events. 'It doesn't help with regards to looking at the footballing side and keeping our focus. We have to deal in real-life situations. We will do our absolute utmost not to get distracted and, hopefully, one day we can talk about the football only.' The delays were caused by, among other things, the fact that Romanov did not speak English and needed everything to be translated, the number of people involved in negotiations and the legal technicalities involved.

Looking back to those days, Levein, who moved to Leicester City a few weeks after Romanov's plans were unveiled, remembers it was a difficult and unsettling time. 'Romanov coming in was a factor for me moving on, although clearly I didn't want to say anything when I was still at the club,' said Levein. 'I did meet him and he tried to get me to stay but I had already made up my mind. I was glad to get out. I needed to get away, as all the stuff with Hearts was getting to me. The budget cuts, the protests. I felt like I was stuck in the middle. I did enjoy my time at Hearts but I knew it was going to be difficult for John Robertson when he came in as my replacement.'

Buying his way into Hearts was proving to be harder than Romanov thought. On 13 September 2004, the conditional sale of Tynecastle to Cala Management for £22 million was agreed, mainly because of the voting power of the big institutions and the club's major shareholders, such as the chief executive, Chris Robinson. It was the first step towards Hearts playing their league football at Murrayfield until a new stadium site was found.

It was a frustrating time for Romanov, who remembers being angry at the delay in his attempts to buy into the club. 'It was good I had the supporters on my side at this time. Although I've been in business for many years, I was naive enough to think that buying shares in Hearts would be a lot simpler and that I would just have to make an offer that was financially viable and that it would be automatically accepted. However, I had to navigate my way through an unbelievable number of intrigues, which, if I'm honest, I still haven't got to the bottom of to this day. I had to think carefully every step of the way.'

Supporters were furious that the plan to sell Tynecastle had got so far and they were close to losing the ground they loved for ever. Their only hope was the fact that the sale to Cala remained conditional upon a number of matters, including the granting of planning consent, and the deal could not be concluded before 31 January 2005. Until that date, Hearts had the right to withdraw unconditionally from the agreement, subject to the payment of 'reasonable expenses' not over £75,000.

Foulkes continued to show faith in Romanov, as he had done from the start. He said he hoped 'major shareholders' would not stand in the way of the sale of the club. His comments were construed as an attempt to put pressure on Robinson, who, it was felt, was holding out for a big price for his shares.

'Hopefully, people will put the club first,' said Foulkes. 'Mr Romanov has some good ideas about the future of Hearts and it is important that the major shareholders are realistic about their expectations when it comes to the possibility of selling their stake.'

As the takeover talks moved forward, Hearts progressed in the UEFA Cup. When Craig Levein and his team were in Portugal to take on FC Braga in the second leg on 30 September 2004, Romanov conditionally agreed to buy the 19.6 per cent stake in Hearts owned by Chris Robinson. The figure of £867,000 was quoted for his stake, with the deal to be concluded by 8 December 2004.

Interest in Romanov grew to fever pitch but even then there was still little known about him. Liutauras Varanavicius said at the time, 'Romanov's approach to business is: "The one who talks much does little."'

Foulkes gave supporters hope that the club could stay at Tynecastle when he said, 'The deal for Mr Romanov to buy Chris Robinson's shares is due to be completed and it would allow us to stay at Tynecastle for a number of years until a long-term solution regarding the stadium situation is sorted out.'

The win over Braga in the UEFA Cup meant Hearts qualified for the group stages of the competition, which was a bonus that Romanov could not have envisaged. With an extra £2 million in the coffers, Peter Houston, the Hearts assistant head coach, made an impassioned plea for money from the club's UEFA Cup success to be diverted to retain some of the 11 players who were out of contract at the end of the season.

It was during this period that Steve Cardownie, the Deputy Lord Provost of Edinburgh, who had met Romanov on several occasions, painted an optimistic picture his friend's intentions for Hearts.

'He's a shrewd business person, and one of his strengths lies in knowing who does what best,' said Cardownie. 'He has an interest in bringing over the best of the players who are operating in the old Soviet Union and who might do a job for Hearts, but they would only be at Tynecastle on merit and that merit would be decided by the manager.

'Romanov sees the potential in Hearts. He regards them as a big club that can compete regularly in Europe. He wants to at least sustain the club at the level they are at the moment, or even take them to a new one.

'I believe he will take them into a new and successful phase of the club's history. It's Vladimir's wish that we can put up stronger competition to Rangers and Celtic. He's an ambitious man and he won't settle for Hearts being the third-best team in Scotland.'

Comments Romanov made to *Izvestia*, the Russian newspaper, certainly backed that up. In an interview he was reported as saying that he would invest £10 million to buy new players and dreamed of 'building a beautiful big new stadium'.

There had been suggestions that as Romanov had a stake in FBK Kaunas as well as MTZ-Ripo Minsk in Belarus, as well as Hearts, there would be problems if all three clubs qualified for the same European competition. However, George Foulkes played down any talk of future problems. Such conflicts of interest had been investigated in the past, with the ENIC business group being checked by UEFA a few years ago after buying into Rangers, Tottenham and AEK Athens. However, Foulkes did not foresee any long-term complications for Hearts, claiming Romanov's attention to detail would have stopped him from compromising Hearts' position. 'I think it is something that anyone in Mr Romanov's situation would have anticipated and looked into,' said Foulkes. 'It is not the type of thing he would be unaware of and I never thought it was likely to create any unforeseen difficulties.'

Romanov sent two senior members of his backroom staff to Edinburgh as his takeover plans for Hearts gathered pace. Sergejus Fedotovas, his senior adviser, and Mindaugas Majauskas, his senior public relations officer, arrived for a series of meetings. But as Romanov continued his preparations to buy into Hearts, one of Scotland's leading football agents warned that the expected influx of Eastern European players could prove a double-edged sword. Raymond Sparkes of the ProStar Management Agency said, 'What my experience tells me is that there will be a technical level in these players that would be at least the same, if not superior, to what we're used to in Scotland. I've no idea why Mr Romanov would want to get involved in Scottish football, so I can only speculate, but I assume there is an ulterior motive and part of that is likely to be that he can see a vehicle to showcase Lithuanian talent. Whatever a player will be earning in Lithuania, it will be considerably less than what he could earn here.

'There's a secondary point that anything which helps a Scottish club get bigger, better and stronger is a welcome change from what we've had so far. If he does well, then maybe it'll prompt other wealthy people from overseas to do something similar.'

The flipside, as Sparkes pointed out, was that a stream of players from the Baltic states would arrive in Scottish football, which would have a detrimental effect on the homegrown players. 'If you accept we really have talented youngsters in Scotland, the reason they're in the Scotland Under-21 squad is that they've actually had the chance in the last couple of years to make their mark in the Premier League by playing first-team football,' said Sparkes.

'If they're going to be curtailed from getting a game at Hearts,

Kilmarnock, Hibs or any other team in Scotland by people who are only marginally better, then it's holding them back from becoming better players.

'From a technical and financial aspect, players from Lithuania will be attractive to Scottish clubs. Instead of a Spaniard or Portuguese player, who might be swayed by weather or climate considerations, for many players from the Baltic states and Eastern Europe, it would be a big improvement coming here.'

There are 39 FIFA-registered agents in Scotland as opposed to just a handful in Lithuania, so it is inevitable some will seek to explore a new market, although Sparkes made it clear he would not be travelling to the Baltic state: 'I won't be out there actively but these are countries which have to be looked at because you will find strong, disciplined, technical players for less money than you will find anywhere else.'

Whatever his motives, Romanov knew he was onto a winner and was determined to invest in Hearts, regardless of the obstacles that were put in his way. He entered into contracts to take over the shareholding of Robinson and around 10 per cent of those shares owned by former club chairman Leslie Deans. He bought only half of Deans' shareholding, which meant the Edinburgh lawyer retained a major investment.

Deans welcomed Romanov's involvement in Hearts. 'I sold 1.3 million shares, which represents 10.3 per cent of the total value of the club and around 50 per cent of my own shareholding,' he said. 'It had been a fraught and difficult time when Robinson was in charge but his [Romanov's] involvement meant there was light at the end of the tunnel for Hearts.'

Romanov continued to put the pieces for his takeover of Hearts into place. Ernst & Young's split from Tite & Lewis, its erstwhile London legal associate, had a fortuitous aftermath for the expanding Scottish law firm Brodies and for Romanov. Former Tite corporate partner Iain Young moved north to join the Edinburgh firm as partner-elect and became the man with the task of helping him buy into Hearts. He led the Brodies legal team, which included Liz Simpson and Michael Mustard.

With everything falling into place, Romanov felt confident enough to turn up officially at Hearts matches. When he watched them play Dundee United at Tannadice Park on 27 October 2004, he jumped out of his seat whenever they attacked.

With Levein leaving for Leicester City a few days after that match against Dundee United, it meant that Romanov had a new manager in John Robertson to deal with. The Hearts legend was appointed on 3 November, before Romanov had a hold on the club, and the Tynecastle legend took over just before the UEFA Cup tie against Schalke 04 at Murrayfield. With his confidence growing that the Hearts deal would go through, Romanov, on the advice of his public relations chief Charlie Mann, started to try and get his ideas across to the Scottish press, most of whom had been very sceptical about his plans.

After Hearts played Rangers at Ibrox, he hired a room in a Glasgow hotel to hold court for his first ever meeting with the scribes. The room was full of the best wine, champagne, beer and a selection of food, leading to jokes from members of the press pack that they were in no hurry for Romanov to arrive in order to give them time to make their way through the spread.

When he turned up, he had an entourage of four, which included his friend Anatoly Byshovets, who sat near Romanov and whispered advice into his ear during the interviews that took place with various newspapers, television channels and radio stations. Byshovets had been lined up to be director of football at Hearts but that plan was soon dropped.

It was fair to say Romanov didn't hide his light under a bushel during the interviews. He claimed that he would turn Hearts into Scotland's number one club. They would have more supporters than either Celtic or Rangers and play in a stadium 'better than any in Glasgow' once his plans were in place. He also hoped they would be Scottish champions 'within three or four years'. Celtic attract around 60,000 people to Parkhead on a regular basis, Rangers have some 50,000 at Ibrox for home games, while both grounds are widely regarded as among the best in Europe.

Despite being asked more than once, Romanov would not

divulge just where the money would come from to bring Hearts up to the standard of the Old Firm. When it was put to him that his plans for the future would be dismissed as grandiose and little more than pie in the sky, Romanov said, 'Nothing is impossible.' He denied that Hearts supporters should be worried that a foreign businessman about whom they knew little was about to become the biggest shareholder at their club. 'We are going to develop the club and bring up the fan base, so why should the fans be scared?' said Romanov.

'You have to understand that it's not just at Hearts and not just in Scottish football but also across the business scene in Scotland that those who come ready to invest money in the country are welcomed. Both the law and the people here are geared towards helping business and I received a good welcome when my plans for Hearts became public.'

He also made it clear that improving Hearts on the pitch was his major concern. 'It was never a question of the amount of money or how many players I wanted to bring to Hearts but the quality. I took a look at football not as a football professional but as a businessman.'

He continued, 'We want a stadium that meets the requirements of today and tomorrow and that is better than any in Glasgow. We need a lot more than currently exists at Tynecastle. We want a stadium with entertainment and commercial facilities to accommodate families, allowing them to spend extra time at the stadium. Mission one for us is to get a bigger fan base at Hearts. Mission two is to get a bigger fan base than Rangers or Celtic.'

Ending on a more personal note, Romanov produced pictures from his wallet of his parents and of his time in the Russian navy. Asked how he had made his millions and the extent of his personal wealth, he laughed and told a story to the assembled press and television crews of how it is always better to tell the taxman you found your money 'in a wardrobe'.

He showed some wit in skirting around the issue when asked about any deadline he had set himself to make Hearts Scottish champions. He simply replied, 'Do you want it in days or hours?'

With that, the man from Lithuania retired, to dream some more about his plans for Hearts.

From that moment on, Romanov made it clear that he was committed to the Tynecastle club. There were some teething problems early on, not least regarding the role of Byshovets. He made his first official appearance with the club as they flew to Switzerland to prepare for their vital UEFA Cup match against FC Basle, which they won thanks to a late Robbie Neilson goal. Byshovets said his main job was to pinpoint new foreign signings and he had already held talks with Robertson about possible targets.

'Anatoly knows a lot of players in the former Eastern bloc countries and we have been going over targets,' said Robertson. 'His knowledge of players in countries I don't know is immense. He has worked in Russia, Lithuania and managed and coached in Portugal and he knows a lot about Croatian football. We want to encourage youngsters to come through and if we can supplement them with quality foreign players, it would be great. However, we don't want to overload and must keep a strong Scottish influence.'

His positive noises papered over cracks in their relationship. The pair fell out over Byshovets' attempts to bring a Croatian centre-half to the club when Robertson was not in the market for a defender. Another flash point occurred after their UEFA Cup win in Basle when he told the victorious Hearts players to turn down the music they were playing.

Byshovets tried his best to play down the incident. 'I didn't mean to ruin their celebrations and by no means wanted to be a spoilsport,' he said. 'I wanted to talk about the game. I was also trying to tell them the importance of focusing on the next game. The professional thing to do once one game is over is to start thinking about the next one. I just wanted to congratulate them but there was a big noise.'

That support for Romanov was slowly building showed when Hearts supporters staged a peaceful protest on 13 December outside the Glasgow headquarters of Scottish Media Group, one of the club's major creditors. The Save Our Hearts campaign claimed the media group were to blame for the two-month postponement of the Lithuanian banker's deal with Chris Robinson the much-maligned chief executive, a point SMG strongly denied.

Romanov was moving forward and ensured the club was given until 28 February 2005 to pull out of the £22 million deal to sell Tynecastle to Cala Management, a month later than the original deadline. The move allowed him more time to become the single largest shareholder by completing the purchase of the stake in the club owned by Robinson.

The date of Tuesday, 21 December 2004 will go down in the history books as a pivotal day in the history of Hearts football club. It was the moment when Romanov, after so many false starts and scepticism surrounding his interest in the club, made his first really big move when he called an extraordinary general meeting to stop the sale of the stadium. Despite claims from Robinson that staying at Tynecastle was not a financially viable option, Romanov told the Hearts board that he wanted them to pull out of the deal to sell the stadium.

'It was a statement of Mr Romanov's intent and showed he was doing all he could to listen to the supporters and help their club remain at the ground they love,' said Gary Mackay, who admitted that it was at that moment he realised the campaign to keep Hearts at Tynecastle might succeed. Romanov's move was designed to allow him more time to consider long-term proposals for the club, including a possible revamp of Tynecastle that would be consistent with his aim of creating a stadium for Hearts that was 'better than any in Glasgow'. If planning regulations strangled his hopes of remaining at Gorgie, Romanov said he probably would have no option but to build a stadium on the western outskirts of the city.

His plans to stay at Tynecastle were given a shot in the arm by a special working group set up by Hearts to find a new home for the club. It recommended that they had to spend just £100,000 on safety measures, mostly on the Main Stand, to ensure the ground was suitable to host Bank of Scotland Premier League matches for the next five years.

Although Romanov's plans were progressing well, the

uncertainty over his buy-out was getting to the players, a point manager John Robertson picked up on. After the 1–1 draw in the Edinburgh derby on 2 January 2005, he gave the clearest indication yet that the off-field problems at Tynecastle were causing him growing frustration and concern.

A bunch of around 20 players from Eastern Europe had been shipped in for a behind-closed-doors trial match in Edinburgh the week before without any input from him. Byshovets ordered the game, which had been sanctioned by Romanov. Asked what input he had into the trial match, and what had been going on at Hearts over the past few months, Robertson shrugged his shoulders and said, 'It's not my club. I'm just the manager.' He sounded like a man with the world on his shoulders. Later, he admitted his mood was simply tied up with the fact he was desperate to do well with Hearts and was feeling real pressure at the time. His spirits weren't improved when Bill McMurdo, the agent for the Scotland striker Stevie Crawford, accused Chris Robinson of undermining a deal to bring the player to Tynecastle. McMurdo, one of the most experienced and outspoken agents in Britain, was insistent that he had agreed a deal with John Robertson for the player. However, he says contract discussions turned sour when they were conducted with the chief executive. McMurdo said he considered the offer Robinson finally came up with to be 'derisory' and believed that he was not interested in doing any sort of deal in the first place. Robinson strongly denied the allegations, as did George Foulkes on behalf of the board of Hearts.

The club was thrown into fresh turmoil when it emerged that the EGM to block the sale of Tynecastle called by Romanov was set to be postponed for three weeks on the orders of the Hearts board, who wanted more time to check his business plan. Although, for legal reasons, the EGM still had to be held, all indications were that it would be adjourned immediately until 27 January 2005, despite calls by senior shareholders for it to go ahead as planned.

On Monday, 10 January 2005, however, Romanov forced the meeting to take place and, in a dramatic U-turn, a vote was taken there and then on the motion to scrap the sale of Tynecastle to Cala Homes.

On a day that was stage-managed to perfection by Romanov, he turned up at Tynecastle at about 10 o'clock in the morning and demanded a meeting with the board, who had been unaware that he would appear. He told them he wanted the Cala deal halted and demanded that an EGM should be held two hours later to discuss the matter as scheduled and should not be delayed for three weeks as the board had suggested. As he had more than a 10 per cent share in the club, the board was bound by Stock Exchange rules to grant him his request.

He entered the Gorgie Suite where the meeting was taking place and received a standing ovation when the 400 shareholders present spotted him and his entourage. At the end of the meeting, he went to the top table and stood only yards from Robinson as Hearts supporters shouted approval at the man they considered the club's saviour.

Sergejus Fedotovas, who was soon to become the interim chief executive at Hearts, read out a lengthy statement explaining why Romanov wanted to invest in Hearts. Fedotovas even used the club song to get his point across.

'Hearts, Hearts, Glorious Hearts, it's down at Tynecastle they bide,' he said. 'I have spent a lot of time in Edinburgh in the last six months and I have learned that "bide" means to stay, remain or live. As the song says, Hearts bide at Tynecastle. Mr Romanov intends that Hearts will continue to bide at Tynecastle.'

His comments brought the house down with the shareholders, some wearing Russian hats in homage to Romanov, and they gave him yet another standing ovation. Deans believed Romanov was the white knight the club were looking for. 'What Vladimir suggested made it a joyous day for Hearts, and I for one went home to crack open a bottle of champagne,' he said. 'The spectre of the club having to move to Murrayfield had disappeared. Tynecastle is saved and we will be playing there for the foreseeable future. That is what the fans wanted and he has delivered. I was in no doubt that he offered the best option for Hearts. I trust the man.'

Fedotovas told shareholders that Hearts would cease to be a

selling club and Romanov would put some of his personal wealth at the disposal of the club.

Asked what would happen if the plans fell flat, Fedotovas said, 'Hearts would still have an asset worth £20 million for which there will be willing buyers. Therefore, the suggestion you will have read that Hearts will go into administration is entirely misconceived. The building blocks are there for the club to break the Old Firm stranglehold on Scottish football and once that has been achieved we can look for greater recognition and glories on the wider European stage.

'I give you Mr Romanov's personal undertaking that he aims to make this club hugely successful. All that remains is to ensure the future of Tynecastle.'

The following morning, Hearts confirmed to the Stock Exchange that shareholders had backed plans to scrap the sale of Tynecastle, with more than 70 per cent of them voting in favour of withdrawing from the planned £22 million deal. The Hearts board brought in financial and legal advisers to scrutinise the multimillionaire's business plans before agreeing it made sense to withdraw from the deal.

Romanov said, 'I was delighted the Hearts shareholders voted so decisively to support the plan to keep the club at Tynecastle. The strength of their feeling for the club and the ground is tremendous and I really do believe that, with that level of support, Hearts can continue to progress and challenge for all the Scottish football honours.'

SMG, who invested £3.5 million and gave the club a £4.5 million loan, and who owned around 19.9 per cent of the shares, did not back Romanov's proposals and wanted the sale of Tynecastle to proceed. A number of small shareholders also voted against, while Halifax/Bank of Scotland, who had a 5 per cent shareholding, abstained.

With another obstacle out of the way, Romanov gave his seal of approval for Hearts to sign three Lithuanians, the first group from that country ever to join the club. Two of them were among the twenty players from Eastern Europe who had taken part in a training camp with the club and were all registered with FBK Kaunas, the club in which Romanov had a major stake. The three players were Saulius Mikoliunas, Deividas Cesnauskis and Marius Kizys. They all started brightly but faded quickly, with only Mikoliunas holding down a first-team place for any length of time.

After the arrival of these players, Byshovets slowly drifted out of the picture at Tynecastle and Romanov made the astute appointment of Phil Anderton, the former chief executive of the Scottish Rugby Union, as the successor to Chris Robinson as chief executive at Hearts. Romanov's niece, Julija Goncaruk, took Robinson's place on the board when he severed all official ties with the club in the summer of 2005. Ukio Bankas, the institution controlled by Romanov, took on most of the club's debt from Halifax/Bank of Scotland.

Once he had his feet under the table, it was clear Romanov wanted his own man in the hot seat at Tynecastle. John Robertson, who many believe was not given enough time to prove himself, left Hearts after just over six months in charge. The club courted Sir Bobby Robson, who was offered a £400,000-a-year salary but despite long negotiations the former England manager rejected their advances. In the end, they plumped for George Burley, who had made his name as manager of Ipswich Town and Derby County, although Nevio Scala, the former manager of Parma, Borussia Dortmund and Shakhtar Donetsk, was also a strong candidate.

Looking back now, Romanov is happy he has bought into Hearts, although tellingly he has admitted he wouldn't rule out buying into other football clubs in the future, possibly back in Russia.

So what does the future hold for Hearts and what are the long-term aims of Romanov?

'For a club that hails from the capital city of Scotland, even second place isn't good enough,' he said. 'We want to be winning the league, cups and competing in Europe on a regular basis. I have interests in other clubs in Europe but for me Hearts is the top one.'

As for the future of the stadium, Romanov is adamant he will do all he can to keep them at Tynecastle.

HEARTS

'Hearts supporters don't want to lose their stadium. That has been their home for over a hundred years. I've developed a good relationship with the local authorities in Edinburgh but there are certain problems at Tynecastle.

'In order to have a large-capacity stadium, you need a sizeable piece of land. There is a shortage of land around Tynecastle and that makes the process of expanding the stadium more difficult but I will try hard to do so as that is what the supporters want and improving the old Main Stand is what I will do first. I may be based in Lithuania but my love is with Heart of Midlothian. I will make this club even greater than it is.'

He certainly invested heavily in players during the summer of 2005. During the transfer window, he brought players like Czech midfielder Rudi Skacel and Takis Fyssas, who won Euro 2004 with Greece, to the club.

'I want quality players at Hearts,' said Romanov. 'I want us to be the most successful team in Scotland and won't rest until that is achieved.'